# Caffeinated PDX

*How Portland Became the Best Coffee City in America*

HFC MEDIA • Portland, OR

Copyright © 2013 by Will Hutchens

All rights reserved. This book or any portion thereof may not be reproduced or used in any manner whatsoever without the express written permission of the publisher except for the use of brief quotations in a book review.

Printed in the United States of America
First Printing, 2013

ISBN: 978-0-9913331-0-3

LCCN: 2014902539

HFC Publishing
6021 SE 56th Ave
Portland, OR 97206

www.caffeinatedpdx.com

*Dedicated to A. Dale Hutchens, my late grandfather, one of the kindest and most generous people I have ever known. Grandpa, I wish you were here to read this book. I think you would enjoy it.*

# Contents

Introduction: Are You Serious? It's Just Coffee, Right?    9

1. Lessons from Brandon Arends, Enthusiast Extraordinaire    19
2. The Waves of Coffee History    23
3. Portland and Its Place in the Third Wave    37
4. Boyd's Coffee: Portland's Longest-Running Roaster    43
5. Kobos Coffee: The Company that led Portland into the Second Wave    49
6. The Long, Winding History of Jim and Patty Roberts, Portland's Original Coffee People    55
7. Mark Stell: Sitting Down with Mr. Sustainability    63
8. Stumptown and the Seismic Shift    71
9. Fresh Pot: A Skip Down Memory Lane    85
10. Phuong Tran: The Godmother of Portland's Third Wave    93
11. Kevin Fuller and Albina Press: Setting the Stage for Portland's Third Wave Explosion    103
12. Billy Wilson: Star Barista and Pioneer of the Multiroaster Café    113
13. Mindy Farley and Keith Miller: The Free-Spirited Founders of the Red E    129
14. Matt Higgins: High Expectations Get Results for Coava    135
15. Rita Kaminsky: Longtime General Manager at the Albina Press    145
16. Devin Chapman: Sitting Down with the Champ    153
17. Sam Purvis on the State of Specialty Coffee    161
18. Matt Brown: Portland's "Let's Get It Done" Guy    177
19. Driven to Perfection: Adam McGovern of Coffeehouse Northwest and Sterling Coffee Roasters    187
20. Ann and Collin Schneider: A Sterling Coffee Family    195
21. Ristretto Roasters: Great Coffee and Beautiful Spaces    201

| | |
|---|---|
| 22. Andrea Spella and the Humanity of Espresso | 211 |
| 23. Water Avenue Coffee: The Synergy of Three Portland Coffee Veterans | 225 |
| 24. Chris Brady: Hitting the Right (Flavor) Notes at Extracto | 235 |
| 25. Wille Yli-Luoma: Carving New Trails at Heart Roasters | 243 |
| 26. Sarah Allen: Supporting Baristas Worldwide at Barista Magazine | 251 |
| 27. Nossa Familia: Keeping It in the Family | 261 |
| 28. Cellar Door Coffee Roasters: Neighborhood Coffee and a Whole Lot of Niceness | 267 |
| 29. Oblique Coffee: The Chandlers' Labor of Love | 275 |
| 30. Case Study: Coffee as a Culinary Art | 281 |
| 31. Speedboat Coffee: The Niemyers Prepare to take Portland Coffee Outside the City Limits | 289 |
| 32. Marcus Young and Nathanael May: Two Portland Coffee Leaders Look at the Present (and Future) of Coffee | 295 |
| 33. Concluding Thoughts | 305 |
| Acknowledgments | 309 |
| Where Coffee Comes From | 311 |
| Barista Jargon | 317 |
| Index | 321 |

Introduction

# Are You Serious? It's Just Coffee, Right?

The first time I remember becoming interested in coffee was on a study abroad adventure in the fall of 2001. My new bride, Shayna, and I went to Italy for a few months as she finished up her university studies. I tagged along, studying the culture, the language, and the guitar. We arrived in Rome in early September and spent a couple nights at Casa Olmata, a small hostel a few hundred meters from the Basilica di Santa Maria Maggiore. Our accommodations included a free breakfast at a café across the street from the church, and that first morning, still tired from the journey, we had to hustle down the narrow streets to make it to the café before the day's breakfast offer expired.

A treasure of sights, sounds, and smells greeted us when we stumbled into the small but elegant café, jet-lagged and a bit doe-eyed about being so far from home. We handed the barista our breakfast tickets, and he handed us two croissants and two small ceramic cups full of a mixture of foamy milk and espresso. At the time, I was not much of a coffee drinker, but when in Rome...well, you know. He called it a cappuccino—my first espresso drink ever. It was tasty enough, and when we came back the next day, I was looking forward to my new ritual.

That fall, I picked up the habit of drinking espresso after dinner—dark and sweet, just like the Italians. Admittedly, part of the attraction was that I was enamored of Italy's food and culture and wanted to feel as Italian as a farm kid from Dayton, Washington (population 2,500), could. I didn't fit in with the locals, but I could at least drink their coffee.

Italy shaped my perception about what espresso should be, a perception that would stick with me for nearly a decade. After returning to the United States, I would order espresso after dinner, finding that it wasn't always easy to get in American restaurants.

I did not understand why the espresso habit had not caught on over here. I later found out that it had, but in a very different way.

## Slinging Coffee at Starbucks

Fast-forward a few years to 2006. I was in Boston, looking for a job. On a coffee run, Shayna saw a sign outside Starbucks saying the company was hiring and suggested I apply. At first, I was skeptical, having never worked in any type of service industry, but the company did offer benefits and I thought it might be interesting. I stopped in one day, filled out an application, and dropped it off with the barista on duty.

A month or two later, a manager of a Starbucks close to our apartment called and invited me in for an interview. When I arrived, the manager offered to buy me a drink, and I ordered a double espresso, which created a mini-stir among the baristas behind the counter. "What else would anyone want?" I wondered. Apparently, most people who came in for interviews were looking for something less direct. So were most Starbucks customers, as I found out after I was hired.

Working at Starbucks was a revelation to me in many ways. I found I enjoyed the service industry. Most customers were great (we were giving them coffee, after all), and the ones that weren't, I would silently imagine them slowly being sucked into Dante's Fourth or Fifth Circle of Hell and then give them decaf. (Side note: Everyone ought to work in food service for a while. It gives you a new appreciation for treating people with respect.)

The best part of my stint at Starbucks was the interaction with my fellow baristas. They were an eclectic group of people who loved to be a little crazy and have fun. Every morning, we would gear up as the morning rush of people started flowing in around seven a.m. For the next couple hours, we were slammed, putting out drinks as quickly as we could, trying to keep up with the line. Some days, chaos reigned, but other days, when the group was in sync, our customers rarely had to wait more than three minutes for their drinks, no matter how many people were in line.

My time at Starbucks gave me a new appreciation for coffee. By 2006, Starbucks had gotten rid of all its semiautomatic La Marzocco

## Introduction

machines in favor of machines that would grind, tamp, and pull shots at the push of a button, so I did not learn anything about the craft of making espresso, but I did get a basic understanding of how to prepare coffee and steam milk. I also learned a little about the different growing regions and some of the subtleties that were commonly associated with them. At Starbucks, you're supposed to try every coffee they offer within the first year you work there, so you have to be deliberate about doing tastings. Kurt, one of my coworkers, and I liked to pull out our company-issued coffee passports and fill them out with the various flavors we recognized. At first, they all tasted like coffee to me, but Kurt helped me out, and over time, a few flavors began to distinguish themselves.

For additional practice, we regularly pulled out the French press and paired coffees with the pastries and candies in the store (the Arabian Mocha Sanani was dynamite with the chocolate-covered cherries). Occasionally, customers joined us as we tried to pick out the fruity notes of an African coffee or the earthiness of the Sumatra, an earthiness we compared to leaves in the fall. Some people might rail against corporate coffee, but working for Starbucks was a great experience for me.

### Stop in Saronno

Though I liked working at Starbucks, another adventure abroad taught me it did not necessarily sell the best coffee in the world. In February 2007, I took a trip to Spain, scheduling a seven-hour layover in Milan, Italy, with the hope that I could get out of the airport long enough to see something interesting. It turned out to be one of the best travel decisions I ever made.

The plane arrived at Milan's Malpensa Airport about seven a.m. After speeding through customs (as fast as is possible in Milan at seven a.m.), I walked to the train station and ordered a round-trip ticket to the first town on the line, Saronno. As I looked out the train window, a surge of emotion welled up inside me. The sun was shining brilliantly in the blue sky that morning, and the light reflected off the morning dampness, giving the passing landscape an ethereal brilliance. It seemed like the northern Italian countryside was showing off just for me. When the train stopped at Saronno, I

## Caffeinated PDX

eagerly jumped onto the platform, where a few passengers waited for the next train into Milan. Lacking a map but not initiative, I plunged into the city with enthusiasm.

Saronno was just waking up for the day when I arrived. The streets were nearly empty — the bars and cafés along the quiet cobblestone streets had only a few early customers. I wasn't ready for breakfast yet, so I wandered around for a while. Soon, I found myself at the center of town sitting on a bench in front of the main cathedral. The piazza was nearly empty, but after a while, people trickled in. Old women passed by with their grocery carts, heading off to catch the best selection at the morning market. Groups of teenagers on their way to school lurched and pushed their way by, their shouts echoing across the open space. The bells of the cathedral rang loudly, signaling a new day had begun.

Despite being famous for its amaretto liqueurs (something I unfortunately found out well after I left), Saronno seemed like a place that does not get a lot of foreign visitors. There were no groups of German or Japanese tourists being herded through the piazza with their matching hats and cameras, nor did I see many foreign laborers. Saronno was a quiet little town that was content with itself, not looking to grow and not expecting to shrink. More than a few people passed by, staring at the odd foreigner, notebook in hand, trying to capture the moment in words.

When the writing inspiration wore off, I decided to seek out two things: a newspaper and a *caffè*. But where to go? I wandered around some more, seeking out just the right spot. Finally, I chose Caffè del Corso, a bar (in Italy, bars are similar to American cafés, though they usually also serve alcohol) on Corso Italia. When you are in a foreign country, entering a new place for the first time is always the hard part, at least for me. You aren't 100 percent sure about how things are supposed to work, and no one wants to make a fool of themselves. In a small town like Saronno, the first step is especially unnerving, since everyone else inside already knows each other. The entrance of a stranger precipitates the simultaneous snapping of necks as heads turn to see who the new guy is. At that point, you feel like you are under a microscope, hoping you don't screw it up.

## Introduction

Caffè del Corso was small and stylish, with a long, gracefully curved, high wooden bar and three or four tables, only one of which was taken. Very few Italians sit in cafés like Americans do. They come in, stand at the bar and quickly drink their coffee, then leave. I, on the other hand, wanted to sit down for a while and soak in the atmosphere. Stepping up to the register, I asked the middle-aged man behind it for a *giornale* (newspaper). He said he didn't have any and pointed across the street toward a newsstand. I walked over, bought a newspaper, and returned to the bar, ordered a caffè (espresso) and a chocolate brioche (croissant), and sat down at the table farthest from the door.

I am sure the setting had something to do with my perceptions, but I recall the espresso was very good and the brioche was fantastic. I couldn't help but wonder why, if Starbucks was modeled after Milan-area cafés, we didn't serve coffee or pastries of the same quality I was experiencing at that moment. As I mulled over that question, I noticed other customers in the café trying not to stare at me. An old woman at the next table, obviously a regular, kept looking over at me and smiling. She asked the baristas behind the bar who I was, but they only shrugged. My Italian was not great, but it was good enough to get the gist of what was being said.

Finally, I got up the nerve to talk to the baristas, asking clumsily if I could take a picture. Once I asked, the old woman realized I spoke some Italian, and she began gesturing and saying all kinds of things to me. The thing I love about Italy is that if you speak even a little bit of the language, the locals embrace you. My new acquaintances were more than happy to chat with me for a while. Bianca and Isabella tended the coffee bar while Alessandro was preparing sandwiches and other small dishes that would be eaten later that day. The tomatoes he was cutting looked delicious. Everything was made fresh each day, with an emphasis on quality.

I told them about my adventure, why I was in Saronno, and where I was going. The trio posed proudly as I snapped their picture for a memento. I promised to send them a postcard from Spain, and I bid them farewell. I would have liked to stay there the whole day, taking in the ambiance and working on the language, but it was time to get back to the train station. Immersing myself in coffeehouse culture would have to wait.

Back in Boston, I tried to employ the same friendliness with my customers that the Italians had shown me. After fifteen months at Starbucks, I felt like a pretty decent barista. If nothing else, I was good at getting the customers what they wanted and doing it quickly (knowing what they were going to order so I could have their drinks ready sooner was the key). Had we stayed in Boston, I might still be working at Starbucks, hopefully managing a café somewhere by now. However, we decided to move back to Washington following the birth of our daughter in 2007. I left Starbucks with much sadness and moved home to a town that was noticeably underserved when it came to quality coffee.

## The First Sip of Portland Coffee

The first time I tried a true Portland coffee, I was less than impressed. I can remember the day clearly. It was March 16, 2008. We had come to Portland so Shayna could run the Shamrock Run with a friend, Katie. After the race, Katie led us to her favorite café downtown, Stumptown on Southwest 3rd Avenue. I hadn't had good coffee for a while, so I was looking forward to some espresso. I didn't know (or care, to be honest) what Stumptown was. I ordered an espresso and sat down.

As usual, I stirred a packet of sugar into the cup and took a sip. My face must have contorted itself because my wife and her friend both laughed at me. The flavors were not what I had expected to taste in an espresso. The shot was tangy and juicy, a far cry from the espressos I had previously encountered.

"What is that, fruit juice?" I asked, grimacing.

"It's Hair Bender," Katie replied. Apparently, Hair Bender was her favorite coffee. She had raved about it to us while we were still living in Boston.

That morning, I received my first indication that there was something unique about Portland's coffee culture. Accustomed to a completely different style, I was not immediately taken. However, I did not give up on Portland coffee, or Hair Bender, the espresso blend that revolutionized coffee in the Pacific Northwest.

# Introduction

## Moving to Portland

We did not stay in Dayton for very long. Small-town life turned out to be a little too quiet, and soon we packed our bags for Portland, where I would enter the Master of International Management program at Portland State University. In terms of coffee, my life would never be the same. When we pulled into town, we did not know that we were in a hotbed of high-end coffee. I was still fairly loyal to Starbucks, having many good memories of my time in Boston. I did not understand how different the two cities' coffee cultures actually were. I would find out once I started writing about Portland coffee.

## Becoming a Writer

In late July 2010, a few months after graduation, I went to Beijing for a month to study the language and culture of a fascinating, rapidly changing China. From my first night in the country, when I stayed in the basement of a cheap hostel, hunkering down in a damp, windowless room resembling a prison cell, to the last day, when I stepped into the vast, airy expanse of Beijing Capital International Airport's Terminal 3, my life was a blur of activity. Between studying for class and spending time with new friends, every day brought something new to see or do. We traveled to the wide-open prairies of Inner Mongolia, danced on the streets in Beijing's old neighborhoods, and wandered through parts of the city where tourists never set foot. I didn't sleep much the whole month, fortifying myself each morning before class with paper cups of bad instant coffee. To keep my friends and family up to date on what I was doing and give them a feel for China, I wrote a blog about my experiences. Unexpectedly, I discovered I liked to write and tell stories. When I returned to Portland, I pledged to keep writing, but I needed a new topic.

Coffee was one of the first subjects to come to mind. As a grad student at Portland State, I had become a regular at Park Avenue Cafe, a spacious café on the Park Blocks just a two-minute walk from my apartment. I spent hours there studying with friends or reading through business cases on quiet afternoons. When I went to China, my coffee routine went with me. Thousands of miles

## Caffeinated PDX

from home, cafés were still my go-to place to recharge and get things done. Whenever I needed to escape the bustle of Beijing, I would duck into a coffee shop with my notebook to write or practice reading Chinese characters. Now back in Portland, writing about Portland coffee and its café culture would allow me to merge my craving for exploration with my affinity for coffee. I renamed the blog *Caffeinated PDX* and set out exploring. What I found intrigued me.

Coffee is one of those topics that the more you learn, the less it seems you know. Coffee is a plant, a seed, a beverage, a drug, a livelihood, and an industry. Coffee is everywhere. According to the National Coffee Association, Americans alone drink around 350 billion cups each year. It has been used as a political statement, as a justification for slavery, as a fuel for troops in faraway wars. Over coffee, intellectuals discuss philosophy, famous authors gather to write, and revolutionaries plot rebellions. You can talk about the agronomy of coffee, the economics of coffee, the culture of coffee — pick your area and there is plenty to discuss.

The area I chose to write about is specialty coffee. Specialty coffee and its subbranch, third-wave coffee — a small but rapidly growing part of the coffee industry — are full of passionate coffee enthusiasts insistent on improving how coffee is grown, processed, traded, roasted, and consumed. In every major city across the United States — and many smaller ones too — third-wave coffee is blossoming. Portland is a microcosm of the movement, and through the stories of the coffee people in Portland, I hope you gain a better understanding of what makes specialty coffee special, not just in Portland but also around the world.

As you read the book, you might notice that sometimes people talk about specialty coffee, and other times they speak of third wave. In most cases, I let the interviewee decide what to call the industry he or she works in. Although people often use them interchangeably, there is a slight distinction between the two terms. The term *specialty coffee* was coined in the 1970s by Erna Knutsen, a well-known coffee importer in San Francisco, to differentiate the high quality beans she was selling to roasters from the commodity-grade beans her competitors sold. The Specialty

# Introduction

Coffee Association of America (SCAA) defines specialty coffees as those receiving a cupping score of 80 or higher (see "Cupping for the People at Portland Roasting" on page 67 to learn more about cupping). Today, it generally refers to coffee that is of higher quality than the mass-market, preground coffees available at the supermarket. Third-wave coffee is a subset of specialty coffee that is even more focused on ensuring quality throughout the entire coffee supply chain, from origin to cup. Company size does not necessarily separate the groups — what matters is the attention to detail and an insistence on doing the best job to purchase, roast, and present the coffees to the customer as possible. The chapter "The Waves of Coffee History" goes into much more detail about the third wave.

## Why Portland?

Portland is known more for its quality of life than for its ambition, but despite the sleepy image, Portland is at the forefront of the third-wave coffee movement. The coffee scene in Portland is very much an extension of the do-it-yourself, geek-out culture that the city is known for. Portlanders like to be nerdy about food, wine, beer, whiskey, and coffee. Their love for coffee runs deep, whether you are talking about the hundred-plus-year-old coffee tradition of the Boyd family or the uncompromising quality of Coava Coffee, which opened its first café in 2009. In 2013, Portland was home to nearly fifty coffee roasters, multiple publications that specialize in coffee, and countless cafés.

This book covers a wide variety of topics. It briefly touches on the history of coffee and how the industry got to where it is today. It will help you understand what makes specialty coffee different from coffee that came before it. The book is also about my own relationship to coffee and how I discovered a culture I had no idea even existed.

When I started traveling around Portland, poking my nose behind café counters, and asking questions, I delighted in the baristas' enthusiastic answers, but I secretly wondered if they really took coffee so seriously. I did not understand what made Stumptown different from Starbucks. I had never heard about

## Caffeinated PDX

barista competitions — in fact, I would have laughed at you if you said you knew who last year's World Barista Champion was. Having since judged multiple barista competitions, I laugh no longer. Coffee captured me with its complexity, community, and worldwide reach. I now understand why people get so excited about it.

Other cities have important coffee cultures too, and critics might find this book a little too Portland-centric. Guilty as charged. However, there are many lessons that can be learned about what is happening in coffee around the country by taking a look at how Portland's coffee industry developed. Furthermore, conventional wisdom says you should write about what you know. After spending so much time traipsing around the city talking to coffee people, I have a good understanding of Portland coffee, and that is what I want to share with you.[1] Part memoir, part guidebook, and part historical record, this book attempts to answer the question, are Portlanders really that serious about coffee?

The answer, I would find, is an emphatic *yes*.

---

1. In addition, three friends and I put together a website to share our favorite Portland cafés with others. The site includes pictures, descriptions, and an interactive map. Check it out at CaffePDX.com.

# Lessons from Brandon Arends, Enthusiast Extraordinaire

As I began my coffee explorations, one of the first people I contacted for an interview was Brandon Arends, a member of my cohort in the Master of International Management program. Brandon had spent several months helping to write a case study about Portland Roasting's Farm-Friendly Direct program,[2] and I knew he would be able to teach me a lot. He began his lessons by taking me on a quick coffee tour.

Our first stop on the tour was Coffeehouse Northwest. As we pulled up to the small café on the corner of West Burnside and Trinity, I realized I had previously walked by the café several times without stopping. *This* was where Brandon was taking me? West Burnside Avenue, to put it diplomatically, is not Portland's best street, and the gritty-looking (at least from the outside) bars residing in the same block as Coffeehouse Northwest had led me to overlook the shop. When we stepped inside, though, the aroma of freshly ground coffee alone made me realize I had made a glaring misjudgment.

Standing in line, I asked Brandon what he usually ordered. He said he didn't go out for coffee much because he had a "crazy setup" at home, but when he did, he would get a double cappuccino. Rather, I *thought* he said a double cappuccino, but when we got to the register, he ordered a double espresso and a cappuccino. Nothing like starting the day with a bang. Brandon explained his order. "You can tell a lot about the quality of a café by the way the baristas make these two drinks," he said. "This is how they judge the baristas at competitions."

"Barista competitions?" I asked, puzzled. "They have barista competitions?"

---

2. The case study, which won the 2010 Oikos Global Case Writing Competition, can be found here: www.pdx.edu/sites/www.pdx.edu.insidepsu/files/portland-roasting-case-study.pdf.

## Caffeinated PDX

Brandon launched into a long story about what competition was like. He had volunteered at the 2009 World Barista Championship (WBC) in Atlanta. "You should go sometime. It's really cool," he said, sipping his cappuccino. "The best baristas in the world all come to the WBC. They do some amazing things, and you can learn so much about coffee. It's incredible."

He told me about some of the celebrities in the barista world — James Hoffman, Michael Phillips, and others, rattling off their names as if they were starters for the Trail Blazers. It was obvious he was a big fan of the competitions. "If you win the WBC, you're set," he said. "You get to travel around the world putting on clinics or teaching baristas how to do their jobs." Listening to his stories, I realized there was way more to coffee than I had ever thought. Even now, after having spent many, many hours in conversation with coffee professionals, Brandon's enthusiasm still stands out.

Brandon wasn't always into coffee, though. Growing up in Austin, Texas, he didn't really care for the beverage, but when he came to Portland, things changed. Interestingly enough, it was not Portland's coffee shops that sparked his interest. Rather, it was the city's Lebanese restaurants, where Brandon, a vegetarian, would visit to eat hummus and falafel. The typical Lebanese meal ends by drinking Turkish coffee — a dark, very sweet coffee made by boiling water, sugar, and very finely ground coffee together in the same pot. "There was this one Lebanese restaurant by PSU, and I went there enough that I got to know the owner pretty well," he recalled. "One day she let me come back to the kitchen and see how she made the coffee. It was cool."

The second step in Brandon's coffee conversion came at a car dealership (yes, you read that right). "I had to take my car in to get the wheel worked on," he said, "so I was stuck at the dealer for a while. They had a place to get coffee, so I tried some — it was very good. I got to thinking about the coffee culture here and that there are so many people here into coffee and drinking espresso, they can't all be idiots. So I figured I'd give it a try."[3] Brandon started

---

3. At one point during the interview, I stopped Brandon and asked him how he could possibly consider going into any industry other than coffee when he finished his graduate business program. I had never met anyone as passionate about coffee

## Lessons from Brandon Arends, Enthusiast Extraordinaire

making coffee at home, a hobby that soon became an obsession as he experimented with different coffees and techniques. He realized that in order to be able to make great drinks, he needed more practice, so he looked for a job at a café. "I could only make so many drinks for myself, and I wasn't going to make a bunch of drinks and just throw them out. Coffee is expensive. I knew that if I could work at a café, I could make a couple hundred drinks each day and I would get better — fast!"

Brandon found a job at PSU's Food for Thought Cafe, a student-run co-op café serving Stumptown coffees. He took it upon himself to bring up the quality of the coffees for the café. Listening to him, I could easily imagine him pushing the other baristas to pull better shots of Hair Bender. He even developed a new barista aptitude test to give to potential hires.

After an hour and a half at Coffeehouse Northwest, chatting about coffee, Brandon asked me if I'd ever been to Barista, a coffee shop in the Pearl District. I hadn't but was planning to go there later in the week. "Do you want to go now?" he asked. Not one to pass up the opportunity to check it out with a coffee guide, I accepted.

Brandon was excited to show me around. "You'll love this place," he said, "especially if you want to learn about coffee. It's an independent café, so they buy the best coffee from whoever they want to. The baristas know a lot and will talk your ear off if you ask them a question." On several counts, he was right. Barista is a unique place — it has three different espressos available every day and different coffees available for regular brewed coffee and for iced coffee. If you want, you can also get a vacuum pot of the coffee of your choice.

Brandon ordered first, another double espresso and another cappuccino. Not to be outdone, this time I ordered two espressos (all three would have been excessive) — one with beans roasted by Spella and one by Sterling. They were very different. The espresso

---

as he was, and his depth of knowledge and experience impressed me — surely any coffee company would benefit from hiring him. Brandon paused to think for a moment and then agreed that he would probably get into the industry eventually, regardless of whether he started somewhere else. And he did. He ended up working his way into a job at Coffee Bean International, Portland's largest coffee roaster.

from Spella was very nutty and smooth, and the one from Sterling smelled and tasted like not-quite-ripe blueberries. Brandon and I discussed why. "More than anything, the origin of the beans is what affects the taste," he said. "Each region, even each farm, has its own flavor characteristics that are typical. It's very similar to wine that way." He gave me a short lesson about the journey the coffee cherry takes as it travels from field to cup as well as about how the processing method affects the flavors in the coffee. I struggled to keep up with all the new information, but I did understand that coffee is a very labor-intensive and complex industry.

After our coffee adventure that day, whenever I had a coffee question, I would always ask Brandon first. Without exception, he always had an answer, or at least an opinion. If I had a theory for why a barista did something a certain way, I would shoot him an email, and he would respond quickly. Occasionally, we would get together and drink coffee. His enthusiasm for great coffee was contagious, and soon I found myself traipsing around the Portland area trying to find the best cafés and coffee shops the city had to offer.

In addition to giving me an introduction to the Portland coffee scene, Brandon also got me involved in the world of barista competitions. He coaxed me into volunteering at the 2011 Northwest Regional Barista Competition in Tacoma, Washington, and then into becoming a judge the next year. Without Brandon's contributions, this book probably would not have been written.

# 2

# The Waves of Coffee History

In conversations about specialty coffee, the term *third wave* is likely to come up. The third wave is a subset of specialty coffee, made up of a group of coffee companies and professionals dedicated to bringing the highest quality coffee from origin to cup. The phrase came into widespread use after Trish Skeie (now Rothgeb) wrote an article for the Roasters Guild newsletter in 2003.[4] Skeie described her understanding of how the coffee industry evolved from the late nineteenth century to where it is today, using three waves as the metaphor.

Some coffee people bristle at the use of the *third wave* term because after it became popular, some small, independent cafés and roasters tried to co-opt it. They tried to make third-wave coffee synonymous with not being tied to a large corporation. The trouble was, these independents failed to put the effort into the coffee that they should have, and a lot of people who called themselves third wave served very poor coffee. While the term is not universally loved, anyone who wants to know more about coffee should know what it means. To understand the third wave, we must first look at what came before it.[5]

## The Early Age

The world's obsession with coffee began more than a thousand years ago. Legend has it that coffee was discovered by a goat herder in

---

4. You can read the original article at http://timwendelboe.no/uploads/the-flamekeeper-2003.pdf. Skeie did not take credit for the term, but it was her article that fixed the use of the waves in coffee lexicon.

5. Several interesting books have been written about coffee's history and effects on the world, and the two I leaned on most heavily for this chapter are Coffee: A Dark History by Antony Wild and Uncommon Grounds: The History of Coffee and How It Transformed Our World by Mark Pendergrast.

what we call Ethiopia. The herder, named Kaldi, let his goats run free one afternoon, and they ended up eating some cherries off the native coffee trees that grew in the highlands. The goats started dancing around in a frenzy, prompting Kaldi to try some of the fruit for himself. He was pleasantly surprised by its stimulating effects, later returning to pick more of the ripe fruits to share with others.

Although the mythical Kaldi was almost certainly not the true discoverer of coffee, he could have been — his goats would have been grazing in the right spot to discover it. Based on the genetic diversity of coffee plants in Ethiopia, scientists believe that coffee evolved there. Then it crossed the Red Sea into the area we call Yemen and began its earnest conquest of the world.

In his book *Coffee: A Dark History*, Antony Wild writes that drinking infusions of roasted coffee as a beverage became popular in Yemen during the fifteenth century. After an encounter drinking tea with the famous Chinese admiral Zheng He, who visited the Yemeni port of Mocha in 1417, a Sufi Muslim alchemist named Gemaleddin began experimenting with infusions of local plants, seeking to replicate the ritualistic experience of tea drinking. Gemaleddin's first attempts were prepared from the coffee leaves and the coffee cherries. Eventually, he roasted coffee seeds, ground them, and made an infusion that turned out to be the drink he was looking for. Coffee caught on quickly among his followers, and by the end of the century, drinking coffee was very popular among the Sufis, a practice that would spread around the world over the next several centuries.

By the early 1500s, Mocha was established as the central port for the coffee trade. As the Ottoman Empire spread down the Arabian Peninsula, the Turks picked up the coffee habit and brought it back to Europe. Within eleven years of its introduction to Constantinople in 1555, more than six hundred coffeehouses were established in the city. Coffee became so popular that subsequent attempts by multiple Sultans to ban it (the rulers did not like how it sharpened the intellectual activity of the populace) were mostly ineffective and did not persist for more than a few years at a time.

Europeans proved susceptible to coffee's allure as well. Wild writes that coffee made it to Western Europe in the early 1600s,

## The Waves of Coffee History

brought by traders to Venice, London, and Amsterdam. Venice received its first major shipment of coffee in 1624, and London's first coffeehouse opened in 1650. In 1683, when the Turks were defeated at the siege of Vienna, they left behind a cache of green coffee that a local entrepreneur, Franz Kolschitsky, used to start his first café, called Blue Bottle.[6] Vienna became a hotbed for coffeehouses, and coffee's conquest of Europe was soon complete.

To meet growing demand for coffee, European traders sought out new sources of coffee. The Turks closely controlled the coffee trade out of Mocha and banned the export of live coffee plants, but they could not maintain control forever. In the mid-1600s, according to Mark Pendergrast's *Uncommon Grounds*, Dutch traders successfully transported a live coffee tree out of Yemen and established coffee plantations throughout their colonies in Southeast Asia from the descendants of that first tree. Holland soon became a worldwide leader in the coffee trade.

Not wanting to miss out on the riches of the coffee trade, other countries established coffee plantations in their own colonies. In 1720, a French naval officer named Gabriel de Clieu brought the first coffee tree to the French colonies in America.[7] With its high altitudes and tropical climates, the Americas had the perfect conditions for producing high quality Arabica beans. Coffee production spread quickly as farms popped up all over Central and South America (especially in Brazil). Millions of acres of rainforests were cleared to plant the new crop, and entire economies of nations were built on coffee production. Slaves provided much of the labor for the industry.

In the United States, coffee became an important beverage during the American Revolution, when leaders such as John Adams encouraged his fellow patriots to substitute coffee for tea to protest unfair tea taxes. By the mid-1800s, coffee was well established on both American continents as both a popular beverage and an important agricultural commodity. Americans' annual per capita

---

6. Wild says there is lack of evidence corroborating the story, but nonetheless, Kolschitsky is the "hero of Viennese coffee."

7. De Clieu was not the first to bring coffee to the New World, but he was one of the most self-promoting. Nonetheless, de Clieu did play an important role in expanding coffee production in the European colonies.

consumption reached five pounds of coffee in 1850, nearly all of which was roasted at home. In the 1860s and beyond, coffee consumption would become more widespread with the growth of the commercial coffee-roasting industry.

## First Wave

During the American Civil War, soldiers on both sides became accustomed to drinking coffee as part of their rations. After the war, demand for coffee shot up, and new companies emerged to meet the demand. Advances in roasting and packaging technology made it easier to produce and ship coffee. At the same time, East Coast entrepreneurs such as John Arbuckle, who roasted and sold Arbuckles' Ariosa Blend coffee across the United States in branded paper bags, changed the industry through new branding and marketing techniques. Their campaigns were effective, and the coffeepreneurs became hugely successful.

Out west, Jim Folger and the Hills brothers established their own fast-growing coffee companies in San Francisco. Maxwell House and MJB, still commonly seen on store shelves today, were also founded in this era. By 1900, Americans consumed twelve pounds of coffee per person per year.

Two innovations during the first wave made coffee more convenient for American consumers. The first was the use of the vacuum sealer, which allowed companies to preserve coffee's freshness for much longer periods after it was roasted. The second was the invention of instant coffee, the coffee-like creation whose positive qualities included its caffeine boost and portability (but not taste). During World War I, US troops drank primarily instant coffee, and they brought their newly acquired taste back home with them.

One innovation during the period that did not get much notice in America was the invention of the commercial espresso machine in Italy in 1901. This quick method of producing coffee spread throughout Europe, creating a new type of coffee culture that would take America by storm nearly eight decades later.

The beginning of the twentieth century also brought large changes in how products were marketed to customers. During this time, national advertising campaigns became common. In the 1920s, coffee companies spent millions on new radio ads to successfully convince the American public they could not live without their products. Even the Great Depression could not stop the spread of coffee. By the end of the 1930s, nearly all American families consumed some form of coffee. In the post-World War II era, they filled their cups with cheap coffees they prepared using stovetop percolators. The method, while convenient, produced cups of overextracted, bitter coffee. For several decades, coffee drinkers quietly accepted this level of quality, unconcerned with or unaware of how good coffee could taste if it were carefully sourced, roasted, and prepared from fresh beans.

## Second Wave

Things began to change in the 1960s, when Alfred Peet started roasting and selling coffee beans in Berkeley, California.[8] Peet, originally from the Netherlands, opened his first store in 1966. The opening of Peet's Coffee & Tea marks the beginning of the second wave of coffee. Unlike the mass-market national brands, Peet roasted coffee in smaller batches and sold fresh beans to customers at his store.

The new business was successful, and Berkeley's resident coffee drinkers flocked to the new store. The coffee was so good that it inspired three early Peet's devotees, Zev Siegl, Jerry Baldwin, and Gordon Bowker to start their own shop in Seattle. Their new company, called Starbucks, started outselling Peet's coffee beans for people to brew at home. To meet growing demand, Starbucks began to roast its own coffee. In 1982, the company hired a home appliance salesman named Howard Schultz from New York to be their company's director of marketing. Few could have guessed how much the hiring would change the coffee world.

On a business trip to Milan, Italy, in 1983, Schultz fell in love with the Italian coffee culture. He came back from the trip believing he had seen the future of coffee. Schultz desperately wanted to bring espresso to Starbucks cafés, but Baldwin, Siegl, and Bowker did not share his vision, so Schultz left the company to start his own

---

8. Much of the story of Peet's and Starbucks comes from Starbucked: A Double Tall Tale of Caffeine and Commerce by Taylor Clark.

chain of cafés, called Il Giornale. This was an attempt to replicate the Italian coffee experience, selling espresso drinks with style and flair.

Schultz's vision forever changed the coffee landscape in America. From the modern perspective, serving espresso drinks to Americans is a rather mundane concept, but in the mid-1980s, when Schultz began selling freshly made lattes and cappuccinos, it was a big departure from the norm.[9] Il Giornale was a hit among Seattle coffee drinkers, and the company expanded to several locations. Schultz and a group of investors eventually bought Starbucks from Baldwin and Bowker (Siegel had sold his interest the company in 1980) and converted the Il Giornale cafés into Starbucks. The company went public in 1992, with plans to expand rapidly. Since its IPO, Starbucks has grown to be a chain of over seventeen thousand stores worldwide, with more than 150,000 employees.[10]

Starbucks and Peet's popularized a better — and just as importantly, a more expensive — cup of coffee among Americans who previously based their coffee-purchasing decisions primarily on price.[11] Starbucks promoted a third-place concept — the idea that coffeehouses could be a place between work and home where people gathered. The company's aggressive growth spread the demand for higher quality coffee throughout the Untied States, and its financial success encouraged copycat cafés to spring up across the country. In almost every city and town across America, you could find some café or kiosk selling some version of espresso, with widely varying levels of quality.

As Starbucks grew, the company moved away from its coffee-centered roots. To increase café throughput, the company

---

9. Starbucks was not the first company to sell espresso to Americans. San Francisco's Caffe Trieste, for example, began selling espresso on the West Coast in the 1950s. However, outside small enclaves like the North Beach district of San Francisco or New York's Little Italy, drinking espresso was not common. Starbucks was where many Americans had their first taste of espresso.

10. As of July 2012, according to Starbucks' 10-K.

11. Lamenting Americans' cost-consciousness, coffee roasters talk of how supermarkets would use coffee as a loss leader, selling it below wholesale prices to attract customers into their stores. Americans became accustomed to cheap coffee, making it difficult to sell better quality, more expensive coffee. Peet's and Starbucks helped change this mentality, to a point.

installed superautomatic espresso machines that ground, tamped, and pulled espresso shots at the push of a button, taking much of the craft of espresso out of the cafés. It promoted new products, like Frappuccinos and Caramel Macchiatos, popular beverages that consisted mostly of milk and sugar. To purists, these drinks were not the way coffee should be experienced. In response, a new type of café and roaster began to sprout up, one focused more on the quality of the coffee than on the quantity being sold.

## Third Wave

The second half of the 1990s marked the beginning of the third wave of coffee. In 1995, Counter Culture was founded in Durham, North Carolina, by Fred Houk and Brett Smith. The same year, Doug Zell founded Intelligentsia in Chicago. Stumptown, founded by Duane Sorenson in Portland, Oregon, opened its doors in 1999. These three companies formed the backbone of the third wave, focusing on a more direct trade with farmers and insisting on high standards of quality throughout the supply chain. No one set of criteria completely encompasses what third-wave coffee is, but the overarching ideal of the movement is to place the highest emphasis on the coffee itself and to respect the people involved in growing it, roasting it, preparing it, and drinking it.

### *Higher Green Bean Quality*

The best coffee starts with the best green beans. First-wave coffee companies did not care so much about what they put in the can as long as it was economical and bore some resemblance to coffee. Mass-market coffees like Folgers and Maxwell House became popular at a time when Americans generally were not wealthy enough to pay more for higher quality coffee. Second-wave roasters purchased better quality Arabica beans, roasted them carefully, and sold them whole or freshly ground to customers.[12] Third-wave coffee roasters start with the best beans, typically high-altitude

---

12. In the United States, we have been led to believe that Arabica beans are always better than Robusta. This is generally true, but not always. Some of the highest quality Robustas are sought after by coffee companies for their body and high oil content. www.freshcup.com/featured-article.php?id=146

Arabica beans, grown at elevations above 3,280 feet. Most of these are selectively handpicked. Coffee cherries ripen at different times on the branch, and unlike some fruits, will not ripen after they are picked. Ripe cherries provide the best flavor and quality, so farmers working with third-wave roasters hire pickers to harvest only the ripe cherries from the branches. Machines cannot selectively pick the ripe cherries (even if they could, most coffee is grown on hillsides too steep to support large machines), so growers must send crews out several times during the harvest season to pick cherries from the same trees, adding significant cost to production.[13]

Once the cherries have been picked, they must be processed within a short time, or the quality of the coffee degrades quickly through uncontrolled fermentation and decomposition. The processes vary (see the appendix for more details), but the goal is generally to get as many of the fruit layers covering the seed off of the seeds as quickly as possible. The coffees are sorted, pulped, washed, and set out to dry within twenty-four to forty-eight hours of harvest.

Careful processing pays off for the farms. When coffee is grown and processed well, it commands higher prices. When Stumptown partnered with an Ethiopian co-op in Gaturiri to install new processing equipment, for example, farmers expected the increased quality to make the equipment pay for itself within five years. To their surprise, the quality improvements were so dramatic that the higher prices for the farm's coffees allowed it to pay off the loan in one year. Growers who work with third-wave roasters have to invest in quality equipment and follow best practices if they want to remain competitive in the specialty market.[14]

---

13. Not all third-wave coffee is selectively handpicked, though. Some companies harvest mechanically or have their workers strip pick (stripping all the cherries off each branch) and then separate the cherries using special equipment. As sorting technology improves, mechanical harvest and separation will likely increase, at least on land that is flat enough to support the machines.

14. There are some downsides to this need for quality improvements, as some farmers can be left out of the market if they are not producing the best coffees. God in a Cup by Michaele Weissman details some of these challenges.

# The Waves of Coffee History

## *Relationships with Growers*

One of the principles of the third wave is fairness to the growers. As much as possible, third-wave coffee companies negotiate prices directly with farmers (or with importers they trust to deal fairly with farmers). Often, they create long-term relationships with farmers, promising to buy a certain farm's coffee for several years in exchange for exclusivity. Counter Culture's Peter Giuliano, Intelligentsia's Geoff Watts, and Stumptown's Duane Sorenson were famously profiled in *God in a Cup*, a story about third-wave roasters' dealings at origin.

In an effort to de-commoditize coffee, roasters emphasize where their coffees come from. When you walk into a third-wave café roaster and ask about the coffees, baristas can often tell you the entire story behind the coffees they are selling. Sometimes they talk about a region within a country or a particular farmer or co-op that raises the coffee. More knowledgeable baristas talk about the coffee cultivar or the processing method used to separate the coffee beans from the coffee cherries. Doing so, companies are able to differentiate their own coffees from others.

Roasters and cafés can charge more for coffees that are differentiated in some way, and the story makes each coffee unique. Ultimately, this differentiation will be good for growers, especially those who produce higher quality coffee, because it will increase demand for their coffee, raising the prices the growers receive and helping them improve their living standards.

## *Smaller Lots and Lighter Roasts*

Third-wave roasters are changing people's perceptions of how coffees should be roasted. Over the past few decades, Starbucks conditioned people to associate a bold, dark roast with quality coffee. From a business standpoint, dark-roasting makes perfect sense. Big business excels at providing the same product over and over, creating economies of scale and large profits. People who regularly walk into a Starbucks in Portland expect to be able to walk into a Boston-area Starbucks and get the same product. By roasting its coffees darker, Starbucks is able to provide this consistency (the dark roast is also why Starbucks critics refer to the company as Charbucks). Following Starbucks' success, other second-wave companies roasted their coffees dark as well. This led to a marketplace saturated with dark-roasted coffees.

By contrast, third-wave roasters tend to roast coffees lighter to bring out the complexities of each coffee they purchase. When roasted, coffee beans contain hundreds of flavor compounds and aromatics (more than wine) that make them unique. Many of these compounds are delicate and volatile and can be lost in the roasting process or if the roasted beans are left to sit for too long before brewing. To preserve these flavors, third-wave companies roast the coffees very gently and then serve them fresh so customers can experience the nuances of each coffee. Portland companies like Heart strive to produce coffees without any hint of roast.

### *Single-Origin Coffees (Espressos Too)*

Espresso has been around for more than a century, and to many people — especially in southern Europe — it is the primary way to enjoy coffee. If you walk into a café in Italy and order a coffee, the baristas will serve you a demitasse of espresso, not a mug (or large paper cup) of brewed coffee like you get in the United States. Traditionally, these espressos are made from a blend of different beans (in Italy, a blend usually has six to eighteen kinds of beans). Blending allows roasters to balance the sweet, sour, and bitter flavors in a cup and to maintain a more consistent profile over time. Blending also reduces the risk that any particular bean will be unavailable. In addition, the roaster can reduce the cost of the blend by adding small amounts of cheaper beans that have little impact on the flavor.

By contrast, third-wave coffee roasters are showcasing more and more single-origin coffees brewed as espressos. Selling single-origin espressos dovetails with the third wave's goal of highlighting particular regions, farms, and varieties. It requires careful roasting and preparation to make a single-origin coffee taste good as an espresso. Baristas must continually monitor and adjust the grinder to ensure the product will be acceptable. Otherwise, the bright notes get blown out of proportion and make the coffee taste like lemon juice or underripe fruit.

## The Waves of Coffee History

### *More Coffee, Fewer Flavor Syrups, and Less Milk*

Over the past twenty years, second-wave cafés convinced Americans that a sign of coffee sophistication was being able to order a beverage in which the coffee is hidden behind loads of milk and sugary syrups (for example, a double grande raspberry white chocolate mocha with whipped cream). Jerry Baldwin, one of the founders of Starbucks, was quoted in *Starbucked* as saying, "Who would have known Americans liked to drink so much milk?"

Third-wave cafés are reintroducing customers to a more transparent coffee. Many have reduced the number of flavor syrups they offer customers (no more walls of syrups behind the counter). At cafés like Portland's Albina Press, for example, baristas explain to confused first-time customers why they do not carry whipped cream in the store. Third-wave cafés also emphasize selling more traditional-sized beverages, in which the ratio of coffee to milk is much higher. The idea is that the coffee they sell stands by itself and does not need to be hidden behind milk and sugar.

### *Skilled Baristas Making a Career Out of Coffee*

Third-wave baristas are a nerdy lot, and I mean that as a compliment. Not content to just serve coffee, they dive headfirst into their craft, learning all they can about the coffees and working tirelessly to hone their skills. They study new technology, read up on what is happening in the industry, and take part in barista competitions. Some travel to origin, where they can see firsthand how coffee is grown and processed. Sometimes they see the same coffees they will serve in their cafés a few months later. Baristas come back from these trips even more enthused about their jobs, a sentiment that creates a better experience for their customers. In other words, these baristas act more like professionals than like people just looking to fill in their free time by slinging coffee.

Over the past decade, the Barista Guild of America and *Barista Magazine* have also helped to raise the status of baristas within the coffee industry. The guild emphasizes educating baristas and offering opportunities for baristas to enhance coffee knowledge and preparation skills. *Barista Magazine* promotes competitions and helps create a strong sense of community among baristas around the United States.

The baristas' work is paying off. At least in Portland, third-wave baristas tend to earn more than minimum wage. At the better shops with busy café locations, the tips alone can nearly double the baristas' hourly wage (it helps that Portland has a generous tipping culture). One café in Portland pays its baristas $15 per hour, plus tips. A few — Stumptown, Ristretto, Heart, and Coava — offer health insurance benefits.[15] Being a barista is seen less as a part-time job and more as a first step toward a career in coffee. Baristas frequently become trainers or roasters, or move on to start their own coffee businesses.

## A Long Evolution

The coffee industry has evolved greatly since coffee was first discovered so many centuries ago. From its origin in the East African highlands, coffee spread across the globe, creating new economies and enhancing the intellects of generations of thinkers. In the late nineteenth century, new methods of roasting and packaging made coffee available to more people than ever before, but quality suffered greatly. Sensing an opportunity, Alfred Peet started his company and rescued Americans from the stale, pre-ground coffees they were drinking. Through Starbucks, Peet's followers spread his message and roasting style throughout the United States and beyond, while also introducing Americans to espresso culture. As the twentieth century came to a close, a new generation of coffee roasters sprouted up with a devotion to quality from seed to cup. They worked with growers to improve the coffees they were raising and invested time and money in helping them advance their processing methods. The roasters experimented with lighter roasts in order to bring out the coffees' inherent properties. Baristas took up the challenge of focusing on each cup they prepared, and customers willingly paid more for a product they believed worth it. The combination of quality (of coffee) and fairness (to growers, roasters, baristas, and customers) is making coffee's third wave the fastest-growing part of the coffee industry.

---

15. Others may offer benefits as well. These are just the ones I know about.

## Streamlining the Coffee Supply Chain

One of the not-so-hidden secrets of the coffee industry is that when someone spends $4 on a latte, the people who grow the coffee only receive a small percentage of the benefits. For years, roasters generated huge profits while coffee farmers lived in poverty. Although economic disparities still exist, the specialty coffee industry is reducing them through the principles of social entrepreneurship. Social entrepreneurship is the idea that business can solve social problems while making a healthy profit. It creates more lasting solutions to poverty and economic inequality than aid programs do (some call it capitalism with a cause).

In the typical coffee supply chain, coffee passes through many hands on its journey from the field to the customer. Coffee farmers sell their coffee to a buyer, who sells it to a processor, who sells it to an exporter, who sells it to an importer, who sells it to a distributor, who sells it to a roaster, who sells it to a distributor or café, who sells it to the end consumer. Each person along the chain has an incentive to keep the price they pay as low as possible, and it is coffee growers who end up getting paid the least.

Several other factors contribute to the farmers getting paid little for their coffee. In many places, farmers do not know what the world coffee market is doing, so they have no idea whether they are selling their coffees at fair prices.[16] This information asymmetry puts farmers in a weakened bargaining position, and customers farther down the supply chain are happy to take advantage of them.

---

16. The spread of wireless communication networks to developing countries helps farmers more easily follow world market prices. Nonetheless, growers still struggle to know what their coffees are worth, so there is a big push within the industry to teach growers how to cup and score their coffees. Cupping is a procedure used by coffee traders (and other people in the industry) to determine the quality of the green coffee beans. For a more in-depth description of cupping, see "Cupping for the People at Portland Roasting." Once farmers know the quality of their crops, they can negotiate fairer prices.

In addition, coffee farmers often come from poor areas and do not have any cash reserves, so they must sell their crops as soon as harvest is over in order to pay their bills. Market prices are generally at their lowest during harvest because the supply of coffee in the market is at its highest point for the year (increased supply = lower price). Farms often lack adequate facilities to store the coffee until prices rebound. Heat and humidity are the two worst enemies of storing a crop, and coffee is grown in places where there is plenty of both, especially during the rainy season. Building proper coffee storage that can preserve green beans for long periods of time is prohibitively expensive for small operators.

An important goal of specialty roasters is to make a profit while making sure that farmers are paid fairly for their products. When Coava pays higher prices for its coffees, for example, it gives coffee cooperatives in developing countries more of an opportunity to purchase better processing equipment and improve storage facilities (and the coffee's quality). Farmers win, roasters win, and coffee drinkers win.

Coffee roasters in Portland (and across the country) are working to buy more of their coffee directly from the farmers themselves. Stumptown, for example, directly negotiates with farmers and cooperatives on coffees and prices and then works with an importer to bring the coffee to the United States. This eliminates some of the middlemen between the coffee farmer and the coffee producer. By streamlining the system, roasters pay less per pound, but the growers still receive more because intermediaries do not take a cut of the price.

# 3

# Portland and Its Place in the Third Wave

The Portland coffee community is a ball of energy, a center of innovation, a cluster of excellence. While there are other cities with advanced coffee scenes (San Francisco comes to mind), no other city has the proliferation of third-wave coffee companies that Portland has.

In many ways, Portland was the perfect place for the third wave to take root. The city has strong culinary and beverage cultures. Food carts flourish throughout Portland, giving residents the opportunity to sample cuisines from every part of the globe. The region is home to many microbreweries, wineries, and craft distilleries. This affinity for exploring flavors naturally extends to coffee. Portlanders are fiercely independent too, and they tend to support local businesses when possible. Further, the city's weather certainly plays its role. Six months (sometimes more) of grayness creates the conditions for a lot of self-medication (caffeine can be quite therapeutic on a winter day).

In addition, coffee has been a long-standing part of Portland culture. P. D. Boyd started his coffee company more than a century ago, and although Boyd's was not the first coffee company in the Northwest, it is the only one that can boast it has been running for more than 110 years, laying the foundation for today's industry to build on. A few years after Boyd began peddling coffee from his red wagon, Fred Meyer also dabbled in coffee before deciding the grocery business would suit him better.

Portland's coffee industry changed significantly in the 1970s. David Kobos, originally from the East Coast, came to study at Reed College, fell in love with the area and its coffee (he regularly frequented Boyd's Little Red Wagon café), and decided to settle here and start his own roaster. Coffee Bean International, Portland's largest roaster, also began in the 1970s.

## Caffeinated PDX

In the 1980s, roasters such as Longbottom, World Cup, and K&F started up, providing even more options for Portland's coffee-drinking community. Jim and Patty Roberts founded the well-loved Coffee People in 1983, a roller-coaster ride that would peak with an IPO in the mid-nineties, the only time a Portland coffee company has gone public.[17]

In the 1990s, the Portland coffee industry helped push the international scene in a new direction, with the founding of Portland Roasting (1996) and Sustainable Harvest (1997). Mark Stell and David Griswold, the companies' respective founders, started their companies with the idea that business could be a force for good, especially in developing countries where coffee was grown. The companies challenged the industry to participate in a more ethical type of commerce, one in which the benefits of coffee were distributed more fairly between producers and consumers.

Stumptown's arrival on the scene in 1999 brought an entirely new energy to Portland coffee culture. Duane Sorenson started his coffee company in Southeast Portland with an obsessive devotion to quality. The company's edgy attitude and focus on sourcing only the best coffees (and being willing to pay more for them) brought higher incomes to the fortunate (and very hardworking) coffee growers who were able to work with the company. Stumptown trained its baristas to make high quality beverages, and its roast profiles retrained customers' palates. The company aggressively courted wholesale accounts, and cafés such as Fresh Pot, founded by Skip Colombo and Matthew "Vin" Vinci, quickly became Portland favorites. Stumptown's growth gave Portlanders a strong local alternative to Starbucks, especially after the demise of Coffee People.

As Stumptown grew, it raised the level of coffee consciousness across the city. A more knowledgeable customer base embraced a purer form of coffee that could be drunk with fewer flavored syrups and condiments. The higher prices Stumptown paid growers also resonated with the city's sustainability ethos. Portland served as

---

17. Coffee Bean International is a public company, but that happened through acquisition by Farmer Brothers rather than an IPO.

## Portland and Its Place in the Third Wave

a base for strong growth, and as of 2013, Stumptown roasts over two million pounds of coffee per year in four roasting facilities around the country.

Hardworking and talented baristas have made major contributions to the industry as well. Just outside of Portland, Phuong Tran purchased Lava Java in 2002 and began selling Stumptown a few months later. Tran and her employee Billy Wilson made Lava Java famous with their success in barista competitions, and they trained a bevy of baristas who would fan out into the coffee community. Kevin Fuller hired Billy Wilson when he opened the first Albina Press, which quickly became known for serving better shots of Hair Bender than Stumptown did. The renowned Albina crew included Mindy Farley and Matt Higgins, who would eventually leave to start their own Portland coffee companies.

The city's progressive coffee culture drew people in from other cities across the United States. In 2005, Din Johnson returned to Portland to open Ristretto Roasters. Andrea Spella opened his cart in 2006, serving espresso praised in the *New York Times*. Chris Brady began roasting at Extracto in 2008. Adam McGovern, who arrived at Coffeehouse Northwest in 2004, brought his perfectionist attitude to the shop and raised the quality of coffee on the west side of I-405. McGovern eventually bought the café and, along with business partner Aric Miller, founded Sterling Coffee Roasters in 2010.

Mindy Farley's Red E Café opened in May 2009, serving Matt Higgins's Coava coffee at the time. Billy Wilson's Barista joined the scene the same year, serving coffees from roasters all over the country. Wilson's café rewrote the relationship between café owner and roaster, breaking the monopoly that roasters typically have over cafés. The multiroaster model proved to be a hit, and Portlanders flocked to the new café to sample coffees from as far away as Europe.

Wille Yli-Luoma, a professional snowboarder from Finland who had settled in Portland, turned his intense focus to coffee, opening Heart Roasters in 2009. Yli-Luoma's efforts to source the finest coffees and his roasting style, inspired by northern Europe's finest roasters, caught many people's attention. His success is pushing the industry toward lighter roasts.

**Caffeinated PDX**

Case Study Coffee opened in 2010 with a passion for culinary coffee and a public-house model that drew diverse crowds. Around the same time, Oblique Coffee's John and Heather Chandler opened their new roastery and café in a Victorian mercantile they had just spent three years remodeling. Oblique slowly but surely built a business through its persistence and attention to building relationships.

With its first retail café, Coava exploded onto the scene in 2010, receiving accolades in the press for its commitment to quality and for its innovative Kone filter.[18] Two of the company's baristas, Sam Purvis and Devin Chapman, swept the Northwest Regional Barista Competition three years running. Meanwhile, a few blocks away, Bruce Milletto and Matt Milletto teamed up with Brandon Smyth, a former roaster for Stumptown, to open Water Avenue Coffee, another small roaster committed to quality.

Behind the scenes, people like Matt Brown, Ricky Sutton, Ryan Cross, and Ann and Collin Schneider — people whose names might not make it into the press — played important roles in opening cafés and maintaining the quality of coffee throughout the industry. In addition to their official coffee jobs, industry veterans like Rita Kaminsky, Nathanael May, and Marcus Young put in extra time supporting barista competitions and bringing more respect to a profession that sometimes gets too little.

In addition to the roasters, baristas, and cafés, coffee publications like *Fresh Cup*, *Roast*, and *Barista* — all founded in Portland — captured what was going on in the specialty coffee industry and created a sense of community among the participants. Sprudge.com, the online leader in specialty coffee news and "frothy gossip," also calls Portland its home.

All of this to say that at the beginning of the third wave, Portland was a city ripe for a new way of experiencing coffee. It had a long coffee history, receptive and adventurous consumers, and just enough social awareness to support a quickly changing culture, bringing Portland to the forefront of the specialty coffee industry.

These days, the Portland specialty coffee scene is not yet saturated, but it is getting crowded. The competition is tough enough

---

18. The Kone is now sold by Able Brewing and is no longer associated with Coava.

that proprietors are seeking out other cities with populations who could benefit from (and support) new roasters. Former Portland baristas have opened their own shops in cities throughout the West. A few Portland roasters are already selling coffees in Canada, Japan, and Korea, while others set their long-term sights on international expansion as well. In the future, other cities will not duplicate what has happened in Portland, but they can use the city as a benchmark for quality.

Portlanders did not invent coffee, but they embraced it more tightly than any other city in the United States did at the time. Accepted by most cultures, and appropriate for almost all ages, coffee is the world's most social drink. It is hard to imagine the time when humans did not drink coffee. It is just as difficult to imagine Portland without its coffee.

## A Note About the Book

The rest of the book is dedicated to the stories of the people who have built Portland's coffee industry. Instead of writing a single chronological narrative for Portland's coffee story, I have included the stories of many of the people who work in the industry. In many cases, their stories intersect, sometimes at multiple points. I tried to let the interviewees' voices come through as much as possible. After all, they know their histories better than I do.

## 4

# Boyd's Coffee
## Portland's Longest-Running Roaster

*Portland's current generation of cutting-edge roasters owes part of its success to a city willing to drink cup after cup of coffee, and one of the companies that helped develop this habit is Boyd Coffee Company (Boyd's). While most of the roasters in the Portland area are younger than twenty years old, Boyd's has more than a century of history behind it. Founded in 1900, Boyd's is the longest-running coffee company in Oregon. It is also one of the most successful. Since its founding, Boyd's has grown from a one-man, one-wagon operation into a 350-employee company that sells coffee throughout the United States and Canada as well as Japan.*

*Three fourth-generation family members are still involved in the business — Katy Boyd Dutt, director of strategic marketing; her brother, Michael Boyd, coffee buyer; and their cousin, Matt Boyd, director of strategic information. They sat down with me to share their perspective on the company and on the coffee industry.* — WH

The history of Boyd's is the timeless American story of an immigrant coming to America, starting a business, and prospering. Percival Dewe (P. D.) Boyd, the founder of the company, was born in New Zealand, the son of a Scottish Presbyterian minister. His parents immigrated to America in 1882 when he was three years old. Although not all the details of P. D.'s upbringing are known, it is clear that Boyd was working in Portland's coffee industry before the turn of the century. "I did a little bit of research at one point," said Katy. "I found that he was working for a coffee company in the late 1890s called Defiance Coffee here in Portland.[19] My assumption has always been that he was like, 'I can do this too,' and started Boyd's."

---

19. Defiance was a Portland coffee company that was purchased years later by Farmer Brothers.

## Caffeinated PDX

By 1900, P. D. had founded Boyd Importing Tea Company, which later became Boyd Coffee Company. In the early days, P. D. delivered his products to customers with a bright-red, horse-drawn wagon. His horse, formerly used to deliver alcohol, had to learn some new habits for the coffee industry. "It would stop at all the pubs around town because it was on a routine," said Michael. "The horse knew it was supposed to stop at all the bars." Within a few years, the wagon was replaced by a red truck, but the image of the red wagon remains an important part of company lore. In the 1960s, Boyd's opened a chain of retail stores called the Red Wagon Store.[20] The fully restored wagon sits in the lobby at company headquarters today.

P. D. eventually turned the company over to his son, R. P. Boyd. R. P. ran the company until he passed it on to his two sons, David (Katy and Michael's father) and Dick (Matt's father). The brothers retired from day-to-day management in 2010, though they remain co-owners and cochairs of the board.

### A Regional Roaster

In addition to having a much longer history than most Portland roasters, Boyd's also has a larger customer base, specializing in serving higher-volume accounts such as hotels, restaurants, convenience stores, and casinos. Timberline Lodge, the Oregon Zoo, the Old Spaghetti Factory, and Spirit Mountain Casino all serve Boyd's Coffee. Diners like Fuller's (in Portland's Pearl District) and Elmer's (around the western United States) are also representative of a typical Boyd customer. As of 2012, the company sold coffee in twenty-nine states and had plans to continue growing. It recently expanded into the Orlando and Atlanta markets and is looking to increase its presence there.

Boyd's size and flexibility helps the company target a unique market segment. "Our customers are looking for a higher quality of coffee," Matt said. "They're not just chasing price. They want to serve something better than some of the huge national coffee

---

20. David Kobos, cofounder of Kobos Coffee, told me that he first tried "real coffee" at one of Boyd's Red Wagon Stores.

roasters. We're serving the customers that want that specialty-type coffee but not as small as the boutique-type roasters."

Customer service is something Boyd's takes pride in. "The level of service we offer to our customers and the way we take care of them is a huge strength of ours," said Matt. "I've always thought of it as something we do with humility — almost to a fault. We haven't promoted the way we care for the customers, and I think we're doing a better job bringing new customers in to show them the passion we have and make sure they have a good understanding for it."

## Contributions to the Coffee Industry

Boyd's was one of the first companies in the country to loan brewing equipment to its restaurant and food-service customers. Today, it is standard industry practice for a roaster to provide and maintain brewing equipment, but when P. D. started doing it in the early twentieth century, it was a novel idea. "Our great-grandfather was a tinkerer," Katy said. "He'd deliver coffee and see someone throwing their equipment out the back door, and he'd say, 'Can I take that from you?' They'd be like, 'Yeah, take it.' So he'd take it, tinker with it, and make it work again. Then he'd loan it to somebody else. That started the whole equipment loan process."

Over the years, Boyd's also came up with some brewing technology innovations. The company was the first to distribute paper coffee filters to its restaurant customers. According to Katy, the company was also instrumental in the invention of another industry standard, the airpot brewer. "In the eighties, my father [David Boyd] and our equipment guy, Mike Johnson, went over to Holland and worked with a company called Bravilor, a coffee brewer manufacturer. They sat together and sketched out what they wanted, which turned out to be the current airpot brewer. They didn't patent it," she said, with a tinge of regret, "but offered it to the industry as an opportunity to take the coffee off the burner. Prior to the airpot, people might take the coffee off the thermal brewer and pour it into something else, but not often."

More recently, Boyd's equipment team created the Coffee Profiler, a programmable brewer that tailors the brewing parameters to the specific coffee being brewed. The goal was to have a brewer that would consistently brew to the Specialty Coffee Association of America's (SCAA) Golden Cup Award standard.[21] Boyd's wholesale customers can use the Profiler to maintain consistent flavors for their customers. "We can put in the profile for the coffee," said Katy. It includes "how much time the coffee is in contact with the water, what the temperature of that water is. We set the profiles here in Portland with the team. Then we send them out preset into the marketplace."

Wholesale accounts like restaurants and hotels want to give their customers similar flavors year-round, and to achieve this consistency of flavor, Boyd's primarily sells blends. With a blend, the company can substitute different coffees to maintain the same flavor profile. "All our coffees are blended before they get roasted," explained Katy. "We want our customers to buy a certain blend, and they want it to taste a certain way all the time. But since coffee is a fruit, it changes with the seasons. It's not quite as easy as it seems it should be. You think, 'It's just coffee,' but no, there's a science and there's an art in coffee."

"It's all just tasting, evaluating everything, and understanding," explained Michael. "You can taste coffees and understand that this coffee is coming in this way. Next year, the coffees from the same origin for whatever reason are not coming in as well, so what can we supplement into the blend so we can keep a consistent flavor profile year-round? That's really a key piece of it, not being tied to a specific origin with the blends. Things do change a lot, so you're dealing with a lot of different flavor profiles and adjusting them."

## Growing Up in Coffee and Finding a Place There

As one would expect, the current generation of Boyds was exposed to coffee at a young age. "Growing up, we always had an airpot of coffee on the counter," said Katy. Her first job was working at

---

21. The Golden Cup Award standard is a range of brewing parameters that the SCAA has determined a majority of coffee drinkers like. In the United States, these include a brew strength of 1.15–1.35 percent and an extraction percentage of 18–22. Meeting the standard requires careful control of factors such as grind, proportion, water quality, and preparation. For more information, visit SCAA.org.

one of the company's coffee shops. "I feel like I was always here. I think I was about fourteen when I started," she said.

"For me, it started younger than that," Matt said of his interest in coffee. "Just being out at the company, seeing what was going on at a young age. You're a part of what's going on. It's what you know so well."

Even though Katy, Michael, and Matt grew up around the family business, it was not certain they would end up making a career there. In fact, Katy's full-time involvement was almost an accident. "I started here in '93," explained Katy. "I was working with our guru of equipment, doing different things, like CAD drawings. I was kind of an office rover too. I was planning just to come back to work here for the summer out of college and then do something else. Suddenly, married and two kids later, I'm still here after nineteen years."

Michael, on the other hand, was fairly certain he wanted to work at Boyd's, but when he got out of college, he first went to work in the insurance industry in San Francisco. "It was too late for Katy," he said, explaining his career detour, "but when Matt and I were in college, [the company] started a rule where you had to go work outside for a number of years. I think for me, it cemented the fact more that I wanted to come back in with everything — really get into it. It made it my choice to come back." In December of 2004, Michael returned full time with the company.

Matt's story is similar to Michael's. He knew he wanted to work in coffee from a young age. "I got interested in software," he said. "So, like Michael, I went off and did something else for a while, but I always had an interest in coming back and being a part of what the family was doing. Eventually, I found the right time to come back, and here I am."

The Boyds have seen many changes in the coffee industry over their lifetimes. One thing that has changed dramatically about the specialty coffee industry is that customers are much more educated than they used to be. "Back in the eighties when I worked in one of our coffee shops," recalled Katy, "I remember somebody coming in and asking for an espresso. In the mideighties, people didn't really know what espresso was. Today, you can't imagine someone not knowing what an espresso is. It would be hard to find someone who didn't know what a latte was." Katy attributed a large part of the customers' increased knowledge to a certain Seattle-based coffee giant. "People say, 'Don't you hate Starbucks?' Well, not really. They've done a lot of marketing for us," she said.

## A Quick Tour

At the end of my visit, Katy gave me a quick tour of the roasting facility, where it has been located since the early 1970s when the company relocated from downtown Portland. The difference between walking into Boyd's facility and most other Portland roasters is like the difference between walking into the Moda Center (where the Blazers play, previously called the Rose Garden) and into a high school gym. Boyd's roastery is an expansive, multiple-story warehouse that seems to go on and on.

When I visited, the facility was stacked high with different products, from green coffee in large burlap bags to cups, lids, and syrups. A troupe of pickers buzzed around on miniature forklifts, guided by handheld computers to put together pallets of products for shipment. Workers unloaded large burlap coffee bags from a container truck backed up to one of many loading docks. Boyd's brings in coffee by the container load and roasts it in one of its four roasters — two Scolaris and two Probats that each roast about five hundred pounds per batch. Seeing the expanse of the facility, I asked Katy about the company's size, but she was loath to give specifics. She said the company has approximately 350 employees and roasts "several million" pounds of coffee each year. Erik Siemers of *Portland Business Journal* estimates the company above $100 million in annual revenue.

As one of the largest and earliest companies to roast coffee in Oregon, as well as a founding member of the SCAA, Boyd's has provided knowledge, training, and talent to the Portland coffee industry. With such a lengthy history, the company that Percival Dewe Boyd started more than a century ago laid a solid foundation for Portland's specialty coffee industry of today.

# Kobos Coffee
## The Company that Led Portland into the Second Wave

*Kobos Coffee, founded in 1973 by David and Susan Kobos, is one of the older roasters in the Portland area. While Boyd's history overlaps both the first and second waves, Kobos Coffee arrived around the same time that Peet's and Starbucks were serving customers with the emphasis on quality and freshness that marked the start of the second wave. Similarly, Kobos helped raise Portland's coffee standards. Still going strong after four decades, the company has a loyal following around the Pacific Northwest.* — WH

When I visited Kobos Coffee's headquarters, located on the southern edge of Portland's Northwest Industrial district, co-owner Brian Dibble[22] and his son, Kevin, first led me on a tour of the roasting plant. We meandered through a warehouse piled high with large burlap coffee bags and into the main production area. Kobos roasts about forty thousand pounds of coffee each month, primarily on its main roaster, a stout gray Probat that looks like a small locomotive. Some of the coffee is sold in Kobos's two cafés, and the company provides full coffee service for offices and restaurants. Kobos also labels some of its coffee for causes, such as the Best Friend Blend, which supports the Oregon Humane Society. All of Kobos's organic coffees, which make up about 30

---

22. During the tour, Brian shared his own coffee story. About thirty years ago, he started dating the niece of another local roaster and got a job working for her uncle. The courtship didn't last, but Brian's love of coffee and roasting did. He worked for the roaster for about nine years before moving to Kobos in 1989 as a production/roasting manager. From the beginning, Brian and David Kobos hit it off well. The first day Brian worked at the company, David came out to watch him roast one batch, realized he was working with someone who knew what he was doing, and went back to his office, fully confident he had hired the right person. A couple years later, Brian also took over the coffee-buying duties. In 2001, he became co-owner of the company.

percent of company sales, are Fair Trade certified by Fair Trade USA (formerly TransFair USA). Brian told me that contrary to the trend among some of Portland's microroasters, most of Kobos's restaurant customers prefer a darker roast. His theory is that over the past couple decades, the ubiquity of Starbucks' coffee has trained people to expect a darker roast. For better or worse, people want the consistency a darker roast offers.

The tour of the roastery finished, Brian and I walked back to the office to meet David Kobos. As we waited, we discussed some of the things happening in the industry. The first topic to come up was the impact that high green bean prices were having on the business. Coffee prices had recently spiked, and Dibble admitted they made him nervous. "It's one thing if you only have to worry about taking care of yourself," he said. "You can always tighten up your own personal budget. But when you have thirty-one employees, with benefits and things, it adds pressure to be profitable. You care about your people, and you want to do as much as you can for them."

Coffee prices have always been volatile, so this was not a new challenge for the industry. In fact, a price spike these days is not as crippling as it might have once been because customers used to be even more price sensitive than they are today. "Back then," Dibble said, referring to his early days in the industry, "you were up against the mind-set of coffee being cheap, mainly because in the fifties and sixties, even into the seventies, coffee was a loss leader for the grocery stores. I don't know why the trend got started, but it was like that. They perpetuated it for so long that people just expected it. Kobos, CBI [Coffee Bean International], and others had to convince customers there was a difference."

### Enter Mr. Kobos

As Dibble and I chatted, David Kobos arrived. He greeted me warmly, and I asked him to tell me the history of his company. With the gleam in his eye of someone who likes to tell a good story, Kobos enthusiastically recounted it.

Originally from Massachusetts, David Kobos spent many of his years growing up in New York. The pursuit of higher education eventually led him to the Pacific Northwest, where he spent four years earning a master's degree from Reed College. After graduating, he taught in Milwaukie, Oregon, for a couple years. During this time, Kobos used to stop in and get coffee from Boyd's Little Red Wagon Store. "That's how I got started drinking *real* coffee," he said.

After his time in Milwaukie, Kobos moved back to New York, where he found a job as a teacher at a school on the Lower East Side of Manhattan. In his free time, he began exploring restaurants in Chinatown and Little Italy, both near the school. He began visiting the shops of the Lower West Side too, where the Shapiro brothers and the McNulty family were famous for roasting coffee.

At some point during his culinary explorations, Kobos met his future wife and got married. After a honeymoon in the Pacific Northwest, they returned to New York, where they spent time exploring the city's restaurants, becoming foodies long before it was popular. Susan was a good cook, David said, so they began to shop at higher quality markets, trying to duplicate at home what they had been tasting in restaurants. The couple also drank plenty of coffee and visited New York's famous cafés. Kobos recalled some of the smells in the neighborhoods where the stores roasted their own coffee. "There was this one little Italian roaster, down in Little Italy, who used to take one kind of coffee and just burn the hell out of it. You could smell it if you went anywhere near that place," he said, laughing.

## From the Big Apple to the Pacific Northwest

Eventually, Kobos and his wife decided they needed a change of scenery. Remembering the beauty of the Pacific Northwest, they decided to move across the country to Portland, where they would indulge their love of food and coffee by starting a cookware and coffee retail store (and a family). It was a lot of change in a short amount of time, and their friends were skeptical. "'You're doing what?' They thought we were crazy," Kobos said, recalling the reactions of his friends and family. "'You've got a job already. Why would you want to do that?'"

Undeterred, the couple moved forward with their plan, a plan that soon had to be modified. The original idea was to sell Boyd's Coffee in the new store, but when David contacted the company, it turned him down. It was a pivotal moment in the Kobos story. Kobos called a Probat salesman from New Jersey, Gilbert Holmberg, and ordered a roaster from the East Coast. He found a small shop in John's Landing and set the roaster up in the front of the store, where he started roasting his own beans. "That's kind of how it was at the Shapiro brothers' and McNulty's," recalled Kobos. "They had the roasters out in the store."

Kobos said that the early days were nerve-racking times, but he never worried about learning the art of roasting. Bud Dominguez, a former Folgers roaster and father of Don Dominguez, cofounder of Portland's K&F Coffee, gave Kobos a roasting lesson one Saturday morning to get him started. Kobos quickly caught on, and even though his roasting technique may not have been refined, his results were satisfactory. "I never had any doubt that the product I was putting out was vastly superior to almost everything else that I was drinking," he said.

## Fire!

What *did* worry Kobos was that he was roasting coffee in an old, three-story wood building. Roasting coffee requires lots of heat, and there were plenty of things in the store that could catch fire. At this point during the conversation, Dibble got up from his chair and disappeared for a few minutes. He came back with a well-worn blue notebook, Kobos's original roasting log. At a pause in the conversation, he started reading out loud a passage that David Kobos had written in the log many years before, after a particularly exciting day at the store:

> *About 9:10, I discovered that I had let the temperature [in the roaster] get up to 250° Celsius. When I let some coffee out, it burst into flames. I called Ken [the shop clerk] over. By this time the coffee in the roaster had caught fire. Ken opened the door while I sprayed the coffee with $CO_2$. I sprayed more into the chaff collector and thought the fire was out.... Then the chaff collector burst into flames.*

Kobos interjected, "This is right inside the shopping center, that was [built out of] wood."

## Kobos Coffee

Dibble continued:

*I sprayed it with powder. I thought that the fire had maybe gotten into the flu[e], so I called the security guard and went up to the roof to spray some down the flu[e] while Ken called the fire department. The fire department arrived and I was still on the roof. I went back to the store and discovered that the chaff burner had burst into flames again.*

Fortunately, the building was not damaged, but the incident made Kobos even more nervous. He got on the phone again and asked Holmberg, who had sold him the roaster, about installing a fire suppression system. Holmberg informed him that doing so would be cost prohibitive. In what Kobos described as a "mellifluous, stentorian voice,"[23] Holmberg told Kobos that "vigilance, eternal vigilance, is the only way" to be safe.

Holmberg did not leave Kobos completely unprotected, though. About four days later, Kobos received a package in the mail. He opened the package to find a Swedish kitchen witch, a small figurine of a witch on a broom that the Swedes traditionally hang in their kitchens to prevent fires. Kobos hung it up over the roaster, and he did not have any more fires.

On a whim, Kobos decided to sell a few of the witches in his store. They sold like gangbusters. Kobos still marvels at how they resonated with customers. "I kept ordering them and ordering them, and people just kept buying them," he said, laughing heartily as he told the story. "We sold a thousand of them in the run-up to Christmas that year. I couldn't believe it!" Today, the original witch no longer hangs over the roaster, but Kobos does have it in his office as a reminder of some of the memories of the past four decades.

When he first started the business, Kobos thought he would need to sell more than just coffee to survive, so in addition to the coffee beans, Kobos sold tea, spices, and cookware. Julia Child was on TV at that time, popularizing the gourmet food movement, and

---

23. **Mellifluous:** flowing sweetly like honey; **stentorian:** very loud, powerful.

people were flocking to stores to buy new kitchen tools. Kobos and his wife seemed to have a good eye for what customers wanted, so they sold a lot of cookware.

While selling cookware was a part of the original store, selling brewed coffee to customers was not. Like Starbucks in its early years, Kobos used to give customers samples of brewed coffee so they would buy the beans. He said his friends back east kept telling him to sell coffee for customers to drink, but he wouldn't listen. He finally saw the light in the 1980s and bought an espresso machine. He was glad he did because the industry took off in the eighties and nineties, with Starbucks leading the trend.

### Speaking of Starbucks…

Our conversation shifted to how Starbucks had really changed the industry. David Kobos knew Starbucks' history fairly well, as he used to get together to do training sessions with Jerry Baldwin and Zev Siegl, Starbucks' original founders. He is still friends with Siegl today.

When Howard Schultz bought Starbucks, Kobos had a feeling he would be successful. He had met the Starbucks CEO when Schultz was working for Hammarplast selling kitchenware. "Howard Schultz is probably the most charismatic person I have ever met," said Kobos. "You could just sit there and listen to him. He had all these stories. [When Schultz first started to expand the company,] I had so many people telling me he's crazy. 'He just spent a million dollars to build a test store just to train employees! The guy's out of his mind. He's going to lose everybody's money!' Zev Siegel later called me up and said, 'You know there are fifty Starbucks stores now, and there's going to be a hundred in a year?'" Both Kobos and Dibble agreed that Starbucks had been very influential in educating customers and teaching them that it was possible to have better coffee, and more importantly, that it was okay to pay more for better coffee.

After hearing a couple more stories, it was time to for me to let Dibble and Kobos get back to work. They had already been more generous with their time than I'd expected them to be. We wished each other well, and I went on my way, a more complete understanding of Portland's coffee history in hand.

## 6

## The Long, Winding History of Jim and Patty Roberts, Portland's Original Coffee People

*Every place has its own personality, its own quirks. Portland has more of both than most. The city is well known for being a center of counterculture and alternative ideas, so it is not surprising that one of the most famous coffee companies to come out of Portland, Coffee People, was a place known less for its hipness than its hippieness. Like Stumptown today, Coffee People was once a beloved local brand trying to expand nationally. At its high point, the company was poised to provide a national rival to Starbucks, raising funds through an initial public offering (IPO) to increase its presence across the country. Unfortunately, things did not ultimately work out for Coffee People, but the story left behind is worth hearing.*

*To find out more about Coffee People's rise and fall, I met with Jim Roberts, who founded Coffee People with his wife, Patty. Roberts shared the long history of Coffee People and also gave me some insights into some of the challenges associated with trying to grow a company into a national brand.* — WH

Speaking with Jim Roberts, you get the sense he is someone who has seen just about everything during his time in business, having had numerous successes and failures, while managing to keep things in perspective. Jim and Patty Roberts, now married for more than forty years, first started selling coffee in Eugene in 1973. At the time, Jim was attending the University of Oregon, so he and Patty sold coffee at Eugene's Saturday Market to raise money for school. In those days, they bought their coffee from a small company called the Coffee Bean, also located in Eugene. Jeff Ferguson, whom Jim called the "coffee pioneer of Oregon," founded the small coffee roaster. "When Jeff started," recalled Roberts, "he had a little counter, 150 square feet, and a roaster. He stood behind the counter and sold his coffee out of a jar. I loved the coffee, so it was what we bought and sold at Saturday Market."

Over the years, remnants of Coffee Bean Roasters would become the huge Portland roaster Coffee Bean International (CBI). At the time, though, Coffee Bean was just a small company struggling to survive. It expanded from Eugene into the Portland market, but in 1976, the company went through bankruptcy. Seeing an opportunity, Jim and Patty bought Coffee Bean's Portland store, moved to Portland, and changed the name of the store from Coffee Bean to Coffee Man. "The *b-e* was easy to change into an *m* and wouldn't cost us much, so we called it Coffee Man," Jim said.

## The Birth of Coffee People

Jim and Patty eventually sold Coffee Man to a relative and moved to the Oregon Coast. In 1983, the Robertses moved back to Portland and started a new café, Coffee People. Over the next decade and a half, Coffee People would take them on a roller-coaster ride of triumphs and disappointments. The company grew from Jim and Patty selling coffee behind the counter in their lone café to having forty-eight shops in cities across the country — reaching as far east as Chicago and as far south as Phoenix.

Early on, however, this growth did not look likely. In 1985, just two years after starting Coffee People, the Robertses found themselves without any money, credit, or coffee beans. The situation was desperate. "One Monday morning, I saw no reason to open," Roberts recalled. "We didn't have anything to sell, and we couldn't buy any more, so I went to CBI and told [Ferguson] that I was done, that we couldn't do it anymore." When he met with Ferguson, Roberts owed CBI $4,000. Ferguson and his business partner, Gary Talboy, offered to buy Coffee People for $4,400. Lacking a better offer, Roberts accepted. "They owned all of it, for $4,400," he said. As soon as Jim accepted the offer, Ferguson and Talboy offered Roberts a job managing Coffee People.

Jim accepted that offer too, and he and Patty began running Coffee People with the hope they could someday buy back half the company. For five years, the couple ran Coffee People but did not own any of it. "Everyone thought we owned it, but we didn't," said Roberts. "We put our picture on the logo for job security. I figured if our picture was on it, they would have a hard time firing us," Jim said with a chuckle. "They didn't object, so there we were, the public face of this company we didn't own." In 1991, just five years later, Coffee People was valued at $2.6 million. The Robertses made a deal with Ferguson to buy half of it, using the earnings of the company to fund the purchase.

## Expansion and Sale

In the mid-1990s, with the economy looking good and Starbucks rising, Coffee People prepared to expand nationally. "Many people thought that there would be a second to Starbucks somewhere — a Burger King to their McDonald's," said Roberts. To fund the expansion, Coffee People started taking small, private offerings, using the money to build new stores. Roberts said he knew what they were getting into when they accepted the outside investments. "The proposition is simple," he said. "You want to own some of a big company or all of a little company. If you want to see the company meet all its goals, you need that money, but if you lose control, it may not be the same company as before."

In 1996, with sights set even higher, Coffee People held its initial public offering on Nasdaq. The owners sold about half the company for $9 million. Expectations for growth were high, but it quickly became obvious that things were not going as planned. "By the second quarter of '96, we found that our expansion was not succeeding," Roberts said. "We'd opened all of these stores across the US, but they weren't ramping up fast enough. They were losing money, and our opportunity to raise more capital was gone. All we could do was seek a buyer."

Coffee People entered into a reverse merger with Second Cup, the number-one coffee chain in Canada at that time. Second Cup also purchased Gloria Jean's, another American coffee retailer. Second Cup struggled to incorporate its new acquisitions, however, and about a year later sold them to Diedrich Coffee. The California-based Diedrich did not have much success with Coffee People either. Diedrich kept the Coffee People name, but in Roberts's opinion, customers could sense the cafés were no longer run like the original Coffee People. In 1998, Roberts left Coffee People, saying he "no longer recognized the company."

After leaving Coffee People, Roberts took a break from coffee. He moved his family to Texas to go to seminary. Jim was planning to become a minister, but after a short time, he decided ministry was not his calling. Tired of the Lone Star State, the Robertses moved back to Portland and opened a barbecue restaurant. The restaurant was "mortally wounded" after 9/11 and went bankrupt, costing the Robertses everything they had left from the Coffee People days. The family moved to a small apartment in Tigard and tried to start over.

## Back in the Coffee Business

In 2002, the Robertses' noncompete agreement with Diedrich expired, allowing them to get back into the coffee business. In November of that year, Jim and Patty opened up a new shop on Northeast Fremont called Jim & Patty's Coffee. Jim & Patty's carries on many of the traditions that started with the original Coffee People. The café has a familiar feel, with plenty of Portland weird thrown in for good measure. The quirkiness extends itself to the café's famed sour cream coffee cakes, which carry names like the Naughty Supermodel Marionberry and Give PEACH a Chance. "People still see us as Coffee People," said Roberts, "and we basically run it as if it were a Coffee People. Somebody called us a post-hippie phenomenon. We have tie-dye here and there. It's our niche." The whole family is involved in the business. Patty is "the boss," the couple's daughter is the baker, and both of their sons work in the café.

Roberts believes that the café's coffee quality is as good as it has ever been. He attributes this to its relationship with Stumptown, which roasts coffee for Jim & Patty's and also trains the café's baristas. "The quality of coffee today at Jim & Patty's, because of Stumptown, is much better," he said. "We're brewing to much higher standards than we ever did at Coffee People."

In addition to Stumptown coffee, Jim & Patty's sells a coffee from Caravan, a roaster based in Newberg, Oregon, that is a throwback to the 1990s (dark, with an edge to it) as well as the Black

Tiger blend, which was Coffee People's most famous brew. The high-caffeine blend (which includes Robusta beans) is anything but subtle. Roberts said appreciating Black Tiger requires a certain type of palate. "It's like country music or thrasher rock. It's not Mozart, but my customers love it. There's sort of a Black Tiger subculture here that comes in and drinks the tiger because they can't get it anywhere else."[24] The variety of coffee offerings makes Jim & Patty's a blend of second- and third-wave coffee culture.

## Bonding with the Neighborhood through Tragedy

In addition to the ups and downs that the coffee business has brought them, the Robertses have also dealt with some personal difficulties. One of their sons, who was a barista at Jim & Patty's, committed suicide in 2006. The incident really shook the family up, and they planned to close the shop for a while, since no one felt like working. In a show of support, people from the neighborhood came to the Robertses and told them they wanted to run the café for them while they were grieving. "Some of the people came out to our apartment in Tigard and said, 'Jim, we'd like to run the store for you,'" Roberts told me. "They asked for the keys and did their best to run the store. People baked things at home and brought them in, made coffee, and stood behind the counters. They covered the place with flowers." The gesture really cemented the Robertses' commitment to the Beaumont neighborhood, where they now live. "The neighborhood has just treated us like family," he said. "We're in a great spot."

## Lessons Learned

I asked Jim if there were any lessons that had stuck with him from his years at Coffee People. He brought up the challenges of trying to grow the business into a national chain. "It's a battle between

---

24. To get an authentic Coffee People experience, I tried a shot of the Black Tiger. The blend, which includes Robusta beans, is about the earthiest (think peat moss in a cup) coffee I have ever had. Most Portland café owners would cringe at the thought of selling anything with Robusta in it, but not Roberts. "We're kind of outlaws for doing it [selling the Black Tiger], but that's why we're not part of the third wave," he said. "We've always tried to have the attitude to give the customers what they want, so if they want the Black Tiger, we'll give it to them."

the experts and accountants trained at a university, and the instinctual entrepreneurs who understand an area and have insight into what the customers want," he explained. "I'm not saying that the MBAs don't [understand], but Coffee People got invaded by lots of people who knew nothing about the industry."

At one point, Coffee People hired a CEO who had run other very successful food companies. The new CEO made some decisions that seemed counterintuitive to Roberts. One particularly telling episode happened when the company hired a research firm to help determine which cities Coffee People should expand into. "I knew we were in trouble," said Roberts, "when after paying $25,000 for this study, we were told that Portland was number thirty-eight on the list of cities where Coffee People could be successful. Vicksburg, Mississippi, was number thirty-seven on the list. If you've ever been to Vicksburg [a rural town with a metro population of less than fifty thousand], you'd know that there's something wrong with that. I knew that if that was wrong, the whole thing was probably wrong."

Although these kinds of problems eventually led to Coffee People's downfall, Roberts does not foresee the same things happening to Stumptown.[25] He believes that the situations between Coffee People and Stumptown are very different. "Stumptown is a more substantial company than Coffee People ever was. We had a lot more stores, but Duane [Sorenson, Stumptown's founder] is an international coffee leader and has created a revolution in coffee across the country."

## Easing into Retirement

During my interview with him, Roberts announced that it was his last day at the café. "The boss took me off the schedule," he said. "I'm done." Any other plans? "I'm not sure. I'll think of something.

---

25. When the news of Stumptown's equity investment from TSG Consumer Partners broke, there was a fair amount of chatter around the Portland area about what would happen to one of Portland's most beloved coffee roasters. Fans of the company's anticorporate, punk rock ethos and high quality coffee worried that once the new owners got hold of the company, the Stumptown experience would change. Their fears were reasonable, as the interests of fast growth and maintaining quality are often not aligned.

## The Long, Winding History of Jim and Patty Roberts

I've always wanted to start some other little type of business, just for the fun of it. Starting businesses and trying to make them work is what I enjoy doing."

Patty walked by, and I asked her what she thought about Jim's retirement. She said that he would still be around, in one way or another. Jim nodded, knowing it was probably true. With the contented smile of someone who is happy where he is, he said, "I'm going to come down here and just enjoy drinking coffee."

After hearing about his life in coffee, it was hard to imagine Jim Roberts doing anything but welcoming people into his café and sharing a cup of coffee with them.

# Mark Stell
## Sitting Down with Mr. Sustainability

*Historically, the coffee industry has a pretty bad reputation when it comes to how it has treated coffee farmers and their communities. Asymmetries of information (especially about coffee prices) and economic power between coffee buyers and sellers made it all too easy to exploit poor farmers in the rural areas where coffee was grown. Not every company treated farmers poorly, but it wasn't until the 1990s that a movement toward more ethical sourcing picked up steam, with roasters traveling to origin to purchase coffees directly from farmers and cooperatives instead of solely relying on importers to find them. The idea that coffee could support all stakeholders in the supply chain, from growers to baristas, became more popular than it had before. One of the roasters that exemplified this new mind-set was Mark Stell, owner and managing partner of Portland Roasting Coffee.*

*The first time I heard Stell speak was when he visited our sustainability class for the Master's of International Management program at Portland State University. During his lecture, Stell told us how his company was using the triple bottom line — a measurement of business performance that includes economic, social, and environmental criteria — to drive company decisions. He described some of Portland Roasting's development projects such as building wells and other water projects in the communities where the company sources its coffees. He admitted that sometimes his company should focus more on profits but was firm in his belief that environmental and social consequences were just as important. A year later, when I met with him in a conference room at the company headquarters, Stell told the story of why and how he got into the coffee industry.* — WH

In an era when it is trendy to be green, many companies stumble over each other to publicize their environmental credentials. Hundreds of products lining the shelves at various supermarkets claim to be natural, green, or earth friendly. Companies know that consumers expect them to care about the environment. Management teams create corporate social responsibility departments and cobble together a few initiatives to make their companies appear more earth friendly. Sometimes the claims are exaggerated or misleading (what, for example, does *natural* mean?), and sometimes the initiatives are meant to distract from failings in other areas (such as BP's Beyond Petroleum campaign).

Not all companies are just paying lip service to being green, however. Portland Roasting is a company that backs up its green talk with actions. It was *Roast Magazine*'s 2012 Macro Roaster of the Year, praised by the magazine for its commitment to sustainability and ethical sourcing. These values come directly from Mark Stell, Portland Roasting's cofounder and managing partner.

### Inspired to Action

Originally from Wisconsin, Stell was studying marketing at PSU when he had a life-changing experience at the United Nations Earth Summit in Rio de Janeiro in 1992. "I was...a student delegate for Portland State," he said. "While we were there, all of these speakers kept coming up to the stage and telling us how their lives were being affected by global warming. It was a powerful moment. You never want to forget how you feel at times like those."

Attending the summit was a watershed moment in Stell's life, and he decided to act based on his new awareness of issues such as poverty and global warming. When he got back to Portland, Stell looked for a job with a local coffee roaster. He chose to work in coffee for a very specific reason. "Coffee is an industry where you can really make a difference," he said. "It is unique in that it is so far-reaching. There are millions of people involved in its production, and it also covers issues like poverty and equity between developed and developing countries."

When he first started at the coffee company, Stell did not even like coffee, though his distaste for the beverage did not last long. "After six months I was completely hooked. I loved it," he said. After a short stint at the local roaster, Stell decided it was time to move on. He and his business partner, Todd Plummer, started

Abruzzi Coffee Roasters, a roastery and café in Northwest Portland. After a couple years, they sold the business and founded Portland Roasting.

Since its founding in 1996, Portland Roasting has grown by leaps and bounds. As of 2013, the company roasts more than nine hundred thousand pounds of coffee each year. Much of its coffee is sold in cafés, supermarkets, hotels, and universities across the United States. Portland Roasting also sells a substantial amount of coffee in Japan. In the second half of 2011, the company opened its first licensed retail café in the Oregon Convention Center, just a few blocks away from Portland Roasting headquarters. A second shop at the Convention Center followed in early 2012. The company's first branded café opened at the company's roasting facility in September 2013.

## Leading in Sustainability

One of Portland Roasting's accomplishments that Stell is most proud of is receiving the SCAA Sustainability Award in 2005 for the company's Farm-Friendly Direct program. In the program, Portland Roasting pays above-market prices for the coffees it buys, and the premiums are used for community projects such as building schools or water purification facilities in the communities where coffee is grown.

In addition to investing in communities abroad, Portland Roasting has also undertaken several sustainability initiatives closer to home. These include implementing recycling programs, contracting with B-Line (a bicycle delivery service) to deliver its coffees, using biodiesel-powered delivery vehicles, purchasing wind-generated electricity, and contracting with Trees for the Future to plant trees to offset the company's carbon dioxide emissions.

One of the biggest initiatives that employees undertake each year is putting together the annual Walk for Water. The event is overseen by Portland Global Initiatives, a nonprofit that Stell founded to raise money for water-related projects in sub-Saharan Africa. Portland Roasting works in conjunction with a capstone class at PSU to organize and promote the event, which in 2011 raised more than $30,000.

Portland Roasting's commitment to the growers it works with has also paid dividends for the company. When bean prices spiked in 2011, Portland Roasting's long-standing relationships with its growers were an asset. "Some of our growers have been helping us out, charging lower prices than they could have, because we have been good to them over the years," he said. "Most of our growers stayed with us. There was one group who decided they had to go for the money. You hope for loyalty in return for working with someone for a while, but it doesn't always work out. It's sad to see that happen, but I understand why it did."

Stell sees quite a bit of uncertainty in the future of coffee prices. "There's going to be a lot more competition for high quality beans," he predicted. "I see that as being a major challenge. As China comes into the market, it could become harder and harder to get the best beans, so there might be more of a price differentiation between coffees, much like there is between wines. I hope that coffee still remains a beverage that everyone can afford. We'll see what happens."

## START-ing a New Movement

Beyond his duties at Portland Roasting, Stell also sits on the SCAA's sustainability council. He helped spearhead the effort to create the recently released START (Sustainability Tracking and Reporting Tool) application, an online program that helps coffee companies monitor their environmental impact. The START project, which took six years to complete, was undertaken with the United Nations Millennium Development Goals in mind. The program, which costs $150 per year for SCAA members, makes it affordable for companies to monitor their social and environmental impacts so they can improve them. Normally, software to do this would cost a company tens of thousands of dollars. The SCAA hopes that enough companies will sign up to make the program self-sustaining.

START will also help the entire coffee industry understand its overall environmental impact. The data that the program collects will be compiled, allowing the SCAA to release it to the public (without releasing individual companies' data) in order to help companies see where they are in relation to industry benchmarks.

## Mark Stell

One of START's key benefits is that it provides a forum for sharing information about development projects. If a project is too large for a single roaster to undertake, the project can be posted to START so other companies can collaborate. Additionally, START helps coffee-growing communities share their needs with roasters. "If I'm in a community that needs help building a school," Stell said, "I can post it on the site so that companies that are looking for projects can work together. It's creating a community for development."

START also includes a certification system for companies participating in the program. To receive the certification, companies must add a certain amount of data to the START system, demonstrating that they are closely monitoring their carbon footprint and social impact. The SCAA hopes that consumers will gravitate toward companies with the START certification, much as they do with the Fair Trade certification.

### More Than Hot Air

As a company, it is much easier to talk about being green than it is to actually do it, but Portland Roasting is a notable exception. Through a focus on action more than on words, Portland Roasting is making a positive difference in communities where coffee is grown. Led by Mark Stell, the company is getting rid of the greenwash and pushing the coffee industry toward a more sustainable future.

> ### Cupping for the People at Portland Roasting
> If you want to learn more about coffee, one of the things you will eventually do is participate in a coffee cupping, a standardized method of tasting coffee to determine its quality. Cupping has been around for hundreds of years and is integral to the industry. Traders use the method to evaluate coffees and negotiate prices based on perceived quality. Roasters, trainers, and baristas cup coffees to identify and communicate aroma and taste characteristics of the coffees they serve.

## Caffeinated PDX

My first cupping experience took place at Portland Roasting headquarters in Southeast Portland. I saw an advertisement on the company's website inviting people to take part in something called Cupping for the People. Curious, I quickly signed up. The event was led by Nathanael May, Portland Roasting's coffee educator and trainer. Only three of us were there to participate — several people had canceled. It was their loss, as we had a very interesting and tasty morning.

Before cupping, we first took a tour of the roasting facility. The coffee storage area was full of large jute sacks of coffee piled high, each bearing the name of a country or growing region. What caught my eye, though, was a pile of sacks labeled *Swiss Water*. Contrary to my first guess, Swiss Water was not some exotic coffee from northern Europe. Rather, it is the name of the company Portland Roasting contracts to decaffeinate its coffee.

May explained that there are two main methods that can be used for decaffeinating coffee. The first is chemical decaffeination, which usually involves spraying ethyl acetate or some other solvent onto the coffee. The caffeine binds to the solvent, which is then evaporated, taking the caffeine with it. Portland Roasting wants to use as few chemicals in producing its coffee as possible, so the company works exclusively with Swiss Water. Swiss Water uses a patented process that submerges the green coffee in hot water, dissolving the caffeine (and other flavor compounds). The water passes through a special filter that removes 99.9 percent of the caffeine. The water is then circulated back to the beans and then evaporated so that the beans can regain their flavors.

After touring the warehouse and roasting operation, our group headed to the training room for the actual cupping. Nathanael explained the cupping process to us, and we were joined for this part of the tour by several Portland Roasting employees. Originally, the cupping process was designed to help commodity coffee buyers find defects in any green coffee they were considering purchasing. The more defects buyers could find, the lower prices they could negotiate. While cupping is still used to find defects, the method is also used to find the good characteristics of the coffees. There are competitions such as the Cup of Excellence, in which multiple growers' coffees are blindly cupped alongside each other. The best coffees receive the Cup of Excellence designation, and the farmers who grew them receive a premium price.

We cupped four different coffees: an organic coffee from Sumatra, one from Colombia, one from Ethiopia (Yirgacheffe), and Portland Roasting's French roast blend. Each type of coffee was weighed and ground into four glass cups (except for the French roast, which was ground into French presses). The first step in the cupping process is to smell the dry coffee to see what fragrances we could pick up. For each coffee we tried, we gave the cup a small tap to stir up the fragrances and breathed deeply with our noses next to the top of the cup. "If you say that each one just smells like coffee, that's fine," Nathanael explained, "but you will probably notice that there are some differences between the coffees, even if you can't say exactly what."

After smelling the dry coffee, hot water is poured over the grounds in each cup and allowed to sit for four minutes. During this time, the grounds float to the top of the cup, forming a crust. While waiting for the timer to go off, you smell each of the four cups of each coffee again to imprint the aromas on your sensory memory.

The third step is to break the crust on top of the coffee. To break it, you insert about half the spoon into the grounds and gently push forward and pull backward, keeping your nose right next to the cup so you can catch the aromas that have been trapped underneath the crust as they escape into the air. The aromas dissipate quickly, but if you can catch them before they do, you are rewarded with a powerful burst of different smells.

After breaking the crust, Nathanael and Stephanie Backus, Portland Roasting's coffee buyer, who had joined us for the cupping, carefully removed the remaining foam from the top of each cup, readying the coffee for tasting. When the coffee has cooled to where it can be drunk without burning the mouth, you partly fill the spoon with coffee and slurp it up into your mouth, trying to make as much noise as possible. Slurping sprays the coffee across the palate and helps you identify where the coffee flavors hit on your tongue (extra points are given to those who can slurp the loudest). I found this part fun, but it was hard to pick out the subtleties. The Sumatra was supposed to be earthy and spicy, the Colombia nutty, the Ethiopia berry-like, and the French smoky. The earthiness of the Sumatra and the smokiness of the French were the two most obvious flavors for me.

In order to help us better detect the flavors, May had arranged some food pairings for the second round of slurping. Sarah Curtis-Fawley, the owner of Pacific Pie Company, brought four different treats for us to try with the coffee — a beef-and-mushroom pie to bring out the spice and earthiness in the Sumatra, a peanut-butter-and-chocolate pie for the nuttiness of the Colombia, a berry pie for the Yirgacheffe, and a sausage wrapped in pastry dough to emphasize the smoky flavors of the French roast. The food was helpful for picking out the flavors and definitely enhanced the whole cupping experience. I left Portland Roasting that day with a better appreciation for coffees, keeping my eyes open around town for more opportunities to practice cupping.

# 8

# Stumptown and the Seismic Shift

*Artists play to the beat of their own hearts. They see things others don't, and they put forward ideas that make you question your view of the world. They are often polarizing figures because they push the limits of what is considered acceptable. Seth Godin, one of my favorite business philosophers, said you cannot interact with an artist without being affected. If their work does not change you or the world in some way, it's not art. It's only imitation.*

*Duane Sorenson, the founder of Stumptown Coffee, fits the definition of an artist. He was not the first to roast or serve coffee in Portland, but his arrival on the scene changed everything. Stumptown's roasting profiles, its purchasing policies, and its commitment to quality from seed to cup set new industry standards. Stumptown radically changed specialty coffee in Portland, and alongside Intelligentsia and Counter Culture, was one of the most important catalysts behind third-wave coffee in America. Unfortunately, Sorenson did not respond to my multiple interview requests. On the other hand, over the past fifteen years, he has done many interviews and there have been enough articles written about him and his company to put together a robust picture of how Stumptown came to be.* — WH

A storm blew into Portland at the end of the 1990s. His name: Duane Sorenson. His passion: serving people great coffee. His company, Stumptown Coffee, turned out to be the roaster that a new generation of Portland coffee drinkers was waiting for. Combining a rock-and-roll attitude, a passion for sourcing the best green coffees (and, just as importantly, a willingness to pay for them), along with a distinctly lighter roasting style than was popular at the time, Stumptown's 1999 opening of its Division Street café marked the arrival of third-wave coffee in Portland.

## Caffeinated PDX

Sorenson has been called many things throughout his coffee career: the "Benevolent Mr. Bean" who is "both unassuming and larger than life,"[26] "Portland's sustainable drug czar,"[27] and "the messiah,"[28] ready to save people from bad coffee. More than one person I spoke with called Sorenson "enigmatic." In 2012, Sorenson came in at #22 on the Daily Meal's list of America's 30 Most Powerful People in Drink, recognized for how he has impacted the coffee industry. Sorenson, with a large build and the personality to match, is an iconoclast, a revolutionary who advances his ideas through coffee and hospitality. People who have worked with Sorenson for many years describe him as very intelligent, passionate, and gregarious. "Duane's like a big bear," said Phuong Tran, owner of Lava Java, a longtime Stumptown wholesale account. "He loves to give bear hugs. He's so funny. He's got an incredible memory. Things I assume he wouldn't remember, he remembers everything, which is so cool. He's super nice. I really, really like Duane. He's super smart."

Originally from Puyallup, Washington, Sorenson grew up in a working-class family. His mother worked in health care, and his father was a butcher and sausage maker at Bavarian Meats in Seattle. The elder Sorenson played a key role in developing his son's palate, regularly bringing home various sausages to taste as well as the spices and other ingredients that went into making them. He also showed Duane the importance of ethically sourcing quality ingredients. The younger Sorenson began working at a young age, picking strawberries to earn extra money. In his free time, he liked to skateboard and listen to hard rock, occasionally hitching rides to Portland to hang out at the Burnside skate park.

In high school, Sorenson got his first coffee job, working as a barista in a local Puyallup café. According to an interview with the *Oregonian*, Sorenson looked for that first coffee job so he could "get out of the specialty sausage business," as he did not want to work in the cold and wet meat lockers and processing plants. He

---

26. By the News Tribune's E. Murrieta.
27. By Willamette Week's K. Clarke.
28. By New York Magazine's M. Altman.

continued to work coffee jobs when he moved north to attend Seattle University. During Duane's sophomore year, Ed Leebrick, who owned Lighthouse Roasters Fine Coffee, offered Sorenson an apprenticeship as a coffee roaster. Duane accepted, dropping out of college to pursue coffee full time. He stayed at Lighthouse for several years, working his way up to head roaster, according to the *Wall Street Journal*.

After a few years in Seattle, Sorenson moved to San Diego to work as a roaster for Cafe Moto.[29] He did not stay in San Diego for long, at least in part because he wanted to pursue better coffees. "I felt I was held back a bit roasting coffee for other folks, as far as the quality of green coffee and the amount I could pay for coffee," he said in a 2005 interview with Portafilter.net. "I had tasted a lot of coffees out there that just weren't in our budget." Duane decided it was time to step out on his own, and he knew Portland would be the place to do it. He spent all his savings on a five-kilo Probat from Calistoga Roastery (the oldest Probat in North America, built in 1919) and headed back to the Northwest.

Sorenson moved to Portland in April 1998. At the time, the Pearl District was undergoing the transformation from a dilapidated warehouse district into the posh, upscale neighborhood it is today, but Portland's renaissance had not yet spread across the city. Mississippi Avenue and Alberta Street were nearly a decade away from gentrification. East of the Willamette River, Hawthorne, Belmont, and Division Streets had a reputation for leftist politics and affordable living, not as growth centers for new businesses. For Sorenson, though, a former beauty salon on Southeast Division was just the right spot to start a coffee company.[30]

---

29. Coincidentally, around the same time, Peter Giuliano, who would later become famous working for Counter Culture, was also working in San Diego at the time. Sorenson said he did not really hang out with Giuliano because any contact with the competition was discouraged. "That's how it was back in the day. As roasters, we were discouraged to go play with the other coffee companies because of the big secrets — which I'm still looking for," he joked in an interview with Nick Cho of Portafilter.net.

30. The salon was called Hair Bender, which later lent its name to Stumptown's espresso blend.

## Caffeinated PDX

It would be a year and a half before his dream would be ready to go. In the meantime, Sorenson worked as a bartender at the Horse Brass Pub, a long-established watering hole on Southeast Belmont. He spent his free time building out the new café. Sorenson and a friend did much of the work themselves, hiring specialists for things like plumbing and wiring when they needed help. In total, the shop cost about $62,000 to build out, which Sorenson funded with his savings and a loan from his sister. Duane's boss at the Horse Brass, Don Younger — a fabled Portland figure himself — played a key role in Stumptown's beginning. The story goes that after a night of heavy drinking together, Younger loaned Duane the money for the espresso machine, the final piece in the company's coffee toolkit.

On November 1, 1999, Stumptown opened its doors, with Duane working behind the espresso bar. The café made $147 in sales the first day. "I thought I was rolling in it," recalled Sorenson in his interview with Cho. "I was excited about the success of the first day of Stumptown." From that first day, sales and quality improved slowly but surely, and the new company became a hit in Portland.

### Stumptown Culture

Sorenson brought an edgy, rebellious attitude to his company. Stumptown was unapologetic about the quality of its coffee, and people could take it or leave it. Chris Larson, owner of Coffee Division, recalled how the company's attitude resonated with Southeast Portlanders. "Stumptown had the perfect narrative," he said. "It was punk rock. It was homegrown. It was really roots." The first shop's location was so far from anything that it almost dared people to seek it out. "People really loved that rebellious aspect," said Larson, "and Duane hired a lot of people who were musicians and did cool stuff. Half the Thermals worked there. Lots of musicians, lots of artists — it really had that vibe."[31]

Stumptown pushed Sorenson's high-end standards for food (sourcing and preparation) while remembering that coffee appeals

---

31. More Portland coffee trivia: Larson met his wife, Sierra Collom, at Stumptown, where she worked as a manager. The couple later inherited the first Stumptown delivery vehicle, a Ford Pinto, which they used to cruise around town.

to people from all walks of life. In an interview with *Entrepreneur Magazine*, Sorenson hinted at his ideals behind the company: "I want Stumptown to be respected as a specialty item," he said, "but also to be the most inexpensive luxury out there. I want it to be accessible to the most hard-core vegan punk rocker and also at the same time to the most successful entrepreneur for whom money is no object."

Stumptown resembled a big family, especially in the early days, when the company was still small. The crew would work together and play together. Sorenson regularly invited employees over to his house for barbecues. He also took them to concerts. In 2006, he chartered a bus to take employees to Salem to see Slayer, one of his favorite bands. Before he put himself on the payroll, Sorenson made health insurance available to his employees. By treating his workers like family, Sorenson inspired loyalty and reduced employee turnover.

## Bringing Together Sourcing, Roasting, and Preparation

One of the things that made Stumptown stand out was Sorenson's commitment to sourcing. He traveled to origin to meet coffee farmers from around the world. Even in the early days, he was committed to working with growers, learning from them, and investing more money in producing better coffees. He paid them higher prices for their coffees and took extra care when roasting them. Each coffee was unique, and Sorenson tried to bring that out. Stumptown also participated in Cup of Excellence auctions, often paying some of the highest prices ever for selected lots of coffee. In 2007, for example, Stumptown paid $19.20 per pound for a coffee from Colombia, $21.20 per pound for one from Bolivia, and $47.06 for one from Nicaragua, all records. The large numbers sent waves through the industry and made people rethink coffee's value.

Stumptown's roasting style was quite different than what was popular in the Pacific Northwest at the time. Starbucks and its contemporaries had conditioned the region's coffee drinkers to prefer darker roasts. Stumptown's lighter roasting style allowed more complexity to come through in the cup. "There are a lot of different delicate flavors in coffee," Sorenson said in an interview with the *Oregonian*. "And we've been a success by catering to people who really give a damn about a good cup." To bring out those flavors and please the palates of discerning customers, Stumptown lightened the roast. "Duane and I feel that too dark, and all you taste is the roast," said Joel Pollock, the former Stumptown roaster who now owns Panther Coffee in Miami, in the same article. "We roast lighter and go for a sweeter, milder profile with more complexity and nuance."

This was especially true for the company's signature espresso blend, Hair Bender, with flavors of lemon, chocolate, and floral notes that came out in the cup. Hair Bender sold well, and just as significantly, created a new perception of what espresso should be. "Hair Bender changed the taste preferences of an entire generation of coffee drinkers in the Northwest," Hanna Neuschwander, author of *Left Coast Roast*, told me. Much of Stumptown's success can be attributed to sales of the espresso blend.

At the beginning, Sorenson focused on developing his own retail business, but he soon saw the opportunity for Stumptown to grow by selling through other Portland-area cafés and outlets. He hired Jana Oppenheimer, who had helped Starbucks enter many new markets in the West, to oversee the growing company's wholesale program. Oppenheimer spent several years visiting retailers in and around the Portland area, winning people over to Stumptown's new profiles, with much success. "One of the biggest turning points for Stumptown's growth was landing New Seasons as an account," she said. "The sheer volume of that, being in bulk, completely changed the dynamic of being able to purchase [green beans] in full containers," a practice that allowed Stumptown to work with farmers to obtain better coffees.

Stumptown took a hands-on approach with its new customers. Ryan Cross, who worked at Haven Coffee,[32] one of Stumptown's first wholesale accounts, recalled what it was like to work with Sorenson. "When I was at Haven," he said, "Duane was in there

---

32. Haven has since closed. Chris Larson bought the café in 2011 and renamed it Coffee Division.

## Stumptown and the Seismic Shift

almost daily. He'd come in and see how everything was going — always smiling, always in a stellar mood." The crew at Haven always told Sorenson things were going well — even when they weren't, just to keep him happy. "It was Duane," he said, "and we wanted to be sure he was stoked about working with us."

Education was a big piece of the Stumptown business model, and Sorenson believed it was important to share what was happening at origin with the people he sold coffee to. Kevin Fuller, owner of Albina Press, told me about the trip he took with Sorenson to Central America. Sorenson gave the group an up-close look at how Stumptown was changing the business of coffee. "Duane was taking us down to farms and saying, 'This is a farm we do business with. This coffee we're drinking is from El Injerto [one of Stumptown's most well-known growers]. I want you to see this farm.' He's like, 'This is why I do business with these guys. This is what they're doing with the money we're paying for this coffee.'"

Sorenson's goal was to bridge the gap between coffee farms and coffee drinkers. He insisted that growers and processors remove overripe or underripe cherries during production, and then he roasted the green beans in a way that would bring out their best qualities. Every step in the entire coffee supply chain needed to be executed well. "Duane was like, 'We need everybody — the guys that were cupping the coffees, sampling it, farmers we're doing business with — working to make sure all this is happening,'" said Fuller. "Then suddenly, you're creating something that had never been experienced before, and that's what was happening at that time."

Billy Wilson, who also went on the trip with Fuller and Sorenson, recognized the differences that Stumptown's buying practices were making at origin. "It is safe to say that Duane is doing some real good and that we are all indebted to the call of relationship coffee," Wilson wrote in a post on Coffeed.com. "You want third wave? Where is the money for your green coffee going? Lining the pockets of farm owners or the pickers? And how do you know for sure? I have only seen half a dozen farms, but you can really see the difference."

Within a few years, dozens of Portland cafés were selling Stumptown coffees. Stumptown also opened more of its own cafés, including Belmont (2001), Downtown (2003), the Annex (2005), and Stark (2007). The Stark café, located inside the Ace Hotel, made the news when it opened with five Clover brewers — an automated (and very expensive) single-cup brew machine that let baristas quickly prepare any of Stumptown's coffees for customers.[33] Stumptown's growth paved the way for other roasters to enter the Portland market, and many did, spreading better coffee throughout the city.

## Stumptown Expansion Outside PDX

Stumptown's success encouraged Sorenson to expand outside Portland. In 2007, Stumptown opened a roastery and its first café in Seattle. In 2009, it opened a roastery in the Red Hook neighborhood of Brooklyn, New York. The location became the base for Stumptown's East Coast operations. New Yorkers undoubtedly rolled their eyes when *New York Magazine* called Sorenson the "messiah" coming to save them from bad coffee, but that did not keep Gotham's residents from flocking to Stumptown's cafés. The expansion to New York gave Stumptown a national influence, and today, Stumptown has hundreds of wholesale accounts on the East Coast.

Sorenson has also mentioned the goal of expanding to Europe, which he did briefly in 2011, when Stumptown opened a pop-up café in Amsterdam for a couple months. Stumptown rented a large house for the fifteen baristas who made the trip, who, in addition to sharing coffee with the locals, were also able to explore the city, another example of how Stumptown has provided a family-like atmosphere for its employees.

Expanding outside Portland allows Sorenson to give the rest of the world a taste of the city he loves. "People say, 'Man, you're not local anymore. You're selling coffee in New York,'" Duane said in a keynote address for Hello Etsy PDX. "Well, I'm sharing Portland. People travel, to do what they like to do, to lie on a beach or surf. I, unfortunately, just make coffee. So I travel to New York, I travel

---

33. When Starbucks bought Clover, Stumptown quickly got rid of the machines because it did not want to have to buy parts or service from Starbucks.

to Amsterdam to make people coffee, and I bring as many baristas as I can. It's probably not the best business model, but I've been able to wing it, and the lights are still on."

## The TSG Investment

Stumptown's growing reputation brought new opportunities, including the chance to bring investors in to help fund the company. In 2011, in an essay for *Esquire* titled, "The End of Stumptown, America's Hippest Coffee Brand," Todd Carmichael, owner of La Colombe Coffee Roasters, a Philadelphia-based coffee company, broke the news that Sorenson had sold Stumptown to TSG Consumer Partners, a private equity firm from San Francisco. Portland's *Willamette Week* soon confirmed the story, and a brouhaha ensued, especially in Portland. The rebellious image of Stumptown's national brand set the company up for criticism. How could it be that Stumptown was selling out?

Stumptown employees were taken by surprise, and they had no response for people asking about what happened. The company lacked a public relations department to respond, and since negotiations had been secret (as is usually the case in these situations), no one knew exactly what was going on. Sorenson sent out a companywide memo several days later, reassuring employees that "Stumptown has found an investor to help us offer opportunities and take care of our employees, farmers and customers like we've never been able to do before." Sorenson also said he would continue to run Stumptown.

The story created quite a stir in Portland, but other than the leaked memo, Duane was notably quiet. Sarah Allen, editor of *Barista Magazine*, remembers the uproar. "Portland people were up in arms — is Duane selling out?" she told me. "Well, he wasn't. He was protecting his company and building a bridge to the next phase." Allen believed there was a double standard in the criticism directed at Stumptown. "Interestingly, it was like two weeks later when Doug Zell [of Intelligentsia] got an extra CEO, and no one said anything about that," she said. "I don't know. Maybe it's because Intelligentsia has a more corporate feel than Stumptown that people were willing to bash Stumptown more."

## Caffeinated PDX

A few months later, Sorenson did open up more about the sale. In a discussion forum held by Hello Etsy PDX at the Pacific Northwest College of Art, Duane said bringing on an investor was a positive and necessary step. He told the audience that Stumptown took on investors "because the bank wouldn't loan me or give me any money that I was begging for, and there's a lot more things I would like to do with Stumptown, for our coffee farmers and for our employees, and I didn't have the dough to do it." Banks, fearful of a slowing economy, had tightened their lending standards, and Stumptown needed a stable way to finance its growth. "I was approached with an opportunity to take some of the financial burden and debt that I've had off of my shoulders," said Sorenson in an interview with the *Oregonian*'s Michael Russell. "We wouldn't have been able to [grow] without bringing on this investor."

Sorenson dismissed the idea that he somehow sold out his company. "I guess my skin has become thicker as we've grown over the last twelve years," he said in his address at the Pacific Northwest College of Art. "Folks are quick to say, 'You're too big, you're huge, you've sold out,' but whatever. I'm in the business to sell coffee and to try to have my coffee taste super-duper, that you buy it every single day because I'm looking to buy the best coffee, and that takes money."

Stumptown lost a few wholesale accounts shortly after the sale, but a couple years after the sale, the company seems to be doing as well as it ever has. Long lines still form in Stumptown's Portland cafés every day. The company was able to consolidate its headquarters and roasting facilities into a large building in Southeast Portland, streamlining operations. It began bottling cold brew coffee and selling what it called stubbies in its cafés and other outlets. Company employees tell me they now have better health and benefits packages. The investment expanded the reach of Stumptown's buyers, who can now bring in more quality coffees from more farmers than ever before. Stumptown hired a new president, Joth Ricci, a longtime beverage industry executive, to help run the company. As of 2013, the company was continuing to grow, with a roastery and café on track to open in Los Angeles in the fall. Chicago is likely to be next.

## Stumptown and the Seismic Shift

For some employees, the new structure improved their lives. "This might sound weird," said Skip Colombo, senior account manager for the company, "but I feel like I have more of a sense of security, in the sense that things are in order and I'm getting to learn and understand the business side of things more. Whereas it used to be, 'Just go out there and do it and learn on the fly and make mistakes,' I have more structure now. Things are more clearly defined."

From a broader perspective, Stumptown's investors represent an example of the company leading the industry again. Other companies have since followed Stumptown's lead by taking on investors. Blue Bottle, James Freeman's San Francisco–based roaster, received $20 million in 2012 to fund its expansion. In 2013, Philz Coffee, also from San Francisco, raised a reported $15 to $25 million in a conjunction with Summit Partners, according to *Tech Crunch*. "The private equity investment that Stumptown got has changed the conversation to like, 'Wow, this is a real, grown-up business model,' which has got people thinking a little bit differently about [specialty coffee]," said Hanna Neuschwander.

### Opening Doors for Others

Since the sale, Sorenson has been able to explore his other culinary interests. He opened four new eateries — the Woodsman Tavern, a high-end American eatery with a menu based on local, seasonal ingredients; Trigger, a Tex-Mex restaurant; Ava Gene's, an Italian restaurant; and Roman Candle, an Italian-style bakery — causing some to question if Duane's heart is still in coffee. In a 2012 interview with the *Oregonian*, Sorenson maintained that his duties have not changed at Stumptown, and talking with people close to the company, it sounds like he is still very involved in the decision making. Perhaps most importantly, Stumptown is still focused on bringing in the best coffees and paying farmers more money for them.

No matter what happens with Stumptown in the future, the company and its famous founder have left an indelible mark on the specialty coffee industry, both in Portland and across the country. "I would say all of us microroasters in the country right now have some credit to give to Duane," said Andrea Spella, owner of Spella Caffè. "He stuck very strongly to his ideologies of his roast profiles and his relationship coffees, things like that. Now we're all around, and we can have our own interpretations. People are more open to trying what everyone is doing."

Without Sorenson's bold stance on how coffee should be sourced, roasted, and prepared, Portland's coffee scene would most likely be a sleepy Seattle knockoff, racing to catch up with other coffee centers, instead of an industry leader.

### Visiting Lighthouse

To get a little better understanding of Sorenson's past, I visited Lighthouse Roasters, in Seattle's Fremont neighborhood. Visiting Lighthouse was a type of pilgrimage (minus the religious connotations) to one of the headwaters of Portland's specialty coffee industry. Lighthouse is where Stumptown's Duane Sorenson learned to roast, under the tutelage of Ed Leebrick. Visiting Lighthouse was a chance to see the environment in which Sorenson forged his coffee skills.

Hopping off the bus at the corner of North 43rd Street and Phinney Avenue North, I first noticed how quiet the neighborhood was. Single-family houses and small apartment buildings lined the streets. Few cars passed by. Had it not been on such a large hill, the neighborhood could have been Southeast Portland.

Inside, Lighthouse's décor was simple. The linoleum was a sage and pale green-gray, durable and functional. The wooden tables were sturdy but plain. A short partition separated the back third of the shop, carving out the roasting area from the seating area. The other side of the low wall was crowded with jute bags of green coffee and stacks of large plastic tubs for roasted beans. Most prominently, a Gothot roasting machine whirred loudly, its gas burner rumbling while beans swished and swashed around inside the drum. From time to time, the roaster opened the door, and dark-brown coffee beans cascaded onto the cooling table, crackling and popping vigorously.

Unlike the neighborhood, the interior of the café was loud and boisterous. In addition to the noise from the roaster, customers contributed a lot of energy. Several people sat around the coffee bar on round stools, talking to the roaster and to the baristas. The majority of people who came in were actually there to converse instead of sitting in front of a laptop, as is so commonplace these days. Since I already stood out as a stranger, I left mine in my backpack and jotted down a few notes on paper.

Sitting at my table, I couldn't help but think of the similarities between Lighthouse and Stumptown's first café. Between the quiet residential neighborhoods, the simple furnishings, the lively atmospheres (Stumptown attracts a lot of Laptopistanis with earphones but makes up for their silence with loud music), and the roasting machines sitting at the front of both cafés, you could see many parallels between the two shops. I felt like I had gained a small insight into Stumptown's origins.

Then I tried my espresso.

For the record, I do not consider Stumptown's Hair Bender to be a delicate espresso. Its lemony brightness and chocolaty finish were made to stand out in milk drinks, something it does well. On its own, Hair Bender has a complex taste profile that takes time to get used to.

However, Hair Bender is almost fragile compared to the Lighthouse espresso. Dark roasted, with a rough, gritty finish, the Lighthouse espresso wanted to force my taste buds into submission instead of befriending them. The profile obviously plays well in that part of Seattle — the traffic in and out the door remained steady throughout my visit — but to my coddled Portland palate, the Lighthouse espresso was almost too harsh to drink. Nonetheless, I'm sure it is something you could get used to if you drank it every day.

**Caffeinated PDX**

My trip to Lighthouse was very informative. These days, as Stumptown grows and changes, the two companies have less in common, but it appears they were very similar at one point. With families, descendants never turn out exactly like their ancestors, but they often share a lot of the same traits. Coffee companies, apparently, can be the same way.

# 9

# Fresh Pot
## A Skip Down Memory Lane

*Skip Colombo, senior account manager at Stumptown, has played a big role in the development of third-wave coffee in Portland. He and his college buddy, Matthew "Vin" Vinci, founded Fresh Pot, one of Stumptown's earliest wholesale accounts. After selling his stake in Fresh Pot, Colombo started working at Stumptown Coffee, where he has mentored hundreds of people in coffee, spreading the knowledge and passion that is fostering the growth of the third wave across the country. — WH*

Skip Colombo's coffee history can be traced back to the early 1990s, when he met his future business partner, Matthew Vinci, during their freshman year at Michigan State University. Both worked at a small café just off campus called Espresso Royale, a small Midwest-based chain inspired by San Francisco's Caffé Roma and Caffe Trieste. "It was an amazing environment," Colombo recalled. "They stressed education and also technical skills — way ahead of the curve."

Skip and Vin worked at Espresso Royale the entire time they were in college. "We used to joke all the time, like, 'We could do this. We could have our own shop.'" After graduation, they saved their money and spent three months traveling around the United States. "I had never really seen anything outside of Michigan other than spring break trips to Florida with the family," Skip said. "This was my first opportunity to be west of the Mississippi." Their trip took them to the Pacific Northwest. "The first time I ever set foot in Oregon was in mid-July," he said, "and I was like, 'How is it that everybody in the country doesn't live here? This place is incredible.'" Portland left an impression on both, and Colombo recalls that they both thought they would return someday. Vin went first, moving to Portland a few months later.

Colombo stayed in Michigan, but less than a year later, Vin drove back to Michigan to a mutual friend's wedding. "He basically pulled me aside and told me I was an idiot for staying in metro Detroit." Vinci's speech convinced Skip to leave. "I quit my job right then and there, packed up my car, and drove back out with him and all my belongings, and I've been living here [ever since]."

## Fresh Pot

In Portland, the friends' earlier premonition about running their own coffee shop would come true, though it did not happen right away. When Skip arrived, Vinci was working for Scott Hartwich, who owned a coffee cart in Lake Oswego, supplying it with beans he roasted in his garage. When Powell's Books on Hawthorne leased out a space for a café, Hartwich got the bid, built it out, and called it Novel Java. Vinci went to work as the only employee at the new café, just a few blocks from his house.

In 1997, within a year of Colombo's arrival, Hartwich decided to sell his shop. Colombo said, "I'll never forget the day Vin came to me and was like, 'Well, we've got to each put twenty-five grand down, and we can buy this coffee shop, and I think it's a great idea.'" Twenty-five thousand was a lot of money for both Colombo and Vinci. "I think I had fifty bucks at that time," Skip said. "I called my dad, gave him the whole pitch, and he basically said, 'I'll tell you what. I'll give you half of the money you put down, pull it out of my retirement, if Mr. Vinci — Vin's dad — puts in the other half.' So Vin went to his dad and was of course like, 'Well, Mr. Colombo said that he'd be willing to put in half if you could.' So Vin's dad agreed and pulled money out of his retirement. They gave us the down payment, and Fresh Pot started."

After securing funding, it was time to get to work paying off the loans. "We worked seven days a week for two and a half years," Skip said. To make the rent and the loan payments, they eliminated all extra expenses. "It was like the Wild West in the early days," Colombo remembered. "Neither of us had a car. We each worked six shifts a week — for a while, seven. We finally got one of our buddies to work one day so we could each have a day off. We got a little red wagon, and we'd lash it to our bike because we

# Fresh Pot

couldn't afford a trailer, and we'd bike to Trader Joe's to get cups and soda and straws, take the towels home and do the bleaching in the washing machine because we couldn't afford a linen service — we basically ran as tight as you could possibly run." The new business survived.

## Meeting Duane Sorenson

When Skip and Vin first started running Fresh Pot, they continued to serve Novel Java coffee in the café, but they soon decided to get their coffees elsewhere. They tried a variety of different roasters. "At one point, we had shade-grown organic coffee from nuns. Longbottom actually helped us out a lot. They were one of the few companies where we actually had an account."

In those days, Fresh Pot's options for where to get the coffee were limited. "Everything was in its infancy," he said. "You know what I mean? Intelligentsia wasn't a national brand. Counter Culture wasn't a national brand. Up in Seattle, there were some pivotal people, like David Schomer. But in terms of wholesaling outside of your immediate area, it really didn't exist unless you were a huge company. And if you were a huge company, your coffee probably wasn't worth shit at that point."

About three years after Fresh Pot opened, a new roaster in town caught Colombo's attention. It was called Stumptown. "I had heard about Duane from my buddies at Jackpot Records, who were like, 'You know what, you've really got to go over to Division and check this guy out. He's roasting his own coffee. It's really damn good.'" Colombo wasn't buying the hype. "I was skeptical. I was like, 'Yeah, whatever,'" he said.

Eventually their paths did cross, when Sorenson showed up at Fresh Pot. "We kept hearing about each other, and one day, he walked in through the door," Colombo said. "I'll never forget it. He got some espresso and was really complimentary in terms of the space. He's like, 'I love your business. I love what you guys do — the vibe, the energy. Your coffee sucks, but I can help you with that.'"

Colombo was taken aback. "Of course, I'm a prideful small business owner," he said. "I'm thinking, 'Who is this clown?'

And then he started to talk about what he was doing and what his vision was." After a five-minute conversation, Sorenson won Colombo over. Skip agreed to visit him at the Division café. When he did, he found Sorenson running the bar, working the register, and pulling shots in addition to roasting in the afternoons. "I remember he went and ripped a couple shots, and we sat down at the bar right by the roaster and drank some espresso, and it blew my mind," Skip said. "I had been doing coffee since I was eighteen years old — at that point, six or seven years — and it was like I had coffee for the first time in my life."

Hyperbole, perhaps? Not according to Colombo. "It had that dramatic an effect — expertly poured, handcrafted on a beautiful piece of equipment," he said. "Incredible. I mean it was just beautiful. It was all of those things that come out of an incredibly well-crafted espresso shot. I was out of my mind. We shook on it right there. I jumped on my bike, biked over to Fresh Pot, went up to Vin, and was like, 'We're switching. We're going to carry Stumptown, and we're never looking back.'"

## Expansion into North Portland

As Fresh Pot's reputation grew, opportunities for expansion came to Vinci and Colombo. One of Fresh Pot's customers, Shane Endicott, who founded the ReBuilding Center (Colombo called Endicott the "forefather of the modern-day Mississippi Avenue"), came to the café one day and tried to get Vinci and Colombo to open up a café in the former Rexall Drug at the corner of Mississippi and Shaver. "He approached us, introduced himself, was like, 'I really want to show you this space,'" Skip said. "'If you can do what you've done here with that space over there, it would be incredible for the neighborhood.'"

Skip and Vin were unsure about the proposition, especially because of where it was located. "Living here and being in Southeast — especially back in the day — it was like, North Portland? Mississippi Avenue? I might as well have been in the state of Washington," Skip said. The neighborhood was far from being the trendy place it is today. "There were prostitutes on the corner. It had been the red-light district of Portland for a long time."

## Fresh Pot

Endicott promised to help with several improvements to the building, and the Portland Development Commission would contribute too. Soon, the two ambitious coffee entrepreneurs had another project. "We were in there, ripping out asbestos, so many nights," Colombo recalled. "Late nights in there just doing crazy shit that we were not qualified to do. Every night, we'd go past the same drug dealers and prostitutes. The first days, sweeping out empty Thunderbird bottles and syringes. There had been people squatting in the space and in the basement that had to get ushered out. It was gnarly, and it was scary."

Duane Sorenson also invested in the new venture, with equipment and other support. "To this day, we owe him a pretty big debt of gratitude for that," Skip said. "I don't know many coffee roasters or small business owners at that point who would be willing to do that for one of their customers."

The new café, opening in 2002, got off to an inauspicious start. Before they had been open two months, Fresh Pot had a drive-by shooting in the middle of the afternoon, an unsettling welcome to the neighborhood. Shortly after the shooting, one of Fresh Pot's regulars showed up at the café in his police uniform, representing the Portland Police Department's Gang Enforcement Team. He sat Skip and Vin down and explained what was going on. "He said, 'I'm really excited for you guys to come into this neighborhood. I'm incredibly happy for you, but here's the lay of the land,'" Skip said. The man told them that Shaver was the dividing line between the biggest rival gangs in the entire city. "Basically, we opened a coffee shop on the front lines, without having any idea," Skip said.

Despite Fresh Pot's rough start at the new location, its presence as an anchor café in the neighborhood helped Mississippi rejuvenate itself. "I never in my life dreamed I would see such a vibrant business district, and it's still one of the funnest neighborhoods in this town," Skip said proudly. The people who live near Mississippi appreciate what Fresh Pot has done for the area. "There's people in the neighborhood to this day that come in there and say, 'Hey, I used to sit at this counter [at the drug store's soda fountain] when I was six years old and get soda and ice cream floats.' That type of history means something."

## Caffeinated PDX

### Transition Out of Fresh Pot and into Stumptown

For several years, Vinci and Colombo successfully ran both Fresh Pot cafés, but they began to have different ideas about how to run the business. "We were up to eighteen or nineteen employees, and I'll be honest with you, it was easier when it was just the two of us," Skip said. Around the same time, Stumptown's wholesale program was growing rapidly, and the company was looking for qualified people to come in and help it grow further. One of the people they called was Colombo.

Colombo and Vinci realized it was time to part ways, although it was hard to let go. "It's like a child that you've brought up from infancy," Colombo said. Skip sold his interest in the business to Vinci, who continues to own and operate it. "It was every moment of every day of my life for a decade, but we were able to work out, probably in the history of selling businesses, the most amicable arrangement you could ever imagine," Skip recalled. "I think we talked to a lawyer for five minutes, our accountant for twenty minutes, and within a week, we were signing papers."

After the sale, Skip took some time off to decompress. Unable to relax for more than a couple months, he called Matt Lounsbury, Stumptown's general manager, to discuss working for Stumptown. Lounsbury said they had already filled the earlier position, but Sorenson called back a few weeks later and asked Colombo to come on board. Colombo started working at Stumptown at the beginning of 2008.

Colombo said his true coffee education started when he got to Stumptown. "All the years I'd been in coffee, from basically the time I was eighteen to the time I was thirty-four, I learned more in the first six months I was at Stumptown than I had in the entire duration before that." He spent time with Sorenson and Lounsbury and also Steve Kirbach, Stumptown's head roaster; Jim Kelso, head of quality control; and Aleco Chigounis, the company's main green coffee buyer. "I was just so incredibly lucky to be amidst some of the best in the industry in their respective positions and all in one room," Skip said. Chigounis made a point to help Colombo with the transition. "Aleco literally taught me how to cup, from the ground up. He would bring me into the lab, and he saw that I was excited but I had a gap and I needed to learn. He would roll out triangulation cuppings, then we moved into delta cuppings, and he just kept pushing and pushing. I owe him a huge debt of gratitude."

In early 2008, Stumptown's Seattle roastery was just opening, and New York City was still a year away. "I came in at one of the craziest and most dynamic times in the company, where we went from this successful punk rock Portland company to multimarket, multicity," he said. The move into New York and the East Coast was somewhat chaotic, but it gave Stumptown a national influence. "It was a wild and wooly time, but it was also incredible fun."

As of 2013, Stumptown has hundreds of accounts on the East Coast. "It's one of the most densely populated areas in the entire country," Skip said. "The New York business is growing exponentially. For as much as we were big with the coffee industry and respected within the industry and the state of Oregon and city of Portland, New York gave us a national presence. That really allowed us to get the national recognition and sort of propel us to where things are now."

## Changes at Stumptown with the TSG Investment

Stumptown's rapid growth and national recognition attracted the attention of TSG Consumer Partners, a private equity firm headquartered in San Francisco. In 2011, Sorenson sold an undisclosed percentage of his company to TSG. When the word of the sale leaked out, many of Portland's loyal Stumptown drinkers felt betrayed. Colombo heard plenty of strong words from his customers. "It was hard, and we didn't get in front of it, you know what I mean? Everybody wishes it had worked out in a little different way, that we could have controlled that message a little bit more. To this day, I get comments that are like, 'How is it now that Starbucks owns you?' and they're dead serious. And these are industry people!"

Since the TSG sale, the biggest thing that Colombo has noticed is that the company runs more like a business than it did before. He laughed as he said that. "I mean that in a very positive way. Stumptown's always been a mom-and-pop sort of business, and

Duane's an amazing visionary in terms of concepts and things like that, but as you grow — just like any business — if you are not tight with things and are a little bit wasteful, the more you grow, the more that waste magnifies. So, frankly, most everybody within the company was happy to see a little more structure."

The sale also made it possible for Stumptown to build its new headquarters on Southeast Salmon Street in Portland. "We're not in the facility we're in right now, with all the amazing things we have in there, without that investment," Colombo said. Fortuitously, the move took place in mid-August 2012, giving the Stumptown crew a few months to get accustomed to its new digs before Superstorm Sandy hit New York two months later. The storm flooded Stumptown's Brooklyn roastery that served all the East Coast accounts. "We hadn't even cleared the dust out [of the new headquarters], and we went from zero to a hundred," Skip said. To keep things running, Stumptown put on extra roasting shifts at the Portland facility, absorbing all of the roasting and customer service for New York.

### Next?

Colombo said things were returning to normal as of May 2013. "Right now is the first time since we started that we've been able to breathe a little sigh of relief and just get a little comfortable in our space," he said. "Granted, LA is going to happen, but we've definitely learned from the past, so, knock on wood, it will probably be the most professional and smoothest transition to a fully functional roastery that we've ever had."

As Stumptown continues to expand, Portland's reputation for specialty coffee will grow as well. Without making predictions about the future, Colombo is optimistic. "It's going to be a very exciting few years for the coffee industry," he said. "That's all I see right now."

# 10

# Phuong Tran
## The Godmother of Portland's Third Wave

*On the way to volunteer at the 2011 NWRBC in Tacoma, Brandon Arends wanted to grab some coffee on the way out of town. Instead of stopping at a café in Portland, as I would have expected, we drove north on I-5 for twenty minutes before pulling off at a small shopping center along the side of the freeway near Ridgefield, Washington. Having grown comfortable in my urban surroundings, I was a bit skeptical about getting good coffee at a strip mall in the middle of nowhere. There didn't seem to be much of anything nearby — no houses (unless you count the RV park that you could see in the distance), only a few stores, and zero foot traffic. My previous experiences with similar out-of-the-way shops had rarely been good, and sometimes were disastrous, so I was less than enthusiastic.*

*As we parked in front of the Lava Java sign, Brandon casually mentioned that the owner of the café, Phuong Tran, won the 2005 US Barista Championship. I should have known better than to doubt my guide.*[34] *— WH*

Phuong Tran is the type of person you would like to sit down with for a cup of coffee. The 2005 United States Barista Champion smiles easily, and she has an agreeable, outsized personality that radiates from her petite frame. When it comes to coffee, Phuong is as knowledgeable as anyone. She has an intense desire for quality that stands out, even in the coffee-crowded Northwest. Tran's small shop, Lava Java, a few miles north of Portland in Ridgefield, Washington, has had an oversized impact on the region's coffee scene. The Lava Java family tree is

---

34. This chapter is based on my initial meeting with Tran and subsequent interactions, including a sit-down interview that took place in early 2013.

as full of well-known baristas and coffee professionals as any in Portland.[35]

Phuong's history begins far from Portland. She was born in South Vietnam in the early 1970s. Her father was killed during the Vietnam War, and in 1979, her family left Vietnam for a refugee camp on a small island in Indonesia. A year later, Phuong's mother and siblings moved to Florida to live near Phuong's great-grandmother, a naturalized American citizen. After working for several months in Florida, Phuong's mother found a better job at a chip factory in Beaverton, Oregon, so the family packed up and headed for the Pacific Northwest.

Tran spent the rest of her formative years in Beaverton. She studied information technology in college and worked in technical and management positions after graduation. In 2002, growing tired of her job, Phuong wanted to start a business of her own. When she met with a developer to discuss leasing space for a boutique in a small commercial center in Ridgefield, he suggested she buy a café he owned instead of starting something from scratch. "I had no prior experience," Phuong told me. "I just thought, 'Hey, I like coffee. I can manage a coffee shop.'" She purchased the café but didn't shake things up too much, at least at first. Phuong kept all of the previous staff and set about trying to figure out how to make the café better.

## Phuong and Billy

In one of the most fortuitous coincidences in the history of third-wave coffee, Phuong's staff included a young barista named Billy Wilson, who had been hired about a month before she bought the business. Wilson and his new boss were both the type of people to throw themselves into whatever they were doing. "I would say that Billy and I — because we ended up having the same passion and same desire to learn about espresso and making coffee — that it was a really good team effort," Phuong said. "I had somebody working here that was into the coffee as much as I was into it. We would trade ideas about what we'd picked up."

---

35. Billy Wilson, Ryan Willbur, Jenny Dorsey, Matt Brown, Charlotte Deason, Cam Kellett, and Ashley Rauch were (or still are) members of the Lava Java family.

## Phuong Tran

In addition to keeping the same staff, Phuong also kept the same coffee, from Coffee Bean International (CBI). She called CBI to introduce herself as the new owner and asked them to come train her. CBI sent Jessica Rice to the café to train Tran, Wilson, and the rest of the staff. "We were asking all kinds of questions, and she was super nice," Phuong said. "She was the one that suggested we consider competing."

The group learned a lot in a short amount of time. "We were learning so fast and absorbing everything — I felt like I was just a sponge," Phuong said. "It was this whole new world of coffee I never knew about." Tran said she was fascinated with coffee, in the same way a child gets excited when learning something new. "I spent all my time trying to find as much information as possible and visiting other cafés." While researching, she started attending industry trade shows. "Those are the things that first started to get me really interested in doing it right," she said. "And then I saw a barista competition and was like, 'Oh my gosh, that's how we should do it!'"

Phuong decided that the barista competition standards would form the backbone of Lava Java's training program. She and Wilson studied the rule book and put together a training program that adhered to the standards of the Specialty Coffee Association of America (SCAA). Wilson became the first Lava Java barista to compete in a regional competition.

At first, Tran left the competing up to her staff. She was still working at her full-time job, coming to the café before and after work, and didn't have time to prepare for the competitions. But she did not stay on the sidelines for long. "It was getting to the point where the baristas were like, 'You haven't competed, so how can you train me?'" she said. "I felt like I should just do it. You can't teach somebody something you haven't done, so I started competing too."

Phuong quickly found success. In 2004, she made it to the US Barista Championships (USBC) and finished second. The next year, she won the USBC and finished seventh overall at the World Barista Championship, missing the finals by only half a point. Phuong would never have to worry about her coffee credibility again.

## Switch to Stumptown

Competing gave Phuong a whole new appreciation for the coffees they were serving in the café. "Once you start learning about coffee," she said, "you start asking questions like, when was this roasted? We went to CBI and checked out the roastery. They were really nice people, but we were asking way too many questions and trying to find out too much. CBI was roasting bigger batches and coding the roast dates on the packages. It was very difficult to get that information back then.

"We learned so much, and then we went back home, and Billy and I discussed how we needed better coffee and we needed a better machine," she recalled. "We did a whole bunch of tastings and checked everything out from Seattle to Portland. When we cupped with Duane [Sorenson] — Stumptown was still small enough that he was still cupping — me and Billy and Jana Oppenheimer, we sat down and we cupped and we talked and I was like, 'This coffee is so amazing! It is so good! I love this coffee!'"

Before Stumptown agreed to bring Lava Java on as a wholesale account, Phuong would have to make some changes at the café. Stumptown wanted to be confident their accounts could take good care of the company's coffees, so each café had to have quality equipment. Tran bought a new La Marzocco espresso machine and soon thereafter, Lava Java began serving Stumptown coffee.

## Success in the Hinterlands of Ridgefield

At a quick glance, Lava Java's Ridgefield venue seems like a tough location for a café. In a strip mall located next to a freeway, Lava Java has zero foot traffic, the lifeblood of most retail businesses. Regardless, customers come to the café from several nearby towns, including Ridgefield, La Center, and Woodland. "Everybody drives here," Phuong said. "Driving is not a big deal for people because they choose to live out here."

Lava Java also gets a lot of customers from Vancouver and Portland who are traveling north to Seattle or Olympia and stop in at the café. "Once people know we're here, they make it a point to stop by all the time. There aren't really many good cafés around here. It's such a good location because it's right at the junction. You can get off I-5, take the exit, and we're right here. Then they can get right back on the freeway." Phuong's reputation as a barista champion brings in customers from around the world. "Even here in Ridgefield, I'll get people coming from Japan, from China, from Vietnam," she said.

It helps that Portland has such a good reputation for coffee. "When people look at Portland, they're like, 'Wow, there's all these great coffee shops there,' and it's becoming a coffee mecca in the United States," she said. "A lot of people flock toward that if they are serious about doing the right coffee." The concentration of good shops in Portland allows people to experience many café styles in a short period of time. "Not very many cities are like Portland. When other people look at how coffee is made, they like to go visit Portland and check out the shops and decide whether that's something they want to take back home."

## Casting a Wide Net

While the trend in third-wave coffee is to reduce or eliminate flavoring syrups, Tran knows her location requires a more open mind-set. "I think it's really cool if you can sell a lot of coffee and make a living without having to cater to everybody — that's awesome! If I could do that, I would totally do it. But given the location, in the middle of nowhere, I have to cater to some other customers to continue having a business." Lava Java offers vanilla, sugar-free vanilla, hazelnut, Irish cream, peppermint, chocolate, and caramel sauce — several, but still fewer than a second-wave shop. "I would love to be a purist and serve only coffee, but you know those [cafés] still have sugar or condiments on their coffee bar. There's no way you're going to be able to just serve purists."

Tran's customers appreciate Lava Java's commitment to quality. "Every day, we still have customers come in and say we make the best whatever they order. Even people who have been coming in forever, to brand-new people who have just found us. We continually get that, and it reiterates that we are doing something right."

## Caffeinated PDX

### Moving into the Portland Market

In the summer of 2012, Tran expanded into downtown Portland, opening a small kiosk inside West End Bikes called Maglia Rosa (the name means "pink jersey," a nod to the jersey the leader of the Giro d'Italia bike race wears). "I'd been thinking about opening a second location, but I've just been waiting for the right one. When that location came up, I was just like, 'Oh my gosh, this is such a great location. I love it, and if I don't take advantage of the opportunity, I might not have the opportunity again.'" Maglia Rosa's espresso-based menu is more limited than Lava Java's. "It's just ten-ounce doubles. We just have vanilla and chocolate, though most of the time, we notice that our customers just order espressos, macchiatos, and cappuccinos."

Phuong praises her staff for the business's success. "I've been really, really fortunate," she said. "My staff has always been amazing. People who love coffee, people who want to stay and make coffee. I hardly have any turnover." She said that most baristas work for at least a couple years, some as long as six or seven. "People like to stay, which is really awesome."

All Tran's baristas work part time. They go to school or just want a part-time job. None of them receive benefits. Like most café owners, Phuong would like to make the barista position more of a career option, but it hasn't happened yet. "My vision would be to be able to afford to pay my baristas more money so they can make it into a career, instead of just offering part-time jobs — to have opportunities for people to grow," she said.

Even though they might not be getting health insurance, Phuong's baristas do gain valuable skills. "I feel like the people who work for me, a lot of them are thinking about opening their own shops, so they're moving in the right direction. They're able to learn, and if they want to create a career, they can. I'm really open to helping people do that. To see somebody succeed in coffee is the most amazing thing that you could offer."

Phuong brought up her most famous former barista, Billy Wilson, who now has three cafés of his own in Portland. "Seeing how Billy's doing right now is amazing," she said. "I wish more of the baristas we have had here would do the same thing. That would be awesome because I know they're doing great things." She did not think bringing more shops into an already crowded marketplace would be a problem. "Even though you think there's a lot of great coffee shops, there's still so much room to improve, even in Portland," she said.

Opportunities abound for those willing to take a chance. "There's still a vast majority of people who have never experienced really great coffee," she said. "There's still so many people going to so many bad coffee shops, so you look at that, and you wonder why people aren't going to the really quality coffee shops. It's because they don't know about them."

Phuong's fame as a barista champion gives her the opportunity to expose people to better coffee. "Once people know I have won a barista competition, they seek [me] out. People who want good coffee will go looking for you. Whenever I'm at the bar in Portland, there's always people coming up and saying, 'Hey, I've heard about you,' or 'I've read about you.' That helps reach out to people who wouldn't have known." Tran said the visitors she sees are not necessarily coffee connoisseurs, either. A lot of them are tourists who come to Portland and read an article in the local press.

## To Origin

While tourists seek out Lava Java because of its reputation for quality, Tran recognizes that quality begins long before the coffee ever gets to her café. In 2007, Phuong traveled with Duane Sorenson and a group of Stumptown wholesale accounts to Finca El Injerto, in the Huehuetenango region of Guatemala. The group included Billy Wilson and Kevin Fuller (both at Albina Press at the time), and Chrissy Hoag (who owned Dog River Coffee in Hood River). Phil Robertson, cofounder of Phil and Sebastian Coffee Roasters in Calgary, also went. "It was an incredible, incredible trip," Tran said.

The trip made it obvious why some coffees are better than others. "You can see the differences between farms that really take care of their coffee plants versus those that didn't do as good a job," Phuong said. "It's like walking into cafés where the steam wand isn't really clean, and then you walk into one that is really nice and clean and the baristas know what they're doing. Farms are like that too. I was really surprised." She also got to see how hard the people who picked the coffee had to work to get by. "You think that baristas don't get paid enough here," she said. "Think about the coffee pickers."

All the efforts to maintain quality at the source push up the prices of Stumptown's coffee. "A lot of people come in here and are shocked to see $14, $15, $16 for three-quarters of a pound of coffee," she said. "I'll say, 'Yes, but it's good, quality coffee.'" The extra price paid is worth it. "There's some people who will always complain, but they will still buy it. Then there are people who say, 'I am willing to pay for this coffee because it is so good.'"

## What Comes in the Next Five to Ten Years

As a longtime Stumptown account, Tran said that any changes at the company since TSG's investment have not affected her. "The quality of the coffee beans is still amazing," she said. "The coffee is really good. The people who I work directly with at Stumptown are still there. Nothing has really changed." Lava Java is one of Stumptown's most low-maintenance wholesale accounts. Many shops rely on Stumptown to train their baristas, at least when they first start working in coffee, but at Lava Java, the boss still does the training. "To me, as long as the quality of the beans is great, I don't have a problem because everything else, I manage myself."

Tran is excited to see the growth of roasters in the Portland area, but she has no current plans to roast her own beans. "Someday, maybe. I won't say no. But right now I'm not ready. Maybe when I'm retired," she laughed. Whether she roasts or not, Phuong plans to stay in the industry for life. "I'll be doing something in coffee forever. That's the thing — you don't have to stay and be a barista. There's so many options to grow in coffee."

Phuong sees a lot of potential outside the United States. She specifically noted the interest she sees from Asia when she goes to trade shows. Tran has traveled extensively as a coffee consultant to Japan, Australia, Colombia, Greece, and Canada, as well as around the United States. She teaches café owners and barista trainers how to create standards manuals for their cafés and how to improve workflows — higher-level thinking that she learned while building her own business. In her travels, she sees the coffee industry quickly changing. "There are a lot of people who see the importance of delivering quality coffee," she said. "The roasters who would hire me to go do training for them, they want their baristas to deliver a high quality cup."

These days, Phuong does not compete, but she stays involved with the barista community by judging the competitions and acting as head judge. In addition to judging, Phuong also teaches classes for SCAA and the Barista Guild in the States and abroad. With an intense focus on quality and a commitment to continuous improvement for both herself and the people who work for her, Phuong Tran has been one of the most influential personalities in the Portland specialty coffee scene over the past decade. Without her drive and determination, the Portland coffee tree would be missing many of its most important branches, and the city would not have the international reputation it has today.

## Kevin Fuller and the Albina Press
Setting the Stage for Portland's Third Wave Explosion

*There is no perfect way to map out a hierarchy of Portland's third wave and all of its connections, but if it were possible, the Albina Press would merit a spot near the top. In the mid-2000s, a group of very skilled baristas converged on the Press, creating a high-energy hub of talent that eventually dispersed around Portland and beyond. Billy Wilson, Mindy Farley, and Matt Higgins, to name a few, are well-known for their contributions to the industry, but before they struck out on their own, they were all integral members of the Albina Press crew.*

*Albina Press continues to thrive, led by its founder and owner, Kevin Fuller. Known for his intense personality, Fuller built Albina Press into one of the most well-known third-wave cafés in the country, recognized for its commitment to quality. AP's success in barista competitions inspired a generation of baristas around the Northwest. Without Fuller's vision, Portland's coffee scene would be much smaller and less interesting than it is today.* — WH

Kevin Fuller grew up in Portland, got his degree in finance and economics from Oregon State, and went to work as a stock broker after graduation. "It's where I cut my teeth on business," he told me on a sunny morning at his North Portland café. Fuller managed his clients' money, buying stocks and bonds for them. "It was a great job, but it was a seven-day-a-week, eighty-[to]-ninety-hour type gig, and there's kind of a life span on it."

After ten years as a broker, Kevin was ready to catch a breath. He moved to Granada, Spain, where he lived off and on for a year and a half. "I was living there for a while, trying to figure out what my next move was, and really trying to force that, 'What am I going to do?' [question]," he remembered. "I found myself pondering these huge questions in European cafés." Fuller gravitated toward busy neighborhood cafés, the type where everybody knows everybody. "It was a completely different environment, from a product perspective, but the scene was something I really enjoyed," he said.

Refreshed, Fuller returned to Portland with the intention of starting his own café. He found a promising location where some of his friends were running an artists' co-op on the corner of North Albina Avenue and Blandena Street. At the time, the co-op was struggling to pay the rent, so Fuller offered to build a coffee shop in the space and let the artists use the walls. "I've always kind of found this space a really magical space, from these old floors, the lights. It has a really unique energy," he said. The group accepted, and the first Albina Press was born, opening in 2004.

The new location had some built-in advantages that would give the café a big boost. Although Albina Avenue does not have a lot of foot traffic, the café sits between two ramps to I-5 and has a large parking lot, making the shop very accessible to commuters. "It had all these structural elements that I wasn't really even aware of," Kevin said. "I got really lucky. It's got all those things going for it.... Over the course of time, it's become the coffee shop for people that live in the area."

While the café was being finished, Fuller hired Billy Wilson, who brought his espresso expertise and competition experience to the shop. That first year, Fuller and Wilson would alternate opening and closing. "Billy would open, and I would close — or I would open, and Billy would close. Billy and I were pretty much the only ones pulling shots." Albina gained a reputation for serving some of the best shots of Hair Bender (Stumptown's espresso blend) in the city.

### Barista Competitions and the Epic 2006 Barista Guild Party

As the shop grew, Fuller and Wilson competed in barista competitions, with much success. Competing for Albina Press, Wilson won both the 2006 and 2007 Northwest Regional Barista Competitions (NWRBC). Fuller finished in third place those same years (he also finished second in 2009). At the time, the competitions were less prominent than they are today. "No one had heard about them," Fuller said. "It was more like a loosely organized thing that was happening at a small level. Which was really nice at the time because we all knew each other. It was still based in the Northwest at the time. Most of the baristas were based in Seattle or Portland."

The 2006 NWRBC changed things. "That was a big year for the barista competitions," Fuller said. "It was a full thirty-five people competing, and we had all this stuff we made up, with parties every night."

One particular evening — Friday, October 20 — stands out as a high point in third-wave history, when Albina Press hosted one of the first Barista Guild parties ever. In the days leading up to the party, Billy Wilson sent out a special invitation on Coffeed.com. "We told everybody that was coming to the party after the competition to bring your coffee and bring your grinder," Fuller said. People responded, in a big way. "There must have been a dozen — fifteen — grinders all the way around this bar with fifteen different companies' coffee blends [that] people were competing with," he recalled.

For someone with an espresso craving, the scene must have been coffee nirvana. "We had baristas back there ripping shots of everybody's espressos, and this counter area was ten deep with people saying, 'I want to try this espresso. I want to try that espresso,'" said Fuller. "It was this really weird, super-epic moment where we had the ability to taste a shot of Black Cat next to a shot of Hair Bender next to a shot of Vita next to Victrola and Hines. As far as I know, that had never happened before."

Fuller continued: "Back in those days, roasters were very protective of their blends, not letting coffee shops carry other roasters' coffees. That didn't go down. Everyone was very protective of their coffees, and the idea of saying, 'I'll let you serve my coffee next to these other dozen coffees,' was really a unique thing."

Albina Press's success at competitions cemented its reputation for quality and coffee knowledge, but the shop also had the reputation for somewhat surly service. Fuller admitted that some of his best baristas (himself included) were not always great at customer service, though no one meant any harm. "It was never intentional," he said. "We never had a really high priority on that kind of customer service. Over the years, I would watch some of [the baristas] become incredibly passionate about what they're doing, and when things get away from you, or things aren't going perfectly — everybody has bad days — without question, it was very obvious to the customer when that was happening."

The crew wanted to get things right. "It was hard for a lot of people to think, 'You're really taking this shit that seriously? You've got to be kidding me,'" Fuller said. The baristas did care that much, a by-product of the expectations Fuller had for his team.

## Espresso Training, the Heart of the Press

The expectations were especially high when it came to how baristas pulled their espresso shots. Fuller still trains the baristas himself, an intensive, lengthy process. "To get these baristas to where I'm comfortable with them working on the bar takes months and months," he said. "To get them to this level where they develop this confidence to own that espresso blend. They know exactly what it's supposed to taste like and what it's supposed to look like."

Achieving consistency in the café is a difficult task. Espresso blends are never exactly the same from season to season, even if they come from the same company. The mix of beans varies during the year, and the beans themselves change from off-gassing and other internal chemical processes, so baristas need to monitor the espresso machine and the grinder closely. Baristas also have to understand milk theory and science and how those affect working with different sizes and different milks, not to mention how to incorporate them for the different drinks on the menu. "For them to get really good and consistent and focused takes a long time and a lot of experience," Fuller said.

One of the reasons Fuller was so demanding about the quality of the coffee is that brewing is the final piece of the seed-to-cup ethos that underlies the third-wave principles that Stumptown helped bring to the industry. Fuller traveled to origin with Duane Sorenson and saw the changes that Stumptown was having on the production side. Sorenson wanted the cafés who served his coffee to commit to brewing and serving the coffees at the highest level. Fuller and his team made it happen.

## Technological Advancement

Along with better green coffee quality, improvements in coffee equipment made it easier to be more consistent. "Technology was changing," Fuller said. "The Robur came out, and all of a sudden, people were going from small, flat burrs [the parts inside a grinder that do the work of breaking up the coffee beans] to these huge new grinders that had conical burr sets turning at low RPM. PIDs were just coming out.[36] Still to this day, we've got this janky little PID that hangs off the side of our machine. That was one of the first PIDs ever. People were like, 'What are these?'"

The PIDs made a tremendous difference in how baristas approached their craft. "We were working on these machines where the variance on the boilers could have a ten-degree swing in water temperature," Kevin said. "This PID came along, we plugged [it] into the machine, and all of a sudden, we were able to maintain this variance of half a degree, plus or minus."

The new technologies made third-wave coffee possible. "All this technology came out, and all of a sudden, the only variance you were dealing with is the coffee in the hopper and the barista that's pulling shots," Fuller said. Baristas had more control over how the coffee tasted, and they had no excuses for poorly brewed coffee, as long as everyone in the supply chain committed to doing everything right. "That's the concept where third-wave coffee came from, where it's like, everybody from the guy that's picking the coffee and trimming the trees to processing it, packing it, and delivering it and receiving it and roasting it and getting it into our hands," Fuller said. "Then our job was not to fuck up what all these people had worked so hard to do."

## Holding Steady as Trends Come and Go
## (Wisdom for New Café Owners)

In early 2008, Fuller opened his second shop, on Southeast Hawthorne. He specifically chose a spot that was away from the

---

36. PID: A temperature control mechanism that relies on proportional, integral, and derivative mathematics to maintain stable water temperatures inside the espresso machine. David Schomer, of Seattle's Espresso Vivace, is often given credit for pushing the industry to use PIDs for temperature control. The PIDs give baristas more control over the quality of each espresso shot.

busiest part of the neighborhood. "If you're on your way to work, running late, you don't have time to park six blocks away and run in to get an Americano to go," he said. Being separated from the touristy areas makes both cafés more intimately tied to their neighborhoods. "I like that kind of European style café where I know the people that come in here and we have these relationships."

Fuller attributes part of his business's success to the ability to be consistent over the years. Albina Press maintains a simple menu that is almost identical to what it was when the café first opened. Fuller sees many benefits to this simplicity. "I think there's this incredible pressure when you open up a new coffee shop and you're new in the business to do something different that no one else is doing," he said, "to try to separate yourself, and at the same time, you're new and you're just hungry for customers and business." For example, new customers might stop by the shop and ask for breakfast sandwiches or multiple espresso blends, something that may be outside the shop's original vision. "When you're new, it's very difficult to say no to people."

Fuller started out with a different mind-set. "We never actually had to go through that process," he said, "because we weren't asking people what they wanted us to do. We were trying to figure out what we wanted to do and how we wanted to do it."

For the most part, Fuller has stayed the course, watching many trends come and go. "At the time when the Clover came out, it was like, 'You either get this piece of equipment, or you become irrelevant,' and it was like, 'Really? We need to do this?' I watched a lot of my friends comp $30,000 they didn't have into equipment. I watched them turn into paperweights six months later. I've seen things come and go and come and go. I've seen people scrape crema off their Americanos — I've seen all these things. Some of them have stuck more than others, and some of them have been total disasters."

The option to add things to the menu is always there, Fuller said, but only if it becomes necessary for the business's success. "I could make a phone call and build a siphon bar or serve eight different types of pour-overs. I could have six different espresso blends or single origins on my espresso bar." Fuller discusses new trends with the staff to decide if they are really worth implementing. So far, the business has been successful sticking to what it does best.

## Roasting? No Thanks, Not Now

Over the years, Fuller has considered roasting, but he ultimately decided it would spread his people too thin. Albina Press has been working with Stumptown since the beginning, and Fuller sees no reason to change. "As long as I have trust and faith in my roaster, that allows me to focus my energies on what we know how to do," he said. Fuller realizes achieving quality is more of a challenge than it appears. "Knowing the whole process from front to back, I know how difficult it is when you're a small-batch coffee roaster to go buy five hundred pounds of coffee and have any idea of what you're actually getting your hands on," he said. To do things right, Fuller would need to send people to source, watching and cupping to monitor quality — an expensive proposition.

Stumptown already has those people at origin. "[Stumptown's buyers] will cup forty different day lots [the green coffees coming out of a processing mill, separated by day] and be like, 'No, no, yes, no, yes.' They can pull out the lots they want, and it's all processed according to their wants," Kevin said. Growers make sure their coffees conform to Stumptown's quality standards to receive premium prices. A new roaster would not have that same type of leverage. "One of the things that's always stopped me from [roasting] is knowing I would have to take this huge, gut-wrenching step down in quality of green coffee," he said, "because I'm not going to have access to these guys and what they're doing and the relationships they have at origin." Without the relationships, Fuller said he could never be exactly sure what he was buying.

## A New Business Model Instead

Instead of roasting, Fuller is working with Stumptown more closely to offer exclusive coffees through Albina Press. When Stumptown's buyers find a lot of green beans that meets their standards but is too small to sell in the company's own retail cafés, they offer it to Albina Press. The café gets a unique coffee to market as its own, and Stumptown gets to purchase (and sell) a wider variety of high-end coffees. Albina Press's first exclusive coffee came from Finca Concepción Buena Vista, in Guatemala's Chimaltenango province.

For Fuller, the model adds a new dimension to his business without significantly increasing risk. He gets to help choose the coffees and how they are roasted, but he does not have to build his own green buying program or buy roasting equipment. "It almost feels like we're roasting coffee, but not spreading us as thin as it would if we were actually roasting coffee," he said. "We have access to their green buyers, their cuppers, their roasters, their infrastructure, shipping coffee and storing and housing without getting caught up in it," Fuller said. "We just get to say, 'That's the coffee we want — you buy it, we'll pay for it. When it gets here, you roast it up, and we'll put together all the marketing for it.'"

The shift gives Fuller more control over the end product. "All of the sudden, we're making some of the decisions," he said. "We're like, 'Okay, this is the one we're going to go with. Buy it. Get it. Let us know when it comes in. We're going to come in, watch you roast it, help you roast it. We're going to really take ownership in the coffee.'"

The new model builds a closer relationship between the farmer and the coffee drinkers. The farmer in Guatemala who raised the first Albina Press coffee knew it was going to be sold only at a certain coffee shop in Portland. "They're buying the coffee, and we're the ones that are serving it, but it kind of takes this direct relationship where it's the farmer and the coffee roaster and now it takes it to the café that's not roasting the coffee." Fuller sees the new relationship as a potential model for the industry. "If it does work, you're going to see Intelligentsia doing it. You'll see microroasters doing it too."

### Legacy and the Skill Set Albina Press Baristas Leave With

As mentioned earlier, several former baristas have left Albina Press to start their own businesses. Fuller praised their success. "I'm proud of Coava, and I'm proud of Red E, and I'm proud of Barista," he said of the businesses run by Matt Higgins, Mindy

## Kevin Fuller and Albina Press

Farley, and Billy Wilson, respectively. Fuller also brought up Josh Hydeman (now head roaster at Heart), as well as Jodi Groteboer and Jason Rhodes, two longtime employees who recently opened a shop — Palate — in Bend, Oregon.

What makes former Albina Press employees successful? Fuller attributes some of their success to the things they learned while working in Albina Press's high-traffic environment. "The people that come out of the Albina Press [who have gone on to start their own companies] — many of who have chosen to take things and expanded their menus [beyond the limited menu they worked with at Albina Press] — still have this very defined core set of skills that were developed here," he said. "They can always fall back on them, and it's where I think a lot of their success comes from. If they had to scrap all these other sparkly side avenues of business, they could always come back to sitting on the La Marzocco and a Robur and pull a billion shots, and every single one of them is going to be nailed. One after the other. They'll crush milks. They'll do it fast and know how to be efficient on the bar."

Albina Press's baristas learn more than just how to make coffee. "Our identity is our back-office part of the business," Fuller said, motioning toward two baristas working behind the bar. "Either one of them," he said, "could tell you exactly where we are in sales right now, within $5, what we're selling and what we're not selling and how this business is managed and organized."

Fuller purposefully brings on people who see working in the café as a step on the path to something else, not just a sideline job. "I have a half-dozen people right now on the staff that I hired with the idea that they were going to open their own coffee shops," he said. "I've always had more luck hiring someone who eventually wants to get into the business on a higher level than just pulling shots for me." The downside to the hiring strategy is that baristas eventually leave to open their own businesses. However, Albina Press's reputation attracts a steady stream of the type of people Kevin likes to hire. "I have people coming from all over the country who say, 'I want to be a buyer, a consultant,'" he said. "They want to come to learn at Albina Press, knowing that several alumni have gone on to start their own businesses."

### Maintaining High Standards

Does anything keep Fuller awake at night? "I sleep pretty good," he said. "I'm like anybody else. I have ideas about what I'd like to do and what I wouldn't like to do. There's a large part of me that would really like to open more cafés, but I know what a toll that takes on taking your staff from fifteen to twenty-five, so I'm very, very careful about the decisions I make at this point." People regularly approach Fuller and ask him to open new cafés. If the right space came up, he would consider opening another shop, but there is no reason to force the issue. "It really has to fit into what I'm doing, and I'm really happy with the business I have right now.... Eventually, I'm sure I will open more cafés, but it has to be done in a way that doesn't sacrifice what I've already built."

# 12

# Billy Wilson
## Star Barista and Pioneer of the Multiroaster Café

*Billy Wilson is one of the most influential personalities in Portland's third-wave coffee scene. Working coffee in the area for more than a decade, Wilson has played a key role in making Portland a destination for coffee pilgrims. He teamed up with Phuong Tran at Lava Java to make the previously unknown shop famous for producing competitive baristas. He helped Kevin Fuller grow the Albina Press into a nationally known café. Along the way, Billy cemented his own reputation through his success as a competitive barista both at the regional and national levels. His original Barista café, in the Pearl District, pioneered the multiroaster concept and is a required stop for any tourist coming to experience Portland coffee.*

*Billy and I sat down over coffee (and beer) at his second Barista café, on Northeast Alberta. During our chat, I was somewhat surprised by his candor. More than once, his gray-blue-green eyes visibly glistened with emotion as he recalled some of the challenges and successes he'd had since he first started in coffee.* — WH

Sandwiched between Interstate 5 and the Cowlitz River, Castle Rock, Washington, is a sleepy logging town that bills itself as the "Gateway to Mount St. Helens." In 1980, the mountain erupted, sending a deluge of mud, rocks, and dislodged trees down the Toutle River Valley toward the town, causing chaos and disrupting life in the region for years to come. The same year, another event received much less attention, one that would later impact the Portland coffee scene in a profound way: Franklin and Delores Wilson had a son, naming him Billy.

Billy Wilson was a fairly typical kid. Growing up, Wilson would mow neighbors' lawns to earn enough money to rent Nintendo game systems from the local video store. His best friend, Matt Brown, describes him as the kind of person who would obsess over something until he learned every detail. From the standard success-model perspective — studying hard, getting good grades, going to college, finding a good job, and so on — Billy looked like he would struggle. He was smart but not really into school. In a high school graduating class of ninety-eight, Wilson finished seventy-seventh.

After graduation, Wilson left his hometown and moved to Alaska, where he worked for a moving company. He later volunteered with Youth with a Mission, an evangelical Christian organization, in Russia and Norway. Wilson said he volunteered because he liked the organization's humanitarian focus. "It was less proselytizing and more ministry to people who didn't have anything," he said. "That's much more my style."

In 1999, while in Norway with Youth with a Mission, Wilson traveled back to Castle Rock just before Christmas to see his father, who was dying of cancer. Franklin Wilson had been fighting cancer, so the death was not a surprise for Billy, but losing his father was a big blow. Billy returned to Norway shortly after his father died but soon came back to Castle Rock, moving in with his mother to support her. He took a few classes at the local community college and worked as a mover to pay the bills.

### Finding Coffee at Lava Java

In early 2002, Billy enrolled at Multnomah Bible College, where he shared an apartment with Matt Brown. In between classes, he worked for the college as a security guard. "It sucked," said Wilson of the job. "I was on the graveyard shift, and it was just awful. It was one of those things where I'd get off work [for the week], and all I could think of was, I had to go back to work in three days. I did not enjoy it at all."

Wilson did not know anything about coffee at the time, but that soon changed. Brown had a part-time job as a youth pastor in La Center, Washington, and Billy would ride along with him to help out. On the drive up, the two regularly stopped for coffee at Lava Java in Ridgefield. Brown stopped so frequently that Lava Java's owners offered him a barista job, but he suggested they talk to Wilson. After a five-minute interview, they hired Billy. A couple months later, Phuong Tran bought the café. "I can say I worked at Lava Java before Phuong," Wilson said proudly.

Inquisitive by nature, Wilson dove into coffee with a need to figure it out for himself. "I don't trust people," Billy said. "I kind of grew up that way." He attributed his distrust to some incidents in his teenage years. "When you grew up in theology circles, where you're around one group of people who believe one set of things, then all of a sudden you're around another group, and you're like, 'Whoa, there's a lot of diversity here.'" Different opinions between the various groups taught him it was best to figure things out for himself. "I got burned pretty hard a couple times — because I trusted people — and that kind of framed my entire outlook, even though that happened in my teen years," he said. "I was like, 'Don't take anybody's word for anything. Find out for yourself.'"

The original owners of Lava Java had trained Wilson how to make espresso, but when Phuong bought the café, she had Coffee Bean International's trainer, Jessica Rice, come to the shop and retrain the baristas. Rice taught Wilson a completely different method. "I was like, 'Okay, here we go again,'" Billy said. Unsure about who was right, Wilson created his own education plan.

Around the same time, a friend suggested Billy check out Stumptown. "So I went into Belmont," recalled Wilson, "and I had my first truly good espresso. I tasted it, and I was like, 'Fuck me! Really? What I'm making is not anything like this!'" Wilson's impressions of espresso were shattered. "I thought espresso was supposed to taste bad," he said. "I thought it was supposed to taste dirty and burnt." Not at Stumptown. "The shot I had from Stumptown — the color was different. It was dark. The crema was like what we see now on espresso. It was sweet, chocolaty. It was smaller — like half the size of what I had been serving."

After the Stumptown visit, Wilson became embarrassed by the shots he had been pulling at Lava Java. He knew he was doing something wrong and began to badger Rice with questions about coffee. She suggested he check out CoffeeGeek.com, an online forum started by Mark Prince for coffee enthusiasts to promote better coffee and share ideas about techniques, equipment, and just about anything else coffee related. Billy also began reading — and commenting, sometimes when he shouldn't have been — at alt. coffee, a user group for home coffee enthusiasts. Wilson recalled being humbled by the rest of the group. "I was young and arrogant, and Jim Schulman [a well-respected amateur coffee geek with a PhD who has studied coffee for years] threw this smack down because I was basically saying how somebody didn't need to listen to home users," said Billy. "He was like, 'Listen, pup, the only reason this dude is doing this is because I did it, and I showed him how.'" According to Wilson, Schulman was PID'ing machines before anybody else.

## Barista Competitions and Landing at Albina Press

Chastened, Wilson continued to learn. He read coffee books, online forums, and whatever else he could get his hands on. "I was learning tons about coffee, all theoretical at that point," he said. "I still had this La San Marco espresso machine, surfing it [to hit the right temperature] as much as possible so I didn't burn the coffee." In September 2002, nine months after he started at Lava Java, Billy competed in his first competition, at North American Specialty Coffee and Beverage Retailers' Expo (NASCORE), held in Portland that year. "I decided to enter that because I thought I was pretty big shit," he said. Wilson had visited Schomer's Seattle café, Espresso Vivace, bought and studied Schomer's book, *Espresso Coffee: Professional Techniques*, and learned how to make latte art. "I'd started doing all these things," Billy said. "I thought I was going to my first barista competition to kick some ass."

Things did not quite work out the way he'd planned. "I went in, and I got disqualified," he said, shaking his head at the memory. "I was the last one to go. I don't think they had an overtime clause back then, but it was so bad, they were just like, 'You can't keep going.' You had fifteen minutes, and I think I was probably twenty-five minutes in by the time they decided to pull the plug." Adding to his embarrassment, the trade show part of NASCORE had already ended and lots of attendees had come over to see what the barista competition was about. "So I'm up there making a fool of myself in front of a couple thousand people," he said.

## Billy Wilson

Not all was lost, however. At the competition, Wilson befriended Bronwen Serna (2004 United States Barista Championship winner), Stephen Vick, and Chris Davidson, three baristas from Seattle who became mentors to Billy. "They really picked me up and held me close," he said. "They were like, 'Okay, this kid's really into it.' They took me in and helped me out. I kept talking to them and asking questions and would go for visits." The three convinced Wilson that Lava Java needed to switch coffees. "I was really in love with Stumptown, so I talked to Duane, and I was like, 'I really want to carry your coffee.'" The decision was not Wilson's to make, but he did convince Tran to try Stumptown's coffees. Phuong liked them, so she agreed to make the switch. Lava Java also invested in a La Marzocco FB/70 espresso machine, and the coffee at the café made a huge leap in quality.

The next year, 2003, the United States Barista Championship (USBC)[37] was held in Boston. Wilson competed using Stumptown coffee and did better, finishing fifth overall. "That was huge because it was approval that yes, I was a good barista," he said. On the plane home, Wilson realized he wanted to work in coffee for the rest of his life. "I was so pumped and excited about it. The fact I took fifth, I was like, maybe I could win one day. I want to win the USBC. That basically became my thing — I wanted to win."

In 2004, Wilson finished fifth again, this time while working for Stumptown. Billy had moved over to Stumptown during the year, to be closer to the person in coffee he looked up to the most. "Basically, I idolized Duane," Wilson said. "I saw what he did. He was a barista, got into roasting, and traveled. I thought the end-all would be buying coffee. That's what I really wanted to do." Wilson first applied to be an apprentice roaster at Stumptown, but he didn't get the job. Sorenson came to the rescue, offering Wilson a barista job — essentially creating a position for Wilson where there was not one. Grateful for the opportunity, Wilson accepted, splitting his time between the Division, Belmont, and 3rd Avenue shops.

---

37. The SCAA started hosting the barista competitions in 2003, calling it the United States Barista Championship.

## Caffeinated PDX

Wilson only lasted about six months at Stumptown before he was fired. "I just didn't fit in," he recalled. "Stumptown has always been incredibly hip, and I am definitely not." Wilson's words struck me as incongruous — Billy Wilson, the rock star barista, not hip? He explained: "Back then, I was in the café, playing emo[38] and other shit, and the other baristas were not having it," he said. "I was so green. I'd never lived in Portland. I'd lived on campus at Multnomah Bible College, but when I got a job at Stumptown living in the city, I was a really sheltered kid, trying to figure shit out in Portland, which was really hip, [while working] at one of the hippest companies. So I stuck out like a sore thumb." Wilson eventually got over the firing, but it was not easy. "Now I get it. I didn't fit the company culture, and I'm okay with that. Back then, I wasn't. I was really mad."

Despondent, Wilson started working part time at Crema — then owned by his roommate, Brent Fortune — while he contemplated his next step. Two opportunities came onto his radar. He could go to work for Intelligentsia in Chicago or Artigiano, the roaster founded by the Piccolo family in Vancouver, British Columbia.[39] "Sammy Piccolo[40] always told me I had everything to be a winner, and he wanted me to win the USBC," Billy said. Wilson's first choice was to work at Artigiano, but he first needed a work visa. However, the Canadian government did not cooperate, and by the time Wilson found out, the position with Intelligentsia had been filled.

Unsure about where to go, Billy was approached by Jana Oppenheimer, Stumptown's sales director, who suggested he talk to Kevin Fuller. Fuller was just about to open a new shop called Albina Press. "I went in there a week or two before he opened, and I was like, 'Hey, my name's Billy. I'd really like to work here. I can train your employees or whatever.'" Wilson had one condition — he wanted to be supported to compete in barista competitions. Fuller hired Wilson, and the two formed the anchor

---

38. A style of melodic rock music from the 1980s and 1990s.

39. After the Piccolos sold Artigiano, they founded 49th Parallel, a high-end roaster and café business, also based in Vancouver.

40. Sammy Piccolo is one of the world's most famous barista competitors, having finished second three times and third once while representing Canada at the World Barista Championships.

## Billy Wilson

for what Sarah Allen, editor of *Barista Magazine*, would later call "the best [café] I've visited in the world." Albina Press was a dynamic shop, with several forceful personalities that pushed the café to the top of the Portland hierarchy.

While Wilson worked at Albina Press, he continued his successful run as a barista competitor. He won the Northwest Regional Barista Competition (NWRBC) twice (2006, 2007) and finished second at the 2006 USBC.[41] Billy's performance at the 2006 regional is still remembered for its espresso pearls, beads of espresso held together with algae extract, inspired by famous chef Ferran Adrià. Wilson's flair for showmanship, his stage presence, and his sleeve tattoos made it easy for the press to call Wilson a "rock star" barista.[42]

Billy stayed at Albina Press for nearly three and a half years, during which time he decided he did not want to be a coffee roaster or buyer. "I just really liked being a barista," he told me, "and I didn't really want to move up. I just wanted to keep making coffee. I got to where I really enjoyed that everyday interaction." Instead, Billy would open his own café. "I was just making someone else money, and I knew I was never going to be the owner of that company, so I was like, 'Okay, I've got to do my own,'" he said. Wilson had seen some of his friends win barista competitions and leverage that to start their own companies, and he wanted to follow a similar path. Though he had not finished first at the USBC, his success gave him plenty of credibility.

---

41. "He's extremely competitive," said Albina Press co-owner Kevin Fuller in a 2008 article on Billy by Imbibe Magazine. "He's extremely intense." After he opened Barista, Wilson also won the 2009 NWRBC. Because of the way the barista competition schedule worked, there were two NWRBCs held in 2009. Alex Pond, working for Fresh Pot at the time, won the first one, held during the first part of the year. Wilson's third regional title came that November.

42. When I asked Billy if there were any misconceptions about him, he told me, "It might be the whole rock star thing, because I definitely don't feel like it. I don't know how cool you can be when you're thirty-three years old with two kids. I'm a dork. I'm a huge geek. I listen to children's music with my kids and dance around the house and act like a fool. I play video games, and I'm a huge Timbers supporter. All these things don't add up to the rock star image I think people want to put on me." Wilson described a typical evening for himself: "Last night, I came home at ten thirty, got all the Harry Potters, and me and my girlfriend did a Harry Potter marathon. That's kind of who I am," he said.

## Caffeinated PDX

### The Transition to Business Owner

Wilson did not have any experience owning a business, but he did have some baseline knowledge. On the advice of a friend's dad, Billy had taken a few business classes at the community college. "I'm such a bad student," he said. "I absorbed the material; I just didn't do any homework. But I learned about small business planning." Though Wilson didn't get any credits, he did get the information. Then, as he readied himself to venture out on his own, Billy dove into the Small Business Administration's website and prepared himself even more.

In between shifts at Albina Press, Billy worked on his new business plan. Once it was finished, he quit his job and temporarily went to work for Coffeehouse Northwest. "I felt it would be underhanded of me to look for financing for my other company while working for Kevin [Fuller]," he said. "I just felt that would have been inappropriate." Coffeehouse Northwest's owner, Adam McGovern, knew Billy was going to open a business when he hired him. The two had an understanding that Wilson would not promote his new café while working and would only stay at Coffeehouse until he signed a lease for his new café.

With a business plan in hand, Wilson found financing Barista to be fairly easy. He approached Jamie Grosse, one of his longtime customers at Albina Press, who, along with his wife, Becky, agreed to invest. Terry Ziniewicz, founder of Espresso Parts in Olympia, also invested in the new venture. Having found his business partners, Wilson's next challenge was to find the right location, which took several months. Early on, Wilson's leasing agent showed him a small space in the Pearl District, previously inhabited by Acorn. "I wasn't sure about it. You had to go up on the dock to go inside the building. It's small," he said. Shortcomings notwithstanding, he ultimately decided to go for it, signing a lease in November 2008.

### The Multiroaster Concept

Wilson called his new shop Barista. When it opened on February 23, 2009, Barista made waves for its new business model. Instead of offering coffees from a single roaster, Barista had three espressos available, each from a different roaster. Wilson told me that barista competitions had given him the idea. Going back to his days at Lava Java, whenever baristas would get together for competitions, they would trade bags of coffees with each other. During his stint at Albina Press, the baristas would use an extra grinder to make the coffees available for customers. "People would come in, and I'd be like, 'Hey, we've got this new coffee on. Do you want to try it?'" Billy recalled. "And before long, people were like, 'Hey, you guys got any of that other stuff?'"

Wilson thought there was enough demand to support a new business model, one more like a bar, where many different beers are served alongside each other, something that had not been done in coffee. Normally, cafés have contracts to exclusively serve a single roaster's coffee. They often lease their equipment through the roaster and receive barista training too, but Wilson's situation was unique. "Since I'd already geeked out and learned about coffee and equipment, I knew I didn't need a roaster to show me how to do anything," he said. "I didn't need the roaster to train my baristas. I knew what equipment I wanted; I knew how to do this. I was like, 'Why are we beholden to somebody? Why can't we do this thing?'"

Prior to opening, Wilson discussed his idea with a few different roasters, who seemed willing to work with him. He also attended Slow Food Nation in San Francisco, a four-day event to celebrate American cuisine that attracted more than fifty thousand people, where he was able to connect with other roasters. "I talked to Peter Giuliano [of Counter Culture] and was like, 'Hey man, this is what I want to do.' And he's just like, 'Um, I don't know…. But I'd sell to you because I know you and I trust you,' and I'm like, 'Exactly!'"

Even Stumptown, which had never been amenable to being just one of several roasters in a café, turned out to be interested. Wilson did not know how Stumptown's owner would respond. Sorenson was fiercely loyal to his company's coffees, and he and Billy had once argued about Wilson using non-Stumptown coffees in competition — even after Wilson no longer worked for him. "I was a little bit nervous asking him about it because I wasn't sure what he was going to say," Billy said. "But when I sat down and said, 'This is what I'm going to do. This is my business,' he was like, 'If you need anything from me, let me know.'" Wilson's eyes gleamed with emotion as he recalled working with Duane. It was clear that he still looks up to Sorenson. "He's been supportive of me for ten, eleven years," Billy said.

Running a multiroaster café, Wilson got back into geeking out about coffee. Billy said he learned more in the first couple months after opening than he had in the previous year or two, when he was almost exclusively working with Hair Bender. "When you have single-origin coffees — and three different ones, you see that, wow, all these parameters you thought were written in stone are not written in stone at all. You cannot treat every single coffee the same way. Every coffee has its own story to tell, its own flavor. I had to destroy so many of my set parameters of how to brew coffee."

Marty Lopes, Barista's former coffee buyer, told me similar things about working with so many coffees. "I was in charge of preparing samples, taste testing, doing the whole gamut of analysis of the coffees and the roasters and deciding which coffees we were going to serve." Lopes's job also included informing the staff about the coffees — who grew them, who roasted them, and so on. "That was pretty much invaluable," said Lopes, who now has his own roasting company, Roseline Coffee. "You got to cup coffees from the best roasters out there, side by side."

The multiple-roaster concept proved to be a hit with coffee drinkers, who flocked to the new café. Within a few months, Barista was turning a profit. Wilson attributed much of the new company's success to the people he worked with. "I'm just really lucky to have the business partners I have," he said, referring to Jamie and Becky Grosse. The Grosses' business background and involvement allow Wilson to do what the does best. "I just do the barista thing," he said. "I come from at it from this angle, knowing how to operate and how to train. They come at it from a business perspective. I've learned so much from them. This business wouldn't be half of what it [is] without them."

Wilson also praised his employees for their contributions. "Honestly, me managing people here is just easy because they're such good people and they work hard. I think they're very thankful not to have people that come in and yell at them all the time," he said. That said, Wilson has very clear expectations of his employees. "It's very much a respect thing," he said. "If you fuck around and you don't do a good job, you're out. If you disrespect me, or Jamie or Becky, you're out. But I don't have to say that. They just know it. It's a given."

## B2 and the Fire

Seeing the success of the first shop, Wilson and his partners soon decided to open another, signing a lease on the Alberta location within six months of the first one opening. B2, as Wilson called it, opened in early 2010. The sequel was much larger than the first, with a long, L-shaped bar and several tables. Dark wood paneling and animals mounted on the walls made it feel like the private study of an English mansion. To attract a later crowd, the shop put a few beers on tap.

Whereas Wilson was very involved in opening the first café — he trained all the baristas and spent a lot of time behind the bar himself, with the second location, he took a slightly different approach. Laila Ghambari, now with Caffe Ladro in Seattle, helped open the Alberta shop. "I think [the second] time around, Billy was a little more hands-off and put more trust in the abilities of those he hired," she said, adding, "He hired a good staff." In addition to Ghambari, Wilson hired other experienced baristas, including Tyler Stevens, Sam Purvis and Matt Brown (who both later worked for Coava), and Joe Suvagian (the current manager), to complete the staff.

Not everything went smoothly with the second shop. Every company has stories about when big obstacles presented themselves and had to be overcome before the business could grow. In the case of Barista Alberta, that story will always be the fire. In the evening of July 4, 2011, Wilson was at home with his kids, lighting fireworks in the street, when his phone buzzed from an incoming text message: *Hey, there's a fire on the roof of the shop.*

Having never received such news, Billy was a little unsure of how to respond. Should he go to the shop right away and see what was going on? "It was funny for me to have those thoughts, like, 'Do I need to come down?' because when I got here, I was like,

'*Holy shit*,'" Wilson said. "By the time the fire department let us in, we had several inches of standing of water on our floor and water coming out of every light fixture. Then there was that realization of, 'We're fucked. We are not opening tomorrow.'"

A stray (and illegal) bottle rocket had landed on the roof of the building and started the fire. Portland Fire & Rescue quickly extinguished the fire, but in doing so, it wreaked havoc inside B2, causing extensive water damage. Contractors would need to tear out the ceiling, the walls, the bathroom — everything would have to be removed except the bar. The timing was terrible. "We'd just started really getting going," Billy recalled. "It was summer — we're starting to turn a profit and then, nothing. It was almost like this thing that died that was really important to me." Stumptown graciously offered the use of the company's coffee cart while the Alberta Barista underwent repairs, and while it helped keep employees busy, it did not sustain the same level of business. Barista lost money for the next four months.

While he waited for the shop to be rebuilt, Wilson found himself drifting. To give more hours to his employees, Wilson cut back on his own bar shifts. He was able to spend more time with his kids — a good thing — but he still felt like he was stuck. "It was almost like the feeling I had when I got fired at Stumptown," he said. "It was a very, very emotionally depressing period of time for me." The personal cost for Billy was very high, and in 2013, he still seemed to be working through what it all meant.

The café was ready to go by the first weekend in November, four months after the fire. It quickly returned to being a popular coffee stop for Northeast Portlanders, and once again, the success encouraged Wilson and his partners to expand. In July 2012, Barista 3 opened on Southwest Third, in downtown Portland. One year later, Wilson announced Barista would open another shop, this one in Northwest Portland's shopping district dubbed Trendy-Third. "One thing I didn't realize is that I enjoy building cafés," Billy said of the decision to keep growing. "I was like, 'I just want to be a barista.' But I really enjoy designing coffee shops and layouts. I have so much fun. It's really hard, but it's so fulfilling to build them." Wilson said he was also keeping his eyes open for opportunities outside Portland. "I'd like to open up a spot in Seattle and LA — wherever there's opportunity," he said. "Even though there's a lot of people out there doing multiple coffee roasters, we're the first. We do it well, and I want to bring that concept to other markets."

## Leaving a Mark

Over his career, Wilson has teamed up with many of the most well-known figures in the Portland coffee industry — Phuong Tran, Duane Sorenson,[43] Kevin Fuller, Mindy Farley, Matt Higgins, Adam McGovern, and others — to create higher standards for coffee in the city. Billy might not have introduced his colleagues to coffee, but he certainly pushed them to make it better. His inquisitiveness and drive meshed with their energy, raising their skills as well as his own. The interactions were not always smooth — Wilson has a reputation for being demanding when it comes to coffee — but they unquestionably made Portland a much better coffee city.

Moreover, by challenging the exclusivity agreements that roasters typically had with their wholesale customers, Wilson and Barista set a new course for the specialty coffee industry, a significant part of Wilson's legacy. "I don't need to necessarily have anybody shout my name from the rooftop," he said, "but I know that this company has changed the way independent café owners do their business. I know that, whether they know or not. I like that. I feel proud of that."

Even though he's now an owner instead of an employee, Wilson sees himself as the same person as he always has been. "It's funny — when you're young, they say you're arrogant, and when you're older..." Wilson paused for a moment. "I'm still the same person. Everybody said, 'He's full of himself. He's got a big head.' I'm still the same guy; it's just that I'm older now and people are like, 'Yeah, he owns his own business. He's got kids. He can walk around the place like he owns it because now he does.'" Nevertheless, after spending years behind the bar serving people,

---

[43]. Although Billy was fired from Stumptown, he has spent nearly all his career promoting Sorenson's coffees in some way, at Lava Java, Albina Press, and now Barista, which generally has at least one Stumptown coffee available.

Wilson has the perspective to connect with Barista's staff. "I still view my employees as friends and as equals.... There's not a single person here that I can't relate to," he said.

As he grows the business, Wilson tries to keep things in perspective. "I want my employees to say they're proud to work here. I want everybody to be happy about that. I want them to go off and be successful and do their own things." Billy was looking forward to what was to come. "I just want to grow old, have fun with my kids, and live a good life.... As long as I can provide for my kids and my employees, that's enough. Life's an incredibly beautiful thing, and I consider myself very lucky."

### The Magic of the Siphon at Barista

When you walk into the original Barista café in Portland's Pearl District, the first thing you notice is what looks like a chemistry lab sitting next to the cash register. Displayed behind glass panels, the chrome-and-glass apparatus is a siphon brewer (also called a vacuum pot). If you're lucky enough that someone in line has ordered one, or if you feel like splurging (twelve ounces of brewed coffee costs $9), you get to see the siphon in action. I splurged — once — to see what the experience was like.

What is so special about the siphon brewing method? For one thing, it's great coffee theater. A vacuum pot looks cool — almost space-age, even though it has been around for nearly 150 years. You don't see them in use very much, so when you do get to see one, it is worth watching. First, the barista adds the correct amount of water into the lower bulb of the vacuum pot. The bulb is then placed over a heat source. It could be a flame or a hot plate, but at Barista, they use glowing halogen heat lamps. While the water is heating, the barista weighs out and grinds the coffee, setting it aside until the water is ready.

When the water reaches its boiling point, the steam travels up a tube to the upper chamber, condensing back into water and arriving at a temperature of about 202°F, just right for coffee extraction. When nearly all the water has reached the chamber, the barista adds the ground coffee and stirs it, making sure all the grounds are in contact with the water, letting them brew for a predetermined amount of time, depending on the coffee. During extraction, a small amount of water continues to flow into the extraction chamber, helping maintain a constant temperature. In this case, the finer grind required an extraction time of two minutes (the coffee was Intelligentsia's Ethiopia Sidama).

The barista told me the shorter extraction time (some shops do up to four minutes) gives the coffee better flavor and helps it retain more of its natural sweetness. When the time is up, the vacuum pot is pulled off the heat source and the lower bulb begins to cool, creating a vacuum that pulls the brewed coffee down through the cloth filter and into the serving pot. The barista held a frozen towel against the lower bulb to strengthen the vacuum and pull the coffee back through the filter more quickly, reducing the possibility of overextraction.

Brewed coffee enthusiasts would likely enjoy siphon coffee. The siphon creates a clean cup of coffee because the cloth filter is very effective at removing the grounds from the water. In my coffee, there was absolutely no trace of grinds in the server or cup, and the method brought out the brightness and complex flavors of the coffee. The coffee left a pleasant sensation in my mouth, similar to what a good tea does. It was very tangy — I thought I could taste green apples or underripe blackberries in it. The reasons that a siphon has such clear flavors are that all of the grounds are fully immersed and the temperature remains constant throughout the duration of the brewing process. Other methods like the pour-over or French press are not as constant with the immersion or temperature.

Would I recommend ordering coffee brewed in a siphon? I certainly enjoyed the experience, and I will say — without any doubt — that it was the best $9 cup of coffee I've ever had.

## Mindy Farley and Keith Miller
### The Free-Spirited Founders of the Red E

*Since the early 1800s, when Lewis and Clark ended up in the Pacific Northwest on their expedition to map the Louisiana Purchase, Americans have seen the region as a land of opportunity. Following the famous explorers, droves of settlers flocked to the area, carving out their own plots of land, working in the logging industry, or seeking fortune in some other way. Whatever they sought, moving to the Pacific Northwest made people feel free, and hundreds of thousands of settlers traveled the Oregon Trail to the Willamette Valley, bringing with them a rugged individualist ethos. In his book,* Brews to Bikes: Portland's Artisan Economy, *Professor Charles Heying cites this individualism as one reason there are so many small, artisan-type businesses in Portland. Portland's relatively low cost of living and accepting nature make the city a haven for young, free-spirited people. Many of these free spirits, such as Mindy Farley and Keith Miller, work in the coffee industry.* —WH

Mindy Farley and Keith Miller, owners of Portland's Red E Cafés, have a story echoing that of the region's early settlers. Two people from the East Coast leave family and friends behind, taking few possessions with them as they seek out a new life in a faraway land. Instead of covered wagons and horses, though, this couple traveled on bicycles. In 1996, they rode from Virginia Beach to Oregon's Pacific Coast, camping their way along the Bikecentennial route.[44]

From the beginning of the trip, Farley and Miller planned to stay on the West Coast, though Portland was not their first choice. "Growing up in the East Coast in the late 1980s, my mecca, being a young hippie kid, was San Francisco," Keith told me as we chatted

---

44. Bikecentennial was a cross-country bicycle tour that took place in 1976 to celebrate the bicentennial of the Declaration of Independence. The route is also known as the Trans America Bicycle Trail.

by the front window of the couple's North Killingsworth café. "I had a roommate who moved there to go to Berkeley. When we finished in Florence [Oregon] — after taking off our clothes and running into the ocean — we spent our last five bucks on a beer and then hid behind a campground to camp for the night. We didn't have any money." The couple called Miller's friend in Berkeley, but she was too busy and did not have space to take them in.

Disappointed but not despondent, Keith called a friend in Portland. "He didn't answer, but he had an answering machine message that said, 'Hey, Keith, I know you're coming out west any day. I just want to let you know that whatever you need and as long as you need it, you got it.' I hung up the phone and looked at Mindy and said, 'I guess we're going to Portland.'"

## Early Coffee Experience with Albina Press

Today, Mindy is known for being the face of the Red E, but it was originally Keith who wanted to get into coffee. "Keith wanted to open a coffee shop. I used to think it was kind of a silly idea," Mindy said, laughing. Keith had helped open a few cafés in Buffalo, New York, but when they first got to Portland, the couple did not have enough money to open their own place. "We found a space, but financially, we weren't ready," said Mindy. "Kevin was a friend, so we passed it off to him."

Farley was referring to Kevin Fuller, well-known around the country as the owner of Albina Press. Fuller had been looking to start a café, and he found the space, then an artists' co-op, to be just what he was looking for. Over the next few years, Albina Press would become one of the top cafés in Portland for both quality of drinks made and quantity of drinks sold. Mindy was on the crew when the café opened in 2003.

Keith, however, was not on the staff. After getting a master's degree in computer science from Portland State University, he found a job in the software industry. Keith helped Kevin with part of the remodeling process, but that was about it. "There was an intention of involvement, but it didn't work out," Mindy said of Keith's association with Albina Press. "It just wasn't the time."

Albina Press quickly developed a great reputation for quality, and it was well-known around Portland that the Press was the best place in the city to get shots of Stumptown's Hair Bender espresso. "Coffee was changing, and Stumptown brought the quality up as far as what people experienced in what they get for roasted coffee," said Mindy. "Then Albina Press took it up to a level that really tweaked it out — like latte art, and focusing on every shot. It was the new flavor, and that made it really unique. There were a lot of star baristas — people that wanted to do more."

The team of baristas continually pushed each other to do better, but it was not always smooth sailing. "In any business," said Mindy, "it's difficult to maintain all the personalities.... It was intense."

The intensity built what some called the best café staff in Portland, and the knowledge they gained prepared several members for starting their own endeavors. In 2008, Billy Wilson left to start his Barista project. Matt Higgins, who had joined Albina Press in 2006, moved on to found Coava. Mindy worked at Albina Press until 2009, when she and Keith opened the Red E.

## Do What You Want, and Harm No One

The Red E launched on Memorial Day 2009, in a large space on North Killingsworth, just down the street from Portland Community College. "We wanted to set down in an area near a community that had disposable income and was not tightly coupled to the economy as far as people with day jobs," Keith said. "For me, that was like, 'Well, the students are here, at least. Maybe we won't hit the big numbers with them, but we're always going to tread water.'" The café space is artsy, with gallery-quality paint and lighting that show off the work of rotating local artists. Farley, who studied art and photography at PCC and PSU, curates the space.

When it opened, the Red E served Coava coffee alongside Intelligentsia coffee from Chicago. Having coffee from more than one roaster was uncommon in those days. "It was only with Billy [Wilson] and me that the multiple-roaster thing existed," said Mindy. "Mostly, it was Billy."

Farley never intended to open a multiroaster café. "I was a little forced into it," she said. "I actually did want to carry Stumptown.

They said no because I was too close to one of their largest accounts." (Red E is half a mile away from the first Albina Press.) Farley admitted Stumptown's decision was hard to take at first, but it taught her a valuable lesson. "After you run a business for a while, you start to understand, 'Oh, that's how business works.' We can't all hold hands in the coffee world like we think we can." Her comments demonstrate an underlying challenge of Portland's coffee industry, where friends often compete with each other for business. Roasters and café owners can remain friends, but they have to leave the business side out of the relationships.

For a while, the Red E carried Heart coffee as well, but in order to save money and have more control over the coffees they served, Keith began roasting for the café in 2012. "We weren't ready to roast when we opened," explained Mindy. "Keith was working. The plan was, he was going to work for three years and keep getting that programming-type money while I ran this, which is what I was already doing." As of 2013, Keith does nearly all the roasting, renting time on a roaster owned by Trevin Miller. (Miller owns Mr. Green Beans, a shop geared to do-it-yourself coffee roasters, on Mississippi Avenue. He has a separate roasting facility off site.) "I feel that Keith really wants to get to quality in the same way I do," said Mindy. "Usually, it's a difficult thing — the roaster and the barista and the owner. Because we're all one, it makes it a little easier."

The couple opened up a second café in 2012, a small espresso stand inside the Ecotrust building in the Pearl District. "This is our flagship," Keith said of the Killingsworth café. "[The other café] is across the river. It shows our brand. Financially, it's never been in the red."

As of early 2013, Keith was roasting around two hundred pounds of coffee each week, all of it sold at the two cafés. Miller learned to roast partly by trial and error, but also by shadowing roasters from Sterling, fellow members of Coffee Roasters United, a group of smaller Portland roasters who pool their buying power. "I guess I just try to accentuate the more fruity aspects of coffee," Keith explained. "Ideally, I try to cover a broad range of options, from bright and fruity to our espressos, which are a little darker and maybe a little more chocolaty. I just try to keep options available — which is tricky."

Green bean quality is where he starts. "My strategy — and I'm still having a lot of fun with it — is, I buy the best green coffee I can afford when I go to the cupping table. When I get it home, I have a general roast profile on it, and I try to push it in whatever direction it needs to go. There's some sweetness and some fruitiness there. I don't always get it." Even though he purchases smaller quantities of coffee than many roasters do, Miller doesn't see a problem getting ahold of good coffee. "Someone's always willing to peel four bags from a container for you," he said. "It's almost nothing for them. And if I handle it right, I can keep it on menu for four months."

To keep things running smoothly, Farley and Miller split up the duties for the business. Mindy spends three days a week on the bar, and on the other days, she works with vendors and does general business stuff. Keith is the roaster and IT/marketing person. "People ask why Keith isn't working in the café, but it's because he's doing other things — things that I don't want to do," said Mindy. "He's the roaster, and I don't want to do that. I went and roasted with him once, and it was amazing, but I don't want to do it. It takes a very specific type of person that can enjoy roasting." Mindy said work is on both their minds a lot. "I constantly ask him, 'How much do you think about work? Do you think it's 90 percent of the time?' He's like, 'Yeah.'"

The couple is determined to make sure they can run the café and still have time for themselves. "From day one," said Keith, "we've wanted this business to be where we can step away from it and it can run itself. We have a really competent manager in place; we've got an assistant roaster."

Keith enjoys being a business owner. "I don't feel as controlled," he said. "When I worked in software, I spent more fucking time in traffic. It was too much. I was working fifty hours a week then spending an hour and a half in traffic five days a week. I was scared to ask for time off because it would always be the wrong time. [Managers would say], 'We're going beta on this product,' even though we weren't going beta for another two fucking years."

"Ooooh," Mindy interjected.

"What, I can't use the *fuck* word?" Keith asked, grinning. "*Fuck* is perfectly good for emphasis, especially when talking about software."

## Red E Expansion and Future Plans

The couple plans to keep growing the business, though they aren't quite sure what that growth will look like. "We have two different visions," said Farley. "My vision is that we stay very special and that we open two more cafés. But I'm also not a roaster, and it's tied to that, and Keith wants growth in a different way. I would love it if only we sold our coffee."

Keith chimed in. "I don't really feel that way. I have multiple fronts I want to go after, which is to expand and service wholesale accounts, to do more catering, contract roasting for private labels or proprietary roasts." The Red E recently got the account to provide coffee for Laughing Planet, a Portland-based burrito chain.

Keith also wants to sell more beans. "I'd love to have a café in a real visible location that has a lot of people with disposable income and a high population density," he said. "We're kind of up here on the lower peninsula. It would be nice to have a roasting and retail location. I'm kind of on the fence about that. I want the draw of having the roaster in the shop, but I don't necessarily want to roast around people."

Whichever path they end up taking, Keith and Mindy will continue to be fixtures on the Portland coffee scene for years to come. Like many pioneers who headed West aeons ago, the couple has prospered in the land of opportunity. "It's kind of fun," Keith said. "Mindy and I came here with nothing, and we've had many lives together."

## Matt Higgins
### High Expectations Get Results for Coava

*Over the years, I have amassed a trove of memories from things I encountered while wandering without any particular destination. One of the first times I walked around Portland looking for coffee, I stumbled upon a little shop nestled into one corner of a bamboo flooring and design company. The café had its large garage door open, and the powerful aroma of freshly roasted coffee poured out onto the street. I had originally planned to wander a little farther, but the smell convinced me I had reached my destination.*

*The café I found that day was Coava. I soon learned that Coava was one of the rising stars in the city's coffee industry, but then, I didn't know that. I only knew that Portland was special and that if you picked a direction and started walking, you were bound to find some good coffee.* — WH

In conversation, Portland's coffee roasters are not always quick to praise their competitors — unsurprising, perhaps, since they started their own companies to provide a better product to the market. When they do compliment other roasters, though, Coava is frequently the first name that comes up. The company's success is a reflection of its founder, Matt Higgins, whose diligent study of every phase of the coffee production process, from seed to cup, is changing the nature of the relationship between roasters and coffee growers.

### Starting in Coffee

Dressed in a fitted black T-shirt, brown Carhartt jeans, and work boots, Higgins looks like he could just as easily be driving an 18-wheeler as producing high-end coffees. He speaks deliberately, punctuating his sentences with precision. Matt was born in Ohio and moved to Portland in 1990. He attended the University of Oregon, studying German and business. He worked in coffee all through college, starting as a barista at Common Grounds, a shop on the UO campus. "Back then, you know, still in 1999, coffee was making advances with regards to the supply chain and quality of the commodity, but I didn't know it," he said. "I didn't have the proper lens to inspect it. To me, a mocha with mega chocolate and whipped cream and a cherry was 'Yeah, I'm a good barista. I did a good job.'"

After graduation, Matt moved to Germany to be a translator for an eco-friendly agricultural company in Hamburg, Germany. He translated chemical documents (all relating to plants) from German to English and English to German. "I had a chance to increase my botanical knowledge and learn about botany, agriculture, and agro-industries," he said. "It started to open my eyes to farming because we were creating eco-friendly pesticidal products — pesticides from plants for plants." Though the material was interesting, Higgins was not a fan of the office culture (or wearing slacks), so he moved back to the States in 2004.

He landed in the East Bay area of California, where he worked for Pacific Bay Coffee. Higgins started as a barista and then transitioned into being a roaster, which exposed him to more than just the retail side of the coffee business. "It had been my passion from day one since returning from my, quote, *career* overseas," he said. "I wanted to hit coffee hard. I had gone through school for four years and had this collegiate debt. Now I wanted to take on a career [without adding to that debt] and have the discipline to create a career for myself." Higgins developed a coffee curriculum for himself, so he could carefully study every facet of the industry.

Working at Pacific Bay gave Higgins the opportunity to learn roasting from a knowledgeable mentor, John Laird.[45] Laird, who founded Pacific Bay, was a mechanical engineer by training who previously worked for Fresh Roast Systems, helping to engineer fluid-airbed roasters. Laird taught Higgins about how roasters transfer heat to the beans as well as the chemistry inside the beans during the roasting process. "It was very fortuitous to be able to

---

45. Laird is currently the wholesale account manager for Verve Coffee Roasters, a Santa Cruz–based company founded by some of his former employees.

study underneath him and see [roasting] through an engineer's lens," Higgins said.

While he studied roasting, Higgins also bought several books relating to growing coffee and scoured online resources to find publications from international agencies that help farmers at origin. "I tried to start pumping up my understanding of farm management, seed to cup, because I really wanted to wrap my mind around the supply chain, wrap my mind around the chemical engagement of roasting," Higgins said. Each new discovery led to more questions and deeper research. In other words, the more you learn, the less you know. "Especially in coffee, that is 100 percent true," he said.

## High Unemployment Leads to Better Coffee

Around 2006, Higgins moved back to Portland, at a time when third-wave coffee was really exploding. "[Third-wave coffee] awoke something in young professionals such as myself who are products of my generation, which is overeducated and underemployed," he said.

When Matt graduated from college in 2003, Oregon's unemployment was the highest in the United States.[46] According to Higgins, the bleak employment picture helped create a new generation of passionate baristas. "You have all these young kids who are smart and have mild embitterment for schooling and can't do anything," he said. "You see them start to really latch on to things that are more their passion than sitting in a cube and earning $9 an hour. I think a lot of people gave up on that, and they're like, 'Well, if I'm going to earn $9 an hour, I may as well earn $30 an hour being a server. Maybe I'll get really good at being a bartender and then split off and [start my own thing].'"

Higgins found a job working for Albina Press, the biggest name on the West Coast for aspiring baristas. "We all sought out Albina Press because we had heard through the grapevine that they were the people who were passionate and loved coffee, the ones that were

---

46. Oregon's unemployment rate for 2003 was 8.1%. Source: Bureau of Labor Statistics. http://www.bls.gov/lau/lastrk03.htm

starting to attend barista competitions," he said. At the Press, the crew Matt worked with was very talented and driven to succeed. "Together, that original crew was effing phenomenal," Matt said. "We did numbers as a human machine that I have not seen replicated elsewhere." Higgins compared the Albina Press crew to the 1992 US Olympic men's basketball team, known as the Dream Team. "It just dominated everybody, and that's what [working at Albina Press] felt like. Literally, there could be a line of thirty people, and we could plow through it in like ten minutes. It was crazy numbers!"

## Moving On

The talented crew could only stay together for so long. "We all worked together, had theories, tastes," Matt recalled. "Eventually that era kind of came to an end. Billy [Wilson] was taking off and wanted to do his own thing, and I knew I wasn't going to be roasting for the company, and that's where my passion and heart lie, so I exited at the same time as Billy." Higgins became a freelancer, doing equipment repair around town for a few months. He also did some consulting for a few café startups, helping with equipment selection, training, installation, and general business consulting. None of the work paid very well.

With his experience in many facets of the industry — as a barista, equipment repairman, and so on — Higgins decided it was time to do his own thing, and in August 2008, he took the plunge. He spent all the money he had, charged up his credit cards, and bought his first roaster, setting it up in his garage. He purchased his first two pallets of green beans and started roasting, selling coffee under the Coava name.[47]

To promote his coffees, Higgins enlisted his friend Sam Purvis to compete at the 2009 Northwest Regional Barista Competition (NWRBC) using Coava coffee. Higgins had carefully selected the coffee for his company's debut. "It was a really good Ethiopia that year that I had been tracking for a while and had sourced it," he said. The strategy worked well. The coffee scored high at the regional competition, signifying a new arrival on the competitive

---

47. Coava is a Turkish word for "green coffee."

coffee scene. "It created this buzz among young professionals that, 'Oh, shit. This coffee's good.'"

Higgins ran Coava out of his garage for a year, strictly as a wholesaler. At the time, he was roasting for Coffeehouse-Five and the Red E Café, shops on Northeast Killingsworth that were two blocks apart from each other. The shops gave Portlanders their first exposure to Coava coffee.

## Out of the Garage and into the National Spotlight

Soon after starting Coava, Matt brought in Keith Gehrke, a good friend from California, to run the company with him. "From day one, I wanted to have a business partner, and I invited him to come up to Portland and gave him half my company," Matt said. Higgins and Gehrke opened Coava's first café on July 7, 2010, inside Bamboo Revolution. Matt said they originally tried to lease their own individual space, but negotiations fell through. Coava's designer and builder worked for Bamboo Revolution, so Matt and Keith were able to rent out space in the showroom that was going to be a model kitchen. Instead, it became a living demonstration of Bamboo Revolution's products and design, run by Coava.

It did not take long for Coava to gain national attention. All of Coava's coffees submitted to Kenneth Davids's Coffee Review website scored over 90 out of 100, signifying their excellence to a wide audience. Another of Coava's first headline achievements was the development of the Kone filter. Keith and Matt developed the product together, going through several prototypes as they tried to perfect the pour-over apparatus. "We had both from day one had an aspiration to create a paperless filter that was proprietary to Coava," said Higgins. Originally, they planned to sell the Kone in the café, and maybe a few online. "The goal was not to mass-produce it because, in my opinion, we did not have a distribution network to make it profitable," said Higgins. When Oliver Strand positively reviewed the Kone for the *New York Times Ristretto* blog, Coava burst into the national conversation. Gizmodo picked up the story and suddenly, Coava became a company people were talking about.

In addition to the Kone, Coava's success in barista competitions also provided lots of publicity. Sam Purvis won the NWRBC in 2011;

Devin Chapman, another of Coava's baristas, won the Northwest Regional Brewers Cup the same year. In 2012, Chapman won regional titles in both the Brewers Cup and the Barista Championship, finishing fourth overall at the US Barista Championship (USBC) in Portland. In 2013, Chapman repeated as NWRBC champion. This success bolstered Coava's reputation for great coffee and great baristas, and the little roaster that started out in Higgins's garage quickly became a national brand.

## A Tough Breakup

Although the sleek, shiny Kone filter helped Coava build its reputation, the brewing products soon turned into a financial liability for the young coffee company. "They were great, but it's supply and demand," said Matt. "If you want to get a proper price point for resale to have a profit margin, you have to do larger runs. Larger runs meaning five, six, seven, ten thousand units at a time. At $25 a pop to produce the filter, we were getting into writing checks for $50,000 at a time." Those checks hampered Coava's ability to source coffee, something Higgins could not live with. "We are a small company. When that starts to interfere with my ability to purchase green coffees, our core product, something has to change."

The business partners ultimately decided to spin off Able Brewing, which focused on equipment, with Higgins retaining ownership of Coava and Gehrke taking ownership of Able (including the Kone). "I didn't want to let [the Kone] go because it was something I helped create, but it didn't make money," Higgins said, "so I had to cut the ties on it.[48]" Although the split was finalized in August 2011, it was clear from Higgins's voice that the separation was still painful a year and a half later.

## What Does Coava Stand Out For?

On the coffee side, Higgins strives for quality and consistency as well as a roasting profile that falls somewhere between light and dark. "I am not by any means a blond, light-roast lover. There's a

---

48. Able Brewing continues to operate after the separation. In mid-2012, the company successfully raised $155,000 through Kickstarter to finance an updated version of the Kone brewing system.

good balance between caramelization of sugars, what's too dark and what's too light."

Consistency is paramount to Coava's success. "We're extremely, extremely consistent, I would say," Matt said. "One thing we really compete with is our consistency, and we're only as good as our consistency with regards to our quality. If the quality is high but not consistent, then it's sort of variable to the consumer."

The first step in reaching consistency involves working with farmers to improve the quality of the green coffee. Higgins regularly communicates with the farmers who raise his coffees. "People at origin have satellite phones now. They have email, access to communication devices they didn't have even five or ten years ago," he said. "I can have live-time dialogue with a mill manager and discuss Brix analysis on their fermentation. I can change values over the phone and say, 'Ferment to this variable,' and really start to have a pulse on the production of the coffee."

The communication pays off for everyone involved. "We're seeing coffees as an industry, in terms of quality, that we have never seen before," Matt said. Every part of the supply chain is changing, from infrastructure to financing to farmers understanding they will get paid more per pound for better quality beans. Farmers in developing countries are used to producing as much coffee as possible instead of focusing on quality. This is changing, according to Higgins. "A lot of the farmers are coming out of, 'Hey, maybe I shouldn't focus on trying to produce an extra fifty quintals[49] or twenty bags of parchment coffee. Instead, I'd like to reduce volume and increase quality.' You have to have a business mind to do that because, as a farmer, you're doing math. 'Well, if I produce less coffee and I can get a higher price for it, I'm actually better off.'"

## Finding New Coffees

When we spoke, Higgins had just returned from Honduras, where he was working on finalizing contracts for the next season's coffees. "You write your financial budget and your growth model,

---

49. One quintal equals one hundred pounds or one hundred kilograms, depending on the country.

what you're going to need, and you come in and do QC [quality control] and start prebooking. Because it's an agricultural product, 50 to 60 percent of it is still on the trees right now, depending on where you're at. It's me QC'ing, making sure that coffee's not dipping three or four points, something that can hurt our brand, making sure we have enough coffee coming in to sell."

Finding new coffees requires a lot of effort on the ground in developing countries because green buyers have to build the contacts necessary to grow the business. "It's hard. A lot of other buyers love to present this image of Indiana Jones-ing the coffee, like, 'I'm discovering it!' But you really have to have a good connection with people on the ground."

A student of every facet of the coffee production, Higgins has taken his coffee studies to the extreme. In the basement of his North Portland home, Higgins has raised more than three hundred coffee trees, including thirty-four varieties, all growing under different conditions. These trials help him recognize problems on the farms such as soil nutrient deficiencies. "I can go to a coffee farm and perform an audit and tell you if you have a nitrogen or boron deficiency, whether or not you're going to be prone to rust, tree spacing — everything, shade trees. That's helped a lot. As soon as I can physically get there, I'll know whether I want to continue asking questions. Sometimes, it will be like, 'I won't be able to turn this farm in five years,' and that's too much of an investment for me to eat through the commodity."

When he finds a farm that looks promising, one of the first steps is to separate the best coffees from the average ones. "In Guatemala, I'm doing a project that produced a general commercial-grade lot," Higgins said. "Two hundred farmers compiled together to make this lot, and it had been going to some of the big boys.[50] They're booking eight boxes, and all they want is eight boxes of 79 [a cupping score]. If you've got eight to twenty boxes of 79 points, you know that some of it is like 60 points and some of it is 85, and a small fraction of that is 88, 89, 90. So we come in, separate everybody in the receiving station, haul it, roast it, cup it,

---

50. Large buyers like Green Mountain and Starbucks.

separate it out, and find the people that are performing, and then develop trends. Then we see how it is comparing to regions, then travel to that area and really separate it out." By getting involved at origin, Higgins is able to find and purchase coffees with higher levels of quality than he could otherwise.

## Coava's Legacy

Higgins has clear goals — for Coava to be a national company, to open a couple more cafés in Portland, and to grow the company in a way that is true to the coffee and the people working with it. "We've got thirteen employees right now. A majority of them are on our health insurance plan. I try to take care of them as much as possible, and anything that offers risk to them, I don't do."

How does Higgins see his legacy? "I want to leave behind farmers that work exclusively with us year-to-year that we support, help, and invest in," he said. "These are a lot of the things Stumptown has done. I'm just competing as the smaller fish and trying to take care of my own employees super, super closely and offer coffees that people have never seen before and not obliterate them on a large production scale." Higgins does not plan to "wallpaper Coava's coffee all over the US," but he does want to grow a national brand, big enough to buy the quantities of coffee necessary to reduce the company's vulnerability to coffee market trends. He plans to open three cafés in Portland before deciding on the next step.

Whatever that will be, Higgins wants to keep everything in perspective. "I don't ever want to say, 'I wish I would have spent more hours at the office.' I want to spend more time with my wife, have children, and be a family man," he said. Nothing too complex, in other words. "I've been working since I was fifteen, and I do what I love, and I want to bring amazing coffees to people who want to taste it. That's it."

## 15

# Rita Kaminsky
## Longtime General Manager at the Albina Press

*Rita Kaminsky is a humble person, at least when it comes to talking about herself. When we met, Kaminsky was the general manager for the Albina Press, overseeing both of the company's locations. "It's not a really glamorous story," Rita said when I asked how she got into coffee. "You're not going to get anything fantastic. My story is really basic." Whether or not she sees her story as glamorous, it does add to the Portland coffee story, and it also demonstrates the career progression of a coffee professional. — WH*

Rita Kaminsky's interest in coffee was originally influenced by her foodie parents. Growing up in Milwaukee, Wisconsin, she remembers them taking her to Northwest Coffee Mills, a small roaster in the Milwaukee area. "It was like Southeast Portland fifteen years ago," she told me. "You walk into this little closet shop, and you had all these glass jars of coffee. Looking back at it, I know it wasn't necessarily quality coffee, but it was very boutique."

Later, while attending the University of Wisconsin-Milwaukee, Kaminsky worked as a bookkeeper for a local grocery store. When the store's owners decided to open a bakery down the street, they put Kaminsky in charge of the project. Opening the bakery gave Kaminsky her first opportunity to manage a café. She was involved in every part of the new opening, including finding the coffee. "I came across Alterra Coffee Roasters and really loved their product," she recalled.[51] "Out of everybody in Milwaukee, Alterra was doing the best thing."

### Coffee, Wow!

Kaminsky signed the bakery up to serve Alterra coffee, which

---

51. In 2013, Alterra became Colectivo Coffee.

allowed her to attend coffee training sessions at the company's headquarters. Visiting Alterra's roastery changed Kaminsky's life. "The first session, they take you back into the bean-packing area, and they open up all these fifty-gallon buckets of coffee and let you smell each one," said Kaminsky. "I remember when they opened up that bucket of Ethiopian Harrar, it was just like this eye-opening experience, like, 'Oh my god! This doesn't smell like coffee. This smells like something else. This is so unique, I've never experienced anything like this before!'"

Kaminsky enjoyed the bakery job, but she longed to know more about coffee. Six months after the bakery opened, when everything was up and running, she left and went to work for Alterra. "I went to Alterra as soon as I could. I never stopped thinking about the coffee," she said. Kaminsky joined Alterra as an assistant manager at the company's original standalone café. She put all her energy into becoming a coffee expert. "I dove into it headfirst. I couldn't learn enough," she said, praising the thoroughness of Alterra's training program. "I really feel like I was taught how to pull espresso correctly from the first time. I was taught amazingly good basics," she said.

## To PDX

Kaminsky stayed at Alterra for two years before moving to the Northwest. Her boss, Ward Fowler, encouraged her to go to Portland, enticing her with stories about the city's coffee scene, especially Stumptown. "At the time, Ward and I were confident I could get a job at Stumptown," Rita recalled. She decided to make the move, having never even visited Portland.

Rita and her boyfriend drove out in April 2003, leaving Wisconsin's bitter cold behind and landing in a much more welcoming climate. "There was literally a rainbow over Portland when we drove in on the freeway," Kaminsky recalled. "I thought, 'Are you kidding me? This is where I'm moving?' I was taken immediately."

Despite her experience at Alterra, Kaminsky soon realized her plan to join Stumptown was overly optimistic. "Unfortunately, it's Portland, so it was really tough getting a job out here — really, really, really tough," she said. (It is important to note that, in 2003, the Portland coffee scene was much smaller than it is today. Albina Press, where Kaminsky has worked for the past six years, did not even exist, nor did many of Portland's better cafés. Stumptown only had two cafés, and Kaminsky was unable to land a job at either one.)

After a few frustrating weeks looking for work, Kaminsky found her first job at a Tully's café in Northwest Portland. "When I walked into that shop, they had a Robur grinder and a La Marzocco machine, and I thought, 'I'll apply here,'" she said. "I was so naïve, I didn't know that Tully's was a corporate chain."

Kaminsky figured it out when she showed up for her first day of work. "I walked in, and they set down this packet [of information about company policies]," she said. "I was like, 'Oh! I had no idea this is a huge, massive chain.' But they pay their employees really well, and they have really good benefits."[52]

Kaminsky worked at Tully's for a little over a year, a frustrating time for her. Every day, she would bring her sixteen-ounce Stumptown coffee to work, discretely slipping it inside a Tully's mug. She longed to get into a Portland-based coffee shop but lacked the relationships she needed to get into the closed scene. Finally, tiring of the corporate culture at Tully's, Kaminsky moved to San Antonio for a year to be a nanny for her cousin's triplets. The move gave her the space she needed. "It was a really good time for me to reassess where I was going," she said. In addition to caring for the triplets, Kaminsky also worked three days a week at a local café, bringing a little bit of Portland style to her job. "In 2005, people in San Antonio had never seen latte art before," she said. "It was really gratifying to serve someone their 'best coffee' ever. I'm really glad I went." Kaminsky's stay in Texas convinced her she wanted to make a career in coffee—just not in corporate coffee.

## Back to PDX, with a Mission

In 2006, Kaminsky moved back to Portland and found a job managing Bakery Bar, a small shop located on Water Avenue, where

---

52. Her statement about benefits was ironic, considering we were speaking one week after Tully's announced it was filing for bankruptcy. Perhaps the benefits were too good.

Bunk Bar is today. Neither of the owners of the bakery had worked in food service, so Kaminsky was able to help them organize the café and improve its scheduling and flow, with good results. "When we started," she said, "we were doing $250 to $300 per day. When I left, we were about $1,200 a day. It was really fun to watch it grow."

Kaminsky's coffee skills caught the eyes of Bruce Milletto and Matt Milletto, whose American Barista & Coffee School was located just behind the bakery. They hired Rita as a barista trainer for the school, and for five years, Kaminsky trained groups of students from around the world. She found the workshops rewarding, often working with people who knew nothing about coffee. "I love getting my hands on somebody who's never made coffee before," she said. "It's great being the first person to teach them how to make coffee and watch their passion and understanding for coffee grow right before your eyes."

## Career Advancement through Competition

In 2006, Matt Milletto convinced Kaminsky to compete in the Northwest Regional Barista Competition (NWRBC), being held at the Wonder Ballroom in Portland. "It was something I had never, ever considered before. I'm not a competitive person," Kaminsky said. Not competitive, perhaps, but definitely driven. Kaminsky's petite frame conceals a forceful determination. Once she decided to enter the competition, Kaminsky threw herself into it. "I've never worked so hard for anything, ever, in my whole entire life," she said. "I had never micromanaged myself so much and looked at every single detail [of what] I was doing, memorizing the performance."

Kaminsky was competing for more than just pride. "The whole reason I did the competition," she said, "was to get hired at a specialty coffee shop. That was the goal — to get noticed by another café to hire me. It was a career move for me. I never wanted to win. I just wanted to prove myself as a barista and prove to myself and other people that I could do what they were doing."

Kaminsky finished tenth, a strong showing for a first-time competitor. More importantly, her strategy to find a better job paid off. "The day that I competed," she said, "was the day that Billy Wilson asked me to work at Albina Press."

## Life at Albina Press

Kaminsky started at Albina Press as a barista and then was promoted to general manager when Billy Wilson and Mindy Farley left to open their own cafés. For nearly four years, Kaminsky oversaw both Albina Press locations. She said that one of her biggest challenges as a manager is teaching people how to be consistent when they make coffee. New people shadow Kaminsky the first three days. She teaches flow, the cash register, and how to pour latte art in a pint glass. Rita has very high standards for her employees. "Everybody involved in coffee knows that it is a micromanaged job. You have to be able to deal with people nitpicking you. There are so many little details that you kind of have to have a thick skin," she said.

Despite the focus on consistency, Albina Press still allowed the baristas some flexibility in how they pulled their espresso shots. Each barista has his or her own ideas about how the coffee should taste, and Kaminsky was fine with that. "As long as you have the intention of making really great coffee all the time, then I'm willing to give you free range to make the coffee how you want to do it," she said.

Kaminsky pointed out how important it is for a barista to develop a good palate. Measuring variables such as mass, temperature, and time is not always enough. "I want all of the new technology, but I think it can be a crutch sometimes and that it's taking away from the idea we're serving a consumer product and experience," she said. "I'd love to have a refractometer to tell me how well I'm brewing my coffee, but we know if it tastes good or it doesn't taste good. There is something to be said for a barista who serves the same coffee every day and can do different things with it."

## Value of Competitions

Rita no longer competes, but she stays very active in the barista competitions as a technical judge. At regional and national competitions, you can see her crouched behind competing baristas, clipboard in hand, closely watching every movement of the baristas as they give their presentations. Rita has also served as a sensory judge, but her years of barista experience and attention to detail make her a natural fit for the technical judge position.

Kaminsky said the competitions inspire baristas to do a better job and learn more about the coffees they serve. "It's a great way to push everybody further," she said. "At the United States Barista Championship (USBC), you've got the badasses of the fifty states that are all pushing each other harder so when they go home to their individual cities, they're going to create a better product."

Baristas get better through practice and through hearing feedback about their performances. "The critiques that I got from my judges as a competitor were extremely eye-opening," said Kaminsky. "It was really nice to have seven different points of view tell me what they thought about my skills and my drinks. It's really rare that you get that kind of feedback as a barista. It's so subjective from customers."

The competitions are also a way to promote new coffee growers. "Sometimes I feel like the competitions are showcasing the farmer as much as the competitor. It's a great way to market different coffees and explain to the audience why coffee is so special and unique for that reason."

Above all, the competitions are about having fun. "The competitions create a great sense of community," Kaminsky said. "These things are like family reunions. I know that the competitors come with the goal to win and it's not to make friends or meet people, but it's something that's inevitable and happens anyway."

## Looking Abroad to the Future

The end of 2012 was bringing big changes to Kaminsky's career. She was planning to leave Albina Press and spend some time outside Portland. Her first stop would be El Salvador, to train one of Aida Batlle's baristas for the El Salvador National Barista Championship.[53] After the competition Kaminsky would attend

---

53. Batlle is a prominent coffee grower in El Salvador. She is well-known for producing some of the world's best coffees.

## Rita Kaminsky

the 2013 World Barista Championship in Melbourne, Australia. After that she planned to move into retail or wholesale training. Wherever she lands, Kaminsky's travels would serve her need for a break from the café floor. "I've been behind counters since I was fourteen, and I'm thirty-two now, so it's time to step aside for a little bit," she said. [54]

Rita also wants to further her coffee knowledge. "It's imperative I work for a roastery next," she explained. "It's really important for me to be close to the coffee. Ever since I've worked for a roastery, I've wanted to work for one again. You can't compare to being that close to the coffee."

Ultimately, her coffee journey may take her even closer to coffee's origins. "My pipe dream would be to work in a coffee nursery. That would be the crème-de-la-crème job, to work with an agronomist in a coffee nursery — anywhere," she said. "When I'm not doing anything coffee related, I'm in my garden. Gardening is just as much of a passion for me as coffee is. It would be the perfect marriage for me if I could grow coffee. I couldn't think of a better job."

---

54. After leaving Australia, Kaminsky's next stop ended up being San Francisco, where she is the retail manager at Linea Caffe, a new café and roastery started by Ecco Caffe founder Andrew Barnett and restaurateur Anthony Myint.

## Devin Chapman
### Sitting Down with the Champ

*Devin Chapman, Coava's retail operations manager,[55] has only worked in coffee for a couple years, but his list of accolades would suggest he has been in coffee much longer. With two regional Brewers Cup championships, two Northwest Regional Barista Competition (NWRBC) titles, and a fourth-place finish at the US Barista Championship (USBC) already in his trophy case, Chapman's rise in the coffee world has been nothing less than impressive.* —WH

Devin Chapman grew up in the Bay Area of California and moved to Portland in 2003 to attend Multnomah University, where he studied learning theory. Outside of school, Chapman was fascinated by the Portland coffee scene. "People would talk about Stumptown as really good stuff," he said, "and I enjoyed it and bought into the product, the quality, and a little bit into the image of it — the classic Stumptown experience."

After graduation, Devin considered becoming a teacher but found a job at Portland Rescue Mission instead. He spent two years at the Mission, doing communications work and coordinating volunteers. In his free time, Chapman started learning about coffee — where he could get better coffee and how to make it. "I was definitely an enthusiast," he recalled.

When he left the Mission, Chapman did some consulting and other part-time work before landing a barista job at Crema in April of 2010. To the new barista, coffee was like a puzzle to be solved. "I wanted to get as good as I possibly could at the mechanics of making espresso," said Chapman. "I've always been a kind of

---

55. Chapman left Coava at the end of September 2013, with plans to start a coffee project of his own.

person that whatever I'm doing, I want to do the best job I can." He went through two training sessions with Stumptown instead of the usual one. "From the very beginning, I was very intent on getting as good as I could as fast as I could," he said. Chapman's stint at Crema was short. He had just started making coffee for customers when Coava hired him to help open the company's first café in July 2010.

## Barista Competitions

When he went to Coava, Devin intended to represent his new company at the barista competitions. "Even when I was interviewing at Crema, I was interested in competing," he said. "Through my training, I was thinking like, 'Yeah, it would be cool to compete someday. I want to get really good at this.'" Chapman prepared a routine and competed at the 2011 NWRBC. He did not make the finals, but he did not leave Tacoma empty-handed. At the last minute, he entered the Brewers Cup, a competition to see who can brew the best single cup of coffee. Chapman won first prize.

Devin said he did not expect to win, but his success was not a complete surprise either. "I was pretty blown away because I'd been in coffee for such a short time," he said. "But at the same time, I came from a café where I brewed coffee to order every day. I'm doing coffee like this and dialing it in every day, and talking to people every day. That first year, I just talked about my job and was very comfortable with brewing coffee that way." Winning the regional Brewers Cup gave Chapman the opportunity to travel to Houston for the US Brewers Cup (USBC). Since he was going to be there anyway, Chapman also entered the USBC, and he made the semifinals.

The extra practice must have paid off because Chapman's second competition season went better than the first. At the 2012 NWRBC, Chapman swept the titles of the Brewers Cup and the Barista Competition. A couple months later, at the 2012 USBC in Portland, Devin made the finals, ultimately finishing fourth in the nation.[56]

---

56. Chapman also won the 2013 Northwest Barista Championship, continuing his remarkable run.

## Devin Chapman

**Competition Preparation**

How does someone become such a good competitor in such a short time? "Competition is interesting because it's like a game," Chapman said. "A lot of people like to harp on the fact that it's nothing like a retail expression — it's not like working as a barista. In some ways, it isn't. But in some ways it is, a lot." Devin welcomes the judges' evaluations, even when they are not all positive. "A lot of people like to argue with the judges, but I'm like, 'No, it's my job to make sure there's no argument,'" he said. "That's part of my job as a professional, just like it's my job as a barista to make sure somebody has a pleasant experience." Figuring out what the judges are looking for is the key to success. "How do I use the subjectivity of the judges to my advantage?" he said. "If I can engage the judges, if I can get them to a place where they're interested, I've done a lot."

Chapman mulls over his upcoming competitions most of the year, but the preparation really ramps up about a month before the competitions take place. Once the practice sessions start, Devin talks to a variety of people about his performances. He invites experienced judges to give him input. People outside the coffee industry also provide valuable feedback. Chapman brings in chefs and bartenders to compare his tasting notes to theirs. For one competition, he invited about a dozen of his regular customers to sit in on a run-through, giving them an opportunity to build an even closer relationship with the café and making the practice sessions more fun. "It gives me really abnormal and completely subjective feedback," Chapman said. "It's just a totally different take on the whole thing."

Preparing for competition pushes Chapman to the limit of his coffee consumption. "I probably tasted twenty-five shots of espresso two nights ago," he told me, referring to one of his practice sessions before the 2013 NWRBC. "I got, like, two hours of sleep. I was blind-tasting five different coffees for competition. It got real weird toward the end."

Succeeding in competitions has not made Chapman complacent. If anything, it makes him work harder. "I have this conversation a lot with people who work as baristas," he said. "Every day at [the] bar I'm like, 'How can I get better? How can I make better coffee? How can I work harder or better? How can I serve people better? How can I respond to an abnormal situation better?'"

Chapman encourages the baristas who work under him to compete as well, even if they have not been working in coffee for very long. "The process of competing puts a magnifying glass on what you're doing," he said. "The accountability you have to have — a mastery of your coffee, a mastery of your craft — is really valuable to develop." Barista competitions have improved the specialty coffee industry. "I think it's creating higher stakes, more drive in people, more professionalism," Devin said. "It creates an opportunity where people are recognized outside the coffee industry for what they are doing. Anytime that happens, I think it's a good thing for them professionally and for the industry at large." The competitions encourage people to stay in coffee too. "A lot of people make the transition from, 'Yeah, I'm kind of interested in working in coffee,' to 'I want to do this with my life.'"

## Service and Hospitality Create Connections with the Customer

Chapman's official title with Coava is retail operations manager, so anything related to retail in Portland is his responsibility. "I'm realizing that in coffee, retail is my passion," he said. "Having the ability to create and regularly make excellent coffee fits [within] the hospitality experience. When somebody comes in, I want them to have the absolute best experience they can possibly have, and I want to connect them to the industry. You do that with really good coffee, by teaching them about the origin or the history of coffee or the specifics of that particular coffee or the farm."

To raise the coffee industry's profile (and to justify higher prices), Chapman suggests the industry take a look at the way coffee is served. "I think a really vital step we as an industry can realize is that hospitality has been neglected," he said. "Hospitality is the widest berth for bringing more people into the industry. If we want to see better and better coffees, we're going to need to get more people involved. It means another 10 percent of coffee drinkers need to switch from drinking Dunkin' Donuts or something they buy at the grocery store to something they can feel more connected to."

When he hires people to work in the café, Chapman stresses the importance of hospitality. He is not necessarily looking for experienced coffee people, but they do need to care about the customer. "Some of our long-standing employees came in without any experience," he said. "They understand the fundamentals of hospitality, where it's your job to work as hard as you can to take care of the customer. That's one thing you can't teach people — the step-by-step process to do that. You can give people tactics about how to read a person or scenario, but you can't teach someone to care. That's the difficult thing."

Chapman sees value in keeping experienced people in the front of the café. "In terms of that connectivity," he said, "I tell all the baristas at Coava their job is to sell coffee and to make really exceptional coffee, but part of being a barista is to connect our customers to what's happening in coffee. That falls on some of the least experienced people in the industry." The more experienced people often work behind the scenes, far from customers. Chapman himself has dabbled in the roasting and production side of the company, including packing and shipping, but that was not his thing. "I realized I didn't really like it that much. I'd much rather be interacting with people," he said, "so I went back into the café full time in sort of a management role."

## Connecting Origin to Oregon

Living so far removed from where coffee is produced makes it difficult for even educated Portland coffee drinkers to understand why some coffees are higher quality than others. "There's no real way to spell it out to somebody," said Chapman. "When you're talking about meat, for example, you can go to Safeway or Kroger and noticeably taste a difference in meat that comes in a plastic package and meat they cut for you in front of you. You can taste the difference, and you can see the difference in what it looks like. But when you start to talk about the same distinctions with coffee, there's no way for people to compare. They're so removed from it." Another thing that adds to the knowledge gap is that baristas, the people who actually have conversations with the customers, have not been to origin to see the differences either.

To help Chapman bridge that gap, Coava sent him to Honduras in October 2012, where he got a firsthand look at coffee farming and processing. "To see and smell and experience that was cool," he said, "because I still hadn't made the connection that this is why our coffee is different than other people's coffees — despite [the fact] that I had been successfully working in coffee for a few years."

Chapman saw stark differences between the coffees Coava buys and the lower grades that larger, nonspecialty roasters buy. "You'd see these coffees coming in off these trucks that had just been harvested, and they're all different colors, with rotten cherries in there," he said. "There was yellow cherry, green cherry, some red cherry, but it was obvious they were stripping off as much as they could. They're throwing them in these big sacks, and the cherries are fermenting."

Chapman's sense of smell also gave him some strong clues as to the quality of the coffee. "The smell of fermenting coffee cherry is so disgusting," he said. "I'd never smelled it, but I was struck by this reality that if people knew the difference — where people were picking only ripe cherries and using clean processes — they would have a clearer picture of why certain coffees taste better than others."

The trip brought the economics of coffee into focus. A lot of farmers are using a varietal called Lempira, a commodity-grade varietal, a cash crop that produces a lot and is resistant to disease. "Chatting with David Mancia [one of Coava's more prominent growers]," said Chapman, "you could tell he was committed to getting rid of as much high-yielding, low quality coffee as possible and just focusing on low yield, high quality." Mancia is raising a couple thousand Pacas[57] trees in his nursery and has planted several hundred on higher elevations on the farm. Coava's Matt Higgins encouraged him to do that, showing how the roasters in the importing countries are affecting the livelihoods of coffee farmers in developing countries. Mancia has taken out many of his lower

---

57. A variety of coffee.

quality trees in favor of the higher quality trees, a leap of faith in some ways, since the new plantings will not produce fruit until several years after they are planted. The farmer takes a big risk by reconfiguring his farm with the hope that things will work out. "The more the farmers know," said Chapman, "the more experience and knowledge they have about the relationship between what they do and how much we pay for coffee, [the more] they're willing to do whatever it takes to make as much money as they can."

For the growers, coffee is a business. "David Mancia was completely clear about it. He said, 'I want to make really good coffee so I can make as much money as I can, so if my kids don't want to be coffee farmers, they don't have to be.'" From the coffee drinker's point of view, this attitude is less romantic because the farmer is dedicating his life to the coffee in order to make money. "What he really cares about is providing for his family," Devin said. "In the end that's definitely the most important thing."

Among the coffee grower community, attitudes about quality versus quantity are mixed. "Some people want to create really great coffee," Chapman said. "They want to provide the best coffee they can and are willing to do whatever it takes to do that. There are some farmers that are just happy making however much they can and selling it to a co-op."

For Chapman, the biggest takeaway from the trip was having a better ability to connect the farmer to the customer, something that isn't always easy for baristas to do. He would like to see a more even distribution of the financial benefits of coffee spread to the farmers. "How is this man [Mancia], who is creating one of the most extraordinary things, how is he living on such a lower wage than everybody else in the chain?" Chapman asked. "What it comes down to is that people don't spend enough money for coffee. People don't charge enough money for coffee. If you actually provided the margin for what the coffee was worth instead of trying to stay competitive with people who sell coffee that's awful, money would no longer be an issue. It would be a game changer for the level of service you could get."

Looking ahead, Chapman said he definitely plans to make a career in coffee. "I think there is still so much potential in this industry," he said. "I've gone from figuring out, 'How can I get the best job?' to 'How can I make the most impact? What's going to be my niche?'" Although that future isn't perfectly clear, Chapman foresees his specialty being related to retail. He wants to help more people feel like they can approach the industry. "I still feel like it's unapproachable," he said. "I've had the experience where you walk into a café and are basically ignored and disconnected for your entire experience. It's not a good feeling, in any sense. It's a particularly bad feeling when you pay somebody to do that to you."

Chapman is pleased with how his career has progressed. "I get to work with some of the best coffees on earth, work with some of the best people in an environment where we're striving to get better and better," he said. "I feel like — I don't know if it's like this in other places, but I can see how once you get to a certain level or status, you'll feel like you've done what you can so you keep doing it. But I just don't feel that way at Coava. I feel like the general consensus is, 'Let's keep getting better — as baristas, as hospitality specialists, [as] coffee people, as roasters, as buyers.' Everything is supercharged with the idea of bigger and better. That's one of the things that makes working at Coava so awesome. I have the freedom to continually ask myself, 'How can I do my job better?'" Such an attitude has quickly transformed Chapman into one of the most well-known baristas in the Northwest.

# 17

# Sam Purvis on the State of Specialty Coffee

*Throughout the West Coast specialty coffee industry, Sam Purvis, who won the 2011 Northwest Regional Barista Competition (NWRBC) competing for Coava, is a household name. However, despite having reached a high level of success in coffee, Purvis chose to leave the industry. In late 2012, he left coffee to work for Epipheo, a growing marketing and storytelling video production company. I wanted to hear why a seemingly successful person would leave the industry for another career, so I reached out to Purvis for an interview. We sat down for a quick conversation, which turned into a discussion about the state of the industry and where specialty coffee is headed.* — WH

Sam Purvis is most well-known for his work at Coava, but his connection to the Portland coffee industry started several years earlier. Originally from Portland, Purvis spent part of his formative years in Sisters, Oregon, before returning to Portland in 2004. After working in land development for a few years, he got his first coffee job as a barista at Cooper's, a shop on the northwest side of Mount Tabor. "I started working in a café and then got intrigued with business growth and continued to hone the craft of making coffee," he said.

Purvis moved from Cooper's to Coffeehouse-Five, where he worked with Matt Higgins, who had recently left Albina Press and was in the process of starting Coava.[58] Purvis later helped Billy Wilson open the second Barista café (on Alberta), and from there, he moved to Coava. He started out working one day a week at Coava, but Matt Higgins and Keith Gehrke (still involved with Coava at the time) soon hired him to train their staff. When Gehrke left the

---

58. Coffeehouse-Five was one of Coava's first wholesale accounts.

company, Higgins wanted to grow Coava's wholesale business, and Purvis stepped into a new role as wholesale director.

## Barista Competitions as Strategy

One of Coava's strategies for growing was to use barista competitions to get the word out about the company's commitment to quality (when he was at Coffeehouse-Five, Purvis competed with Coava coffees at the 2009 NWRBC). Purvis polished his competition skills when he moved into a full-time position with Coava, working side by side with Devin Chapman. "We've got a really cool dynamic," Purvis said of his former colleague and fellow barista champion. "We were friends long before we started working together. We both, I think, have a draw toward everything that was involved in competition and how it translated into our day-to-day at Coava. We learned a lot from each other. We pushed each other a lot, and it was a really fun couple years competing together."

Training together was a big part of the friends' success. "Competing with someone and training with someone is a major foot up," said Purvis. "Having an additional set of eyes on your presentation and having people to taste coffee with — it's priceless." Luck also played a role. "In competition, you just never know what's going to happen," he said. "I've walked away from presentations where I thought I knocked it out of the park, and my scores weren't as good I thought they were. And then you walk away thinking you did all right, and then you score really high. I always try to go in with — I don't want to say low expectations because when you're competing, you're definitely competing to win — but there are so many things that can happen."

Even the smallest detail can make the difference. When Purvis won the NWRBC, he edged out Ryan Willbur by one half point — 688.5 to 688, or 0.0073 percent. "Everything has to line up," he said. "We just all took a really hard swing at it. Matt [Higgins] from the sourcing side, Matt [Higgins] and Keith [Gehrke] from the roasting side. Devin [Chapman] and I were training together a lot. We spent a lot of time just tasting coffees and building presentations. We just fed off each other really well."

## Sam Purvis on the State of Specialty Coffee

Besides being an effective marketing tool, the competitions benefitted Coava in other ways. The preparation generated enthusiasm among the staff members and helped them focus their energy on learning more about coffee. "You have people that are working with coffees leading up to competition very intensively for months at a time," Purvis said. "As a barista, your skills really get honed in terms of pulling coffee, making coffee, talking about coffee. And then, there's a ton of value in the camaraderie."

### Specialty Coffee's Social Benefits

One of the prizes Purvis received for winning the NWRBC was a trip to Brazil to tour coffee farms. He came away impressed with what he saw. "When you go to Brazil, you see these large farms, and they're obviously making it," he said. "They have millions of dollars in investment in processing equipment. Then you go to the farmer producing two hundred bags of coffee, and they're totally making it too. They're selling their green coffee for $4 to $4.50 a pound, and they've got a two-bedroom house, a kitchen, air conditioning, two happy kids running around, a microwave and a refrigerator. It's a cool environment. You definitely feel good about buying coffee from Brazil because even the small farmers are able to make a living. It's awesome."

Brazil's economy is more developed than many coffee-producing countries, meaning that farmers there have an easier time selling their products to roasters. "At the end of the day, coffee people want the specialty industry coffee to get to the point where they're able to buy from small farmers in all growing regions in all countries," Purvis said. "It's not happening right now. It's happening in some places, but specialty is still a very small industry, and there's still a lot of pieces of it that are not sustainable." The world's leading coffee producer is on the right track. "It's cool in Brazil because you see it working, and you can feel good about it."

Not all countries are doing so well. In Guatemala, said Purvis, you see a dramatic contrast between a large farm that is "totally making it" and a small farm producing two hundred bags of coffee each year. "You can be a farmer in Guatemala and be farming phenomenal coffee and, depending on the size of your farm, it can still be really hard to make a living doing that," Purvis said. "A lot of these farmers aren't just growing coffee. They're growing corn and soy and a number of different things just to make it."

## Improving Lives for All Stakeholders

Moving more small farmers into the middle class is not going to be easy, according to Purvis. "There's a ton of players in that question.... You're talking about governments, subsidies, importers and exporters, labor, and commodity [coffee] — even though specialty is not commodity, the health of the specialty market is tied very closely to the health of the commodity market." Ultimately, the key will be to get more people to buy more specialty-grade coffee. "To continue to build demand is really important," Sam said. "The way in which specialty roasters and buyers engage farmers is really important."

Purvis mentioned how Geisha (a coffee varietal famous for its quality as well as its record-setting prices) exemplifies some of the contradictions within the industry. Although stories of $7 for a cup of Geisha make a splash in the media, it's not so clear that its high prices actually help the growers. The farmers who grow Geisha do get paid more per pound, but the reality is more complicated. "Geisha sells for a ton of money in the States, but it's a really low-yielding varietal that's not disease resistant," Purvis said. "There would be roasters that are head over heels in love with Geisha. They want to get their hands on Geisha. Well, if you told a farmer, 'Hey, we can get you this price for this coffee. Just tear out all your Catuai and plant Geisha,' that's a terrible thing to tell a farmer because they're probably going to lose most of their crop to disease, and the yield they do get will never recoup the income they lost based on taking out high-yielding varietals. That's been one of the darker pieces of the relationships between roasters and farmers."

The farmers' well-being is just as much the responsibility of the buyers, importers, and roasters as it is of the growers. "Farmers don't necessarily know the demand for their products," he said. "Specialty coffee can continue to build purchasing relationships and do a good job figuring out how to buy and how to sell coffee in a way that's really sustainable for farmers."

## Sam Purvis on the State of Specialty Coffee

Purvis believes many coffee drinkers do care about the social and environmental issues surrounding coffee. "Coffee, like anything else, is incredibly complex in terms of social structures that are in place." Purvis compared the coffee industry to diamonds and oil as examples of industries with unsavory reputations. "All of us know about those things to a certain level, and it's easy to make large, sweeping statements about the validity or the evil or the good that's involved in these different scenarios, but when you dig down underneath, these are very complex situations that involve myriads of people and players and stakeholders. People care, and they would be totally open to caring and understanding more as information came out. Like in any situation, everyone continues to learn as they go."

The situation is dynamic. "I don't think there's anyone who would say we know exactly how to get specialty coffee to a place to where every farmer raising specialty coffee is putting food on the table." Despite the challenges ahead for the industry, Purvis was optimistic. "Coffee as a whole wants to go in a direction where things continue to get more stable for all the stakeholders involved," he said.

### Scaling Specialty Coffee

Microroasters are proliferating around Portland and across the country, but these new entrants in the market may be facing some tougher times ahead. "Wholesale specialty coffee roasting isn't seeing the margins it was six years ago," Purvis said, "so you don't have people that are making the margins on being a wholesale roaster that they used to. There's more competition and the rising cost of raw products."

There are still plenty of opportunities in coffee, though. "If you look at stand-alone cafés," Sam said, "I think you'll see the growth of the café model for years and years and years, not just in major metropolitan areas." He cited Bend, Oregon, as an example. "Five years ago you couldn't get anything close to specialty coffee, and now you have three specialty coffee roasters in Bend. That development, where people buy homes, where there's money but there's not good food or beverage — that will continue to develop in metropolitan areas and in areas where you have people that care."

## Caffeinated PDX

Existing companies will look to scale up even more in the future. "You have some really focused projects like Barista or Madcap [a specialty roaster based in Grand Rapids, Michigan] or Coava — the list goes on — and they're small businesses that might have three or four locations and haven't really figured out how to scale, and you have very large enterprises that have really scaled and have lost a lot of quality as they've scaled."

According to Purvis, the ability to scale up while maintaining quality might be the biggest opportunity in coffee right now. "You have this really huge gap between quality and scalable businesses, and I think somebody's going to fill that gap, sooner than later. Someone needs to figure out how to scale quality a little more." I asked what company is most likely to do that. "Stumptown is trying, and we'll see how that goes," Purvis answered. "I think they have the team to do it. They have an amazingly talented team, so for them it really comes down to commitment and making decisions that are based on long-term growth as opposed to just bottom line."

Purvis spoke more like a businessperson than most people I have talked to in coffee — they usually seem more interested in the coffee itself. With a bachelor's of science degree in financial analysis, Purvis came into coffee with a business mind-set. "At the end of the day, people need to make money," he said. "We're not doing anybody any favors if we haven't figured it out. Specialty coffee obviously isn't a trend. It's a healthy, growing industry, but within that industry, there's a lot of inefficiency that doesn't need to be there, like any craft industry."

The inefficiencies create opportunities. "When you figure out how to become more efficient and how to scale, you do a lot of people a lot of good if you can do that without losing the heart and soul of why people started in coffee. That's always the challenge. I think this industry is definitely on the soft side of that tension, in terms of really caring about the craft and really caring about people doing it 'for the love of the game' as opposed to really pushing in and pushing back.… If these people can't make living wage and raise two kids on this job, I don't know if we've done anybody any favors. If this is just a young man's game, or a pay-for-college gig, whatever it is."

## Sam Purvis on the State of Specialty Coffee

### Leaving Coffee (for Now)

In late 2012, Sam left Coava to work for a marketing firm called Epipheo, a storytelling firm that builds interactive websites, videos, and other types of marketing promotions. He wanted to make it clear that his decision to leave coffee was not strictly financial. "What I'm doing now was a great opportunity for me, but I was making a living at Coava," he said. "Coava is a really phenomenal story for me because, as frustrating as small business startup is — we went through a ton of highs and lows — when I stepped away from the project, we had done a really good job of growing and ironing a lot of that out in terms of process, sales, and revenue growth. It felt like it was time to move into a new project." Matt Brown took Purvis's spot, and Purvis felt very comfortable leaving his position in Brown's hands.

Purvis enjoys the startup environment, and Epipheo is entering into an aggressive growth phase, one reason Purvis took the job. Still, he will miss certain things about working in coffee. "I was really intrigued — and am still intrigued — by the craft of making coffee," he said. "It has a unique beauty to the sensory aspect of it. For sure, I'll miss cupping coffees and roasting coffees and figuring out what coffees we wanted to buy and if there was a market for that. Coava was a really nice marriage of sensory and business development. I'll definitely miss that."

Purvis still has many friends who work in coffee. His wife, Christine, has worked at Barista in the Pearl District since it opened, and the couple has no plans to leave Portland, so he'll have plenty of good coffee within reach for the near future. Sam left open the possibility of returning to coffee someday. "For me, I've experienced a lot of different things in coffee, and for me to go back, it would probably be my own project or it would be something that was really aggressive in terms of scope, in terms of the challenge it offered."

### Competition Coffee: Get Your Coffee On

Before starting this whole coffee project, I had never heard of barista competitions. When Brandon Arends first told me about them, to be honest, I kind of thought he was nuts. "Competitive coffee," I thought, "who cares?" Many people, I found out. The competitions have become a large part of the specialty coffee industry. Many companies use competitions to build their baristas' skills and spread the word about their coffees. Although competitors have the most harrowing role in competitions, volunteers and judges play an important part as well. In 2011, I volunteered to bus tables at the NWRBC, furtively sneaking a few sips from several drinks before placing the cups into the wash tubs. In 2012, I volunteered at the NWRBC again, this time as a sensory judge, a role for which sipping the drinks was required. The following story is an overview of competition from the judges' side of the table.

After the 2011 NWRBC, Brandon Arends spent much of the next year convincing me to try judging. For a long time, I was reluctant because I thought I lacked enough coffee experience. It's one thing to regularly drink and write about coffee and quite another to be working with it all the time. He finally persuaded me, which is why I found myself rolling northward on I-5 at 6:15 a.m. the Thursday before the 2012 Northwest regional started so I could attend the required daylong judges' certification workshop.

I was a little nervous about the day ahead. I didn't know what to expect at the training because I had waited until the last minute to register and never got the email with the day's schedule and instructions. Brandon, who had registered on time, had given me a little advice the night before, when we discussed our travel plans.

"Make sure you check out the rules and the score sheet," he told me.

"I'll do it," I replied, not really intending to do much studying.

I should have heeded his warning a little more closely.

## Sam Purvis on the State of Specialty Coffee

### *Ready or Not*

We arrived at the Tacoma convention center just in time, scooting in through the doors precisely at nine a.m. and taking our places at the only available seats in the room (the training was kind of like going to church — if you arrive at the last minute, you sit up front). The head judges welcomed everyone and introduced themselves before going over the protocol for becoming a judge. Each of the head judges had worked in the coffee industry and had years of experience judging competitions all over the world.

Most of the aspiring judges in the room worked full time in the coffee industry as trainers, café managers, baristas, marketers — all types of roles. However, not everyone had years of experience in the industry. One woman was a writer from Seattle. Another had only worked in coffee for a year. She had never been to a competition before, but her manager had encouraged her to judge.

After introductions, the head judge said it was time to take the certification test and that we had to get an 80 percent on the exams to be certified to judge. "Test? Already? Eighty percent?" I thought. I felt a whoosh of air around me as the test takers gasped in unison. Apparently, I wasn't the only one who didn't get the memo about knowing the rules beforehand. Could they really expect us to know how to judge before we even got to the training? Somewhere in the back of my mind, I recalled Brandon's advice from the night before. At least I had read through the rules in the car on the ride up from Portland.

### *How Much Do You Know?*

I started working my way through the exam, which consisted of multiple-choice and fill-in-the-blank questions about both technical and sensory elements. The test took nearly an hour to complete and covered the USBC rules and the official competition score sheet. It had questions like "How do you judge the integrity of an espresso's crema?" and "How thick does the foam on a cappuccino have to be for the drink to be eligible to receive a 'Very Good' score?"

I pictured myself back in college, sweating my way through an English literature exam I hadn't prepared for. I employed every trick in the book I could think of, eliminating obviously incorrect answers and leafing through the different sections of the test for clues. When everyone had finished the exam, we took a short break before resuming our training. Multiple people I talked to during the break were pessimistic about their results on the test.

### It's Not Getting Easier

After being tested for our knowledge of the rules, we moved on to actually figuring out what made a good drink and what didn't. One of the most difficult things about competition is to get all the judges to grade consistently between competitors. This process is known as calibration. The head judges showed us slides of what to look for when we evaluated an espresso's crema (the foamy layer that sits on top of an espresso, formed when the steam is forced through the coffee grounds, emulsifying the oils inside). In each slide, the crema looked a little different. As a group, we discussed how they differed and which deserved good scores and which did not. We then took a quiz, scoring several espressos of varying quality based on their photos.

After the espresso quiz, we did a triangulation test to check our palates. A triangulation test is an exercise in which three coffees are set out on a table together. Two of them are the same, and the other one is different. The testers sip each one and mark down which of the three is different.

If I felt fairly confident about the capabilities of my palate before that day, I finished the triangulation test wondering if I had ever tasted coffee before in my life. We did six groups of three, and I was confident about only two of the groups. The rest of them were similar enough that I ended up guessing. I figured I had failed the test and would end up washing dishes the next day instead of judging.

Everyone seemed relieved when lunch was served. As we gathered around the buffet table, I overheard several people in shock at the difficulty of the triangulation test.

### *The Real Calibration: Testing Drinks*

After lunch, the head judges gave us our test results. By some miracle, I had passed. Shortly thereafter, we went to the competition hall for calibration. Technical judges grouped up at one machine, and the sensory judges divided into two groups and gathered around the other machines. Each machine was staffed by a barista who made us a variety of drinks. Our barista tried to vary the quality of the shots he made, attempting to make the calibration more like the competition.

We began by evaluating espressos. Espresso is the main focus of the barista championships, as it is the most difficult type of coffee to consistently make well. To score well, baristas need to make great espresso, not only in the espresso course but also in the cappuccino and signature beverage course. As the training barista pumped out the espressos, the trainers let us write down our impressions, reminding us to follow the regulations in the rulebook.

Each drink gets one of the following scores: Unacceptable=0, Acceptable=1, Average=2, Good=3, Very Good=4, Excellent=5, or Extraordinary=6. You can give scores with half-point increments, but no scores of 0.5 are allowed, and the head judge must approve any scores of Extraordinary. As we practiced judging, we were encouraged to use the words instead of the numbers in order to accustom ourselves to the official scoring language. The language helped us score the drinks more accurately.

The calibration was fun but challenging. All of the judges who were new to the certification process were reluctant to make a definitive score for each of the drinks we tried.

We would taste a drink and then look to our trainer for guidance instead of writing down the score we thought it deserved. After a while, when we had evaluated shot after shot and cappuccino after cappuccino, we began to get a pretty good sense of what was good according to standard and what was not.

We finally finished up the calibration about quarter to six. The head judges sent us home and told us to be back at eleven the next morning. My fears about being deemed unworthy to judge had not been realized. When we got the schedule, I was assigned to the first, third, and fifth competitors of the day. I would be nervous, but thanks to our trainers, I felt confident that I would do a good job.

## *Judgment Day*

When I woke up the next morning, the first thing that popped into my mind was the espresso category's four elements and what I should be looking for in each one. You could say I was focused. At least I hadn't dreamed about cappuccinos.

After a hearty breakfast, Brandon and I returned to the convention center an hour before the start of the competition to do a little more calibration. We tasted a few espressos and cappuccinos and returned to the judges' room, waiting for the first competitor. At noon, we got the call to come judge. We filed out into the competition hall, were introduced, shook the competitors' hands, and sat down at the judges' table (presentation table). It was time to see if our training had prepared us.

The protocol for SCAA-sponsored barista competitions is standard throughout the United States. Baristas have fifteen minutes to prepare their competition station. The station is set up with a machine table (where the espresso machine sits), a preparation table (for storing milk and other ingredients), and the judges' table (where the four sensory judges sit). As the baristas prepare, they calibrate their grinder and carefully lay out the utensils they will need to make the drinks. Usually, they set out plates, napkins, water glasses, and spoons at the judges' table too.

After the prep time, the judges enter, and the main part of the competition begins. Each barista must make three types of drinks during fifteen minutes: an espresso, a cappuccino, and a signature beverage, one for each of the four sensory judges. That's twelve drinks in fifteen minutes, a challenge for baristas anytime, let alone with the pressure of competition weighing on them. Baristas must be efficient and fluid with their movements, and they are expected to talk about the coffee they are using, describing the origin and the characteristics that make their chosen coffee special.

Seven judges evaluate each competitor's performance. This includes four sensory judges, two technical judges, and a head judge. The technical judges hover over and around the competitors while they are presenting, watching how the barista grinds, tamps, uses towels, keeps the station clean, and a myriad of other details. The head judges watch the other judges to make sure they are judging consistently. They taste many of the drinks, often writing down their own scores. These scores do not count toward a competitor's score, but they help head judges resolve any major score discrepancies between the sensory judges' scores.

I chose to be a sensory judge for several reasons. First, I had done a lot of sensory evaluation (drinking espresso) over the previous year and a half, so I knew I would feel comfortable as a sensory judge. Second, technical judges have a large number of small things to watch, and it helps to have a lot of barista experience, which I lacked. Most importantly, the sensory judges get to taste the drinks.

### *Put Your Tastes Aside*

As a sensory judge, one challenge was to put my biases aside and base my observations on the rules set by the competition committee. When I go to cafés, most of my observations are highly subjective, which doesn't make for good competition scoring. To be a good judge, you have to be able to discard your own preferences and judge the espressos against the standards in the rule book.

For espresso, this means you evaluate the crema, first for its presence, then for its persistence and consistency.[59] Next, you mix the espresso three times from front to back, using the small spoon that the barista is required to provide. For the competition, an espresso should have a balance of sweetness, sourness, and bitterness, and these reside at different levels in the cup. Mixing the espresso allows you to detect all three flavors in each sip (assuming they are present).[60] In addition to the taste balance, you also evaluate its tactile characteristics, or what coffee people often refer to as mouthfeel. These characteristics test the barista's skills at pulling shots.

Cappuccinos are judged in a similar manner. The first criterion is visual appeal, which doesn't necessarily mean the barista is skilled at latte art. Instead, judges are looking for contrast, sheen, balance, symmetry, and whether or not there is a complete brown espresso ring around the outside of the milk in the center. Once the judges have evaluated the visual aspect, they take a spoon and push back the foam of the cappuccino to check the persistence and consistency (per-con, in the judging lexicon).

After evaluating appearance, the judges sip the cappuccino to determine its taste balance. The judge should be able to detect a pleasant balance between the sweetness of the milk and the espresso flavors. The temperature should also be such that you can drink the cappuccino immediately, without letting it cool.

The third category of drinks, the signature beverage category, has criteria that are less strictly defined. The baristas

---

59. Some of the competition rules were changed for the 2013 season. Crema color was eliminated as a scored evaluation criteria.

60. Also for 2013, the baristas had to predict the flavors the judges would taste in the espresso, and the judges would gauge the predictions for accuracy.

get to express their creativity in making a drink, so some of the drinks are very complex. Baristas add coffee reductions, gum syrup, star fruit juice, a raspberry ganache, an infusion of hops — you name it and a barista has probably tried it (no alcohol or banned substances are allowed). Calibrating is somewhat harder for the signature beverages because they are different from competitor to competitor, but no matter what, the drink should be designed to feature the espresso.

One of the keys for baristas who want to score well in the sig bev category is to clearly explain what they are doing so the judges know what to expect. They should also remember that the espresso is central to the drink — that is, whenever they are thinking about how to compose the drink, they should also think about how all of the additions showcase the espresso. It is easy to forget that. The beverage can be delicious, but if the judges cannot taste a strong espresso presence, it will receive a lower score.

Throughout the training, the head judges had drilled the procedure and evaluation criteria into our heads, constantly reminding us to remove our own tastes and biases from the evaluation process as much as possible. They had us focus on describing what we saw so we could justify the scores that baristas would receive.

Speed is important when you are a sensory judge. You need to quickly evaluate the drinks because any time lag negatively affects the quality of the beverages. The crema on the espresso is its thickest and most stable when it is first served. So is the foam on the cappuccino. A judge cannot hesitate. With an espresso, for example, the judges' thought process is something like, "Color, tip forward, tip back, stir, stir, stir, sip once, sip twice, give it a score." Then you take a couple notes to support the score you give it. You have to do this in a few seconds. At first, you go slowly, trying to remember everything, but the process becomes automatic over time.

These protocols floated around in my head as I sat at the table, trying hard to concentrate on what the barista was saying. After each competitor finished, we went back to the judges' room to finish the notes on our score sheets before we discussed the scores as a group so that there were no glaring outliers. Our head judge gently pushed us to correct them, when necessary. Instead of first telling us to change our scores, he had us justify the score we gave the competitors. If we had good justification for what we experienced, he let the score stand. If we did not, he helped guide us in adjusting either upward or downward.

### Competition Takeaways

Each of the competitors put in a lot of work preparing, and I felt honored to be a part of the team that judged them. As the head judges told us in the beginning of our training, one of the main roles of a judge is to support the baristas as professionals. We were there less to judge them than to give them feedback for all their preparation and make the competition as much fun as possible. Everyone wants to help raise the specialty coffee industry's profile, and these competitions are an opportunity to do that.

The baristas who competed were very professional. I like to joke about the tattoos and interesting fashion choices that baristas are known for, but when it comes down to it, a barista's skills make a huge difference in the way your drink tastes. They are the final step in a very long, complex process that brings the coffee from where it is grown to your cup. As Brandon told me one time, if baristas think about how complex the process is to produce high quality coffee beans, they should feel an obligation to prepare it in the best manner possible. The baristas who care enough to compete take that responsibility seriously. After judging a competition, I could see why.

## 18

# Matt Brown
## Portland's "Let's Get It Done" Guy

*Matt Brown, Coava's director of wholesale, may not be as well-known as some of the more prominent names in the Portland coffee industry, but if you look at where he has worked, Brown has played an integral role in making Portland's coffee scene what it is today. Prior to working at Coava, Brown spent significant time working at Lava Java, Coffeehouse Northwest, Barista, and Stumptown — all prominent area coffee companies. I caught up with Brown at Coava's headquarters, where we ducked into the green been storage room — about the only quiet place in the whole facility — for our meeting. (Side note: Coava's green bean room might be the only green bean storage area in Portland that has a chain saw sitting on the shelf. Brown told me Coava had just purchased a used delivery van, and owner Matt Higgins, the ultimate DIYer, was remodeling the back of the van to make it better for coffee delivery. Brown said the chain saw was integral to the demolition of the shelves inside the van.) — WH*

In his flannel shirt and baseball cap, with a cropped red beard and tattoos on both arms, Matt Brown looks like he could have been a lumberjack, although his propensity to say "dude" makes that seem less likely. Brown grew up in Kelso, Washington, about an hour north of Portland. "Kelso is a depressed lumber town," he said. "There's no coffee there. We all grew up without coffee." Starbucks opened its first café in Kelso when Brown was a senior in high school, but he never went there.

Brown likes to tell the story of how his best friend elevated his interest in coffee. After high school, Matt moved to Portland to attend Multnomah University, and he convinced his friend to move from Kelso to Portland to room with him and go to school. The friend found a part-time job as a security guard, working nights, and he absolutely hated the job, so Brown made it his mission to find him a better one. An opportunity arose at a small coffee shop in Ridgefield, Washington, called Lava Java. The café was about halfway between Portland and La Center, where Brown was working, and he spent so much time studying there that the manager eventually offered him a job. Matt suggested the manager talk to his best friend. "I said, 'I don't need a job, but my roommate, he's a bum. He needs a job,'" recalled Brown, pausing for dramatic effect. "So Billy Wilson took the job."

Wilson getting a job at Lava Java was transformational for both friends. Neither were heavily into coffee at the time, but Brown said Wilson jumped in with enthusiasm. "The thing about Billy is, he's the guy in elementary school who got the yo-yo and learned the ten thousand tricks," said Matt. "It didn't matter what it was going to be. If he was going to do it, he was going to do it really well." A short time later, Phuong Tran bought Lava Java. "She buys it," Brown said, "and you end up with two people [Tran and Wilson] who are very competitive in their hearts, pushing each other. They make Lava Java this factory for barista competitors."

As Wilson developed his coffee skills and began competing, his enthusiasm rubbed off on Brown. When Billy left Lava Java to work at Stumptown, Brown filled his spot, eventually becoming the café's operations manager. Brown later left Lava Java to play in a band full time, but before long, the industry called him back. He worked at Paradise Cafe in Vancouver, Washington, streamlining operations and helping return it to profitability. When the owner, Philip Search, offered to sell Brown the café, Matt declined. "I'm not the dude who wants to own his own thing," he said. "My nature is, 'Let's get it done.' Others can be the dreamers. I love dreamers. I'm not that guy. I'm the guy who makes it happen."

## Coffeehouse

As Brown considered his options for what to do next, Wilson, now working at Albina Press, took Brown on a tour of the Portland coffee scene. They talked about where Brown could find a job. "I didn't want to work for Billy, in case something happened between me and Kevin Fuller, who owned the place," Brown said.

## Matt Brown

In addition, Matt was unsure if he would fit in at the café. "The Albina kids at that point were like the cool kids, and I come from a lumber town, you know?" Wilson saved the best stop on the tour for last. "Billy takes me around to all these shops," said Brown, "and at the end he tells me, 'Now I'm going to take you to where I go to get cappuccinos.' I'm like, 'Dude, we're going to all these places, and we haven't been there yet?'"

The two friends stopped in at Coffeehouse Northwest, where Adam McGovern made Brown a cappuccino. "Blown away" by the cappuccino, Matt offered his services to McGovern. "If you guys need anybody," he recalled telling McGovern, "I would love to work here." Adam hired Brown, who spent the next three years working at Coffeehouse. He took on the management duties — hiring people (and firing them, when necessary), paying the bills, and so on. "That's where most people know me from," Brown said of his time at the West Burnside Avenue café.

Hearing Brown's stories from his time at Coffeehouse Northwest gave me a better appreciation of all the obstacles the shop has overcome to become one of Portland's best. Back then, the café was far from the beautiful space it is today. "When I started working at Coffeehouse," said Matt, "the walls were dark blue and kind of a mauve-burgundy crappy color. There was an old couch in the back, no back door."

Located on West Burnside, the café needed more than just cosmetic changes. "We had fun with it, but we also had the hobos," said Brown. "They would come in and lock themselves in our bathroom and pass out. We had people setting up offices in our bathrooms and selling drugs. We'd have to clean up blood and needles. It constantly blew my mind, but that's how it was. We became the stewards of the corner, which meant that if anything was going on, we'd call the cops."

The baristas even got a few self-defense tips from the Portland police. "The cops told us to get them before they got into the building," Brown said. "One officer said, 'When you see someone who is obviously drunk about to come in, charge forward and start telling them to get out. Point your finger out the door and yell at them saying, 'You're not allowed in here!'" The staff took the officers' instructions. "It kind of startled our customers, but that was our rule. We were going to protect our customers at all costs."

Brown made sure that when women were scheduled to work, they weren't working alone. "We had to do something," said Brown, who stands over six feet tall and weighs about two hundred pounds. "There were points when it wasn't safe. We ended up having to buy Mace because a guy got physical with me." The neighborhood has improved quite a bit since then, though it still attracts its share of unruly characters.

When Matt arrived, McGovern had lots of ideas about how to improve the café, but paying for the changes was going to be a challenge. Brown knew he could help. "I'm listening to Adam's dream, but he's like, 'Where are we going to get the money?' I told him, 'Dude, I did remodeling at one point. We can build it. Why not? You dream it — let's get it done.'" Brown helped McGovern rearrange the café space, repaint it, redo the bathroom, and even put in a glass door at the back. There was plenty to do. "You worked the shift; then you worked on the space," he said. "Sometimes that's what you've gotta do. It was exciting because I found someone with this vision."

Changing the café's look helped the business, but it was the employees' commitment to quality and service that made Coffeehouse Northwest stand out in Portland. "We made sure that if you made it into the shop, our motto was to meet your need before you knew you had it," said Brown. "If you came in, we knew if you'd never been there, so we would invite you into our world. That became the mark of what that crew was. Everybody had the same attitude about it — hospitality first."

Pretentiousness was not allowed. "It didn't matter if you wanted a sixteen-ounce vanilla latte. We were going to make it work. That attitude overcame the crappiest corner in Portland," Brown said, describing the obstacles to success. "There was no parking. It's a one-way street that doesn't really go anywhere. It's easy to miss. The whole establishment went from being this dank, nasty hole in the wall to being something that you would have rock stars and movie stars coming in there who didn't want to be noticed, but they wanted a good drink."

Brown called Coffeehouse Northwest a "star in Portland that only coffee lovers knew about for a really long time." As the shop's fame grew, McGovern planned to launch a second café. However, the economy didn't cooperate. After trying unsuccessfully to raise enough capital to build a second Coffeehouse Northwest, McGovern and business partner Aric Miller decided to start a new roaster and coffee kiosk called Sterling.

As preparations to open Sterling got underway, Brown's daughter was born. He was going to have to manage both cafés, something he was reluctant to do because he wanted to spend more time with his newborn daughter. "I was already working fifty to fifty-five hours a week," he said. "To add another business that also involved bringing in green coffee was going to be too much." Brown reluctantly left Coffeehouse to go work for Billy Wilson and help launch the second Barista, on Northeast Alberta. (Brown had earlier declined to work for Wilson when he opened his first Barista because of its proximity to Coffeehouse Northwest. "Leaving Coffeehouse was really hard for me," he said. "To leave, if I went to the Pearl, customers could have followed too, and I didn't want any part of that. I wanted Coffeehouse to grow. But to go to the other side of town—I was fine with that.") Brown felt more at home at his new shop. "It's in a neighborhood, and it serves beer—that helps," he said. Matt and Billy worked well together. "Because there was no other boss, we felt like we could deal with any problem between us, if there ever was one. Of course, there never was one."

## Stumptown

The economy disrupted Brown's life again, about a year and a half after B2 opened. Brown's wife was laid off, and shortly thereafter, the couple found out they were going to have another child. The family had been getting health insurance through Brown's wife's work, and Barista's employees did not have insurance. "It became very apparent I had to find a different job," Brown said.

Brown was bummed at the prospect of leaving coffee. "I thought that to make the kind of money I needed to, I was going to have to leave the industry," he said. "I started taking interviews with companies that were just crushing my spirit." Wilson encouraged him to use his network of contacts. "Billy's like, 'Did you call Stumptown? I've known them forever.'" Brown did not want to leave coffee, but he was still hesitant to take his friend's advice. "I'm not one to ask for favors, but he told me I had to [call Stumptown] or I would regret it forever." Somewhat reluctantly, Brown called Skip Colombo, his Stumptown account manager. "I've known those guys forever, and they knew my reputation, so when I called, they said, 'Let's talk,'" Brown said.

Despite having worked with most of the Stumptown crew already, Brown was still nervous as he walked into the meeting at the Horse Brass Pub, a bar on Southeast Belmont known as a favorite hangout for Stumptown employees. "We go to the Horse Brass," said Brown, "and there's Aleco [Chigounis, Stumptown's coffee buyer at the time], Matt Lounsbury [general manager], Chrissy Hoag [director of sales], and Skip. I'm like, 'There's four of you here!' I told Aleco, 'I didn't know you'd be here,' and he's like, 'Yeah, I just wanted to see what they'd do to you.' It was kind of intimidating to be at that table when you need a job, you know?"

Brown had no reason to worry. The meeting was mostly just a formality. "Because it was Billy's idea," he said, "they sat down and asked me what I wanted to do, work on the wholesale side or in one of [the] cafés." Brown told the group he wanted to keep learning, working on the wholesale side. "While I'm talking, Matt Lounsbury interrupts me and says, 'If you could do any job at Stumptown, what would you do?'" Brown replied that he wanted to do be an account manager. "I told them, I want to be the guy who helps people like he helped me," said Brown, pointing to Colombo. "Skip would come into Coffeehouse Northwest, and after he left, myself and Charlotte Deason would talk about how we wanted him to stay and mentor us." Stumptown created a new position so Brown could do just that. Brown was named the second account manager in Oregon. "It was a huge honor to be able to be a part of that family," he said.

Brown loved his new job, and not just because it included health insurance. The position encompassed a wide variety of responsibilities, from helping out with machine maintenance to doing business and cost analysis. Sometimes, he said, his accounts just needed a shoulder to cry on because business was bad.

## Changes at Stumptown

Brown was working for Stumptown when news broke that Duane Sorenson had sold part of the company to TSG Consumer Partners, a private equity firm based in San Francisco. Brown said that around Portland, the reactions to the news were mixed — but not mild. "Skip and I spent seven or eight months having people do everything from saying, 'Congratulations, that's awesome!' to them screaming at us. That was rough, but the advantage we had was, we could say, 'All we're going to do is to hire more people.'"

Brown thought the way the news got out had a lot to do with Portland's reaction. "The story broke in a really crummy way, at a time where Stumptown wasn't ready to talk about it," he said. "Stumptown doesn't have a PR department, so all of a sudden, the employees were caught not knowing anything the press is talking about, and immediately they're put in the spotlight, and they haven't even heard about it yet because the deal wasn't done."

Clearly, though, some things had changed. From Brown's perspective, most of the changes were positive. "With the employees, everybody that needed help, got help. Everyone who was doing the job of three people got someone to help carry the load. So quality of life went up. We [already] had amazing insurance, but we got better benefits. We also established — instead of doing a 401(k), where only people who worked forty hours a week get it — they made a profit-sharing program where every person who works for Stumptown gets a chance to be a part of that profit sharing." The company held classes to teach employees how to invest and do a 401(k) if they chose.

## Coava

Brown stayed at Stumptown for two years before he got a call from another friend, Sam Purvis, Coava's director of wholesale. Purvis was leaving Coava to work outside the coffee industry, and he wanted to know if Brown had any recommendations for his replacement. Purvis described Coava's plans to open two more

Coava retail shops in Portland and to grow the wholesale business outside Portland.

Brown realized that the director of wholesale position might fit himself. He knew many of the people working at Coava, and he liked the feel of working for a smaller company. Everyone at Stumptown was so busy, they rarely had time to talk to each other. "All of a sudden, a lightbulb goes off in my head," recalled Brown, "and I say, 'You mean this position isn't going to be competing with my friends at Stumptown? I wouldn't have to be trying to fight for business with them?'"

As with previous departures, Brown vacillated about leaving Stumptown. "I thought that I would be at Stumptown for the long haul," he said. "When the Coava position came up, it was good to have Duane look me in the eye and go, 'I would take that job,' which made me feel okay about it. Matt Lounsbury, bummed that I was leaving, told me he understood why. Others were like, 'You have to go.'" The fact that everyone at Stumptown liked Coava's coffees helped. "Coava's not doing something super strange and weird. We're in the same tradition as Stumptown."

The transition has been good for Brown. "It's really been nice to shrink my world a little bit, to lay the groundwork where, instead of me waiting at Stumptown for someone to retire to move into another role, I get to be a part of every bit of it here," he said.

## Future of Specialty

Brown was positive about the future of specialty coffee. "I think that quality coffee is just going to increase," he said. "There are a lot of ridiculous fads in our industry as well as trends with the product we call specialty coffee, but what you'll still see is people longing for a better drink than they had before. That, we see spreading. The rise of Stumptown is a really good example of that." Brown sees the diversity of styles as one of the industry's strengths. "Now we have the super-fancy end of it. The Sterling kids are very sharp. Then you come in here [to Coava], and we've got our trucker caps and our boots. We're like, 'Is it time to go fishing yet?' You can find a thing that fits each person. The industry is expressing itself in many different avenues."

## Matt Brown

Brown brought up See See Motorcycles, a combination motorcycle shop and coffee-centric café as an example of how specialty coffee was spreading to other demographics. "That's a café!" he exclaimed. "It's a killer café, and there's got to be a whole bunch of people who didn't drink anything but black diner coffee that go in there for bike stuff and are now exposed to awesome coffee."

Having seen the rise of Portland's specialty coffee scene firsthand, Brown has played an important role in advancing the industry. He plans to stay in coffee for now, filling in wherever he is most needed. Brown is going to keep pushing it forward from behind the scenes. You might never see him on the front page of any magazine, but you can be sure he will be somewhere making sure we're able to experience the fruits of his efforts. "I'm not the rock star," he said, "but I will get it done."

# 19

## Driven to Perfection
### Adam McGovern of Coffeehouse Northwest and Sterling Coffee Roasters

*Coffeehouse Northwest was one of the first specialty cafés I visited in Portland. Brandon Arends introduced me to the shop in the fall of 2010. I asked him to show me the best cafés in town and let him pick the spots. The first shop he took me to that day was Coffeehouse Northwest. More than a year later, I interviewed Adam McGovern, owner of the café on West Burnside Avenue.* — WH

When you sit down to chat about coffee with Adam McGovern, co-owner of Coffeehouse Northwest and Sterling Coffee Roasters, you feel the fiery intensity burning inside a man driven to succeed. Fueled by caffeine and determination, McGovern has little time in his day to sit and chat. "My day is typically doing as much as I can while I'm awake," he said, sitting across from me in his Burnside café. "Occasionally, I'll have meetings, but most of the time I'm just trying to not get tired so I can keep working until I go to bed."

McGovern moved to Portland from Sacramento in 2004, and he said when he arrived, he was sure of two things. First, he wanted to work in coffee. Second, having worked at the "first café in Sacramento to think it was doing a really good job with coffee," which was the Naked Lounge, he "knew" what he was doing when it came to coffee. "The last part was wrong," he told me, admitting his ignorance about Portland's coffee culture. "I didn't know about Stumptown — I didn't know about anybody. In fact, I lived near the Belmont Stumptown, and when I went in there, I was not impressed."

Instead of landing at a local café, McGovern found his first coffee job in Portland at Starbucks. His five-month stint with the industry giant shaped his perceptions of what a café should be. While some Portlanders would balk at the thought of working in corporate coffee, McGovern said the experience taught him a lot about the industry. "The thing I learned more than anything was that people generally care more about the location and the quality of service than they care about the quality of the coffee," he said. "That's been a lesson I've learned again and again and again. Working at Starbucks was very helpful because I got a sense of how they deliver consistent product and service. It was a really good experience overall."

## Becoming a Café Owner

After leaving Starbucks, McGovern went to work at Portland Coffee House, a café at the corner of Southwest Broadway and Alder Street, where Public Domain currently resides. Working at Portland Coffee House was the first in a complicated set of events that led McGovern to where he is today. At the time, Portland Coffee House's owner also owned Coffee Time (a small café on Northwest 21st Avenue) and was in the process of opening a second Portland Coffee House on West Burnside, where Coffeehouse Northwest is today. While covering shifts at Coffee Time, McGovern met Brian Brooks, a fellow employee who eventually bought the Burnside Portland Coffee House location and renamed it Coffeehouse (the Northwest would be added later). When Brooks bought the café, McGovern tried to help him out. "Because I had this weird idea I knew what I was doing, I started coming to Coffeehouse on a regular basis and trying to offer suggestions to Brian," said McGovern.

Brooks ultimately hired McGovern to manage the new shop. "I told him, 'I can change this. I can make it better,'" Adam said. "Even though I didn't know what I was doing, I did bring that confidence that I could do a good job and that things would improve." In those days, Coffeehouse was open until two a.m., making the café a destination for people stumbling out of the nearby bars. McGovern smirked as he recalled the café's clientele: "We had a mixed crowd, let's say."

At that time, the café space lacked the refinement you see when you walk into Coffeehouse Northwest today. The room was dark, with high-backed Gothic furniture. It lacked a back door, so the rear of the café was cave-like. McGovern called the shop a typical Portland café from the time period.

## Adam McGovern

Business was slow, but the work schedule was not. McGovern's job was to run the morning shift, something he did continuously. Although they had a few employees, Brooks and McGovern nearly worked themselves to death. At one point, McGovern worked 140 days in a row. "It was brutal, just brutal. Brian was working at least that much too," said McGovern, shaking his head at the memory.

Optimism kept Brooks and McGovern from fretting too much over what the shop was really like ("bad and slow") as they kept working to improve things. Then fate intervened in McGovern's life. Brooks had a "brush with mortality," after which he decided to give McGovern half the shop. Once the two became business partners, McGovern said he drove Brooks nuts with his quest for perfection, so much that Brooks soon decided it was time for him to sell the business. McGovern told Chris Crase, a software engineer who had come to Portland to get into the coffee business, that he should buy the other half of the shop. Crase agreed and subsequently bought Brooks's share of the business. According to McGovern, Crase's involvement came just in time. "It was a miracle. That was the first miracle that kept the shop going," he said. Aric Miller, a friend of Crase's who would later become McGovern's business partner, joined McGovern behind the bar, working as a barista.

Crase's investment brought some much-needed capital, which helped the struggling business in two very important ways. First, it was able to buy a high quality Synesso espresso machine, and second, it could to start serving Stumptown coffee. Up to that point, becoming a Stumptown wholesale account had been impossible because Coffeehouse Northwest could not afford to buy the high quality equipment Stumptown requires of its accounts. "We had no money — we had *no* money at all," stressed McGovern. "It was unbelievable how little money we had."

With the coffee and equipment upgrade, Coffeehouse became a place where people could expect quality. "We got the Synesso and we got Stumptown, and that was when our whole quality program started taking off," McGovern said. "We finally had the tools where we could deliver what we had been trying to deliver."

## Caffeinated PDX

### Inspired by Albina Press

Adam looked around Portland for ideas on how to improve his café. He found a source of information at Albina Press, a popular coffee shop he thought was "way cooler than Stumptown." At the time, Albina Press was run by Kevin Fuller and Billy Wilson, the person who brought celebrity to the Portland barista culture. McGovern was impressed by the quality of the drinks they were serving, and he strove to learn what he could from them. "I was young — only twenty-three — and really impressionable," he said. "I had no idea what I was doing, and they apparently did, so I was willing to listen to them."

As McGovern applied his newfound knowledge, Coffeehouse Northwest's coffee quality improved — and so did the café decor. The team slowly remodeled the space and added some outdoor furniture. About the same time, construction wrapped up on the Civic, a large condominium complex across the street, giving the café some peace and quiet. Things were shaping up in the way McGovern envisioned. "About 2007, we started building a reputation for doing a great job with the Stumptown coffee and being super nerdy about the coffee," he said.

That same year, *Willamette Week* wrote up Coffeehouse Northwest in a feature article, subsequently attracting more press to the café. Food magazines and writers would come by regularly, writing about the up-and-coming café. Just as important, Billy Wilson and other Albina Press baristas started coming by Coffeehouse Northwest, giving the shop more credibility among Portland's coffee community.

While McGovern's intensity and commitment to perfection helped improve the café, he said they also made it difficult to maintain business relationships. In 2007, Crase sold his interest in the business to Brennan Novak. Six months later, Novak decided he couldn't work with McGovern, so in late 2007, McGovern bought the other half of the café.

In 2008, Coffeehouse added the back door to the shop, ridding itself of the cave-like atmosphere. "Getting light back there was huge!" said an emphatic McGovern. He painted the café walls white with dark trim, cut up the coffee bar, and rearranged the decor to free up space in the café, giving the shop the look it has today. In addition to improving the ambiance, the streamlined design also contributed to the efficiency of the shop. "We finally got some flow," said McGovern. "People could get drinks, pick them up here, and go all the way to the back for condiments, where before it was impossible." Coffeehouse Northwest could deliver the quality product and service McGovern had been seeking.

By 2008, Coffeehouse Northwest seemed to be doing well. It had a talented team of employees and was regularly receiving press as a top-tier Portland café. It changed its hot chocolate, which also showed up in the press. People began seeking out Coffeehouse Northwest as a destination café. In the second half of the year, a touch of star power boosted the café's fortunes even more. Billy Wilson left Albina Press and came to work at Coffeehouse Northwest that summer, staying through the fall while he prepared to open his first Barista, in the Pearl District. Wilson's presence gave the shop additional prestige.

## Setbacks and a New Strategy

Just when it seemed like Coffeehouse Northwest was on a roll, the Great Recession hit, causing a huge drop in business. At the same time, competition in Portland really escalated. Barista, Coava, Water Avenue, the Red E, Courier, Heart, Ristretto's Williams Avenue location — all quality shops — opened within a few months of each other. The abundance of quality cafés and new roasters made it difficult to get more than a couple sentences in the coffee press. Everyone was vying to be the alternative to Stumptown, but media stories often mentioned each of them as one of several alternatives.

McGovern was frank as he recalled the café's difficulties during the time. "We got fucked. We got fucked. It was scary." He leaned in closer and said in a hushed voice, "Scary. In October, we were steaming. We were doing better than we have ever done. But the market crash plus press driving people to Barista really hurt us."

The crash forced McGovern to innovate. Coffeehouse began offering different brewing methods to attract customers, but these did not fully make up for the loss of business. McGovern decided he would have to roast his own coffee to keep Coffeehouse

Northwest profitable, so he asked Miller, who had left Coffeehouse to paint full time when Crase exited the business, to come back and help him start a new roaster. Miller, after a year out of coffee, was ready to return, and the new business partners began work on their latest project, Sterling Coffee Roasters.

McGovern took on the challenge of roasting with the same determination he'd had when reworking the café. For most people, roasting coffee is something that takes years to learn how to do well. They start by working with an experienced roaster, learning the method and the subtleties involved with roasting good coffee. McGovern and Miller began roasting without any real experience. "We learned how to roast by roasting and just fucking up," said McGovern. "The coffee was good because we were buying the most expensive coffee we could afford, but it was a little dark by our current standards."

Miller and McGovern systematically applied themselves to learning how to roast well, recording what they did with each batch to avoid repeating their mistakes. To compensate for their lack of technical knowledge, they bought the best coffee available and treated it with as much respect as possible. "It's the most expensive green coffee you can buy, except for Cup of Excellence lots," McGovern said.

Adam said he still does not know all the chemistry behind the roasting process, but he does understand how to make sure the coffee is good, or at least how to "not fuck it up." Most of the time, the perfectionist inside McGovern is pleased with the results. "We make sure that the coffee is not sour and not bitter, and it usually turns out okay," he said.

While roasting helped the company's margins, it did not immediately solve the profitability issues. About the time Sterling started roasting, the market for green coffee shot up, doubling prices. "It didn't kill us, but it opened our eyes more to the value of careful planning and being fiscally responsible when times are good," McGovern said.

### Sterling: A Precious New Jewel

Looking to grow the business, McGovern and Miller considered opening a café in the Pearl District, but creating the environment they wanted would require $250,000. Believing it impossible to finance such a large investment, they rewrote their business plan to raise $50,000 from a group of small investors. When a small space next to Trader Joe's on Northwest Glisan opened up, McGovern and Miller opened Sterling Coffee's retail kiosk in a cart lodged in the alcove, roasting coffee on a one-kilo roaster sitting in the window of the kiosk. While it produced good coffee, the roaster's small size left little margin for error. To keep up with demand, the machine needed to run for six to seven hours each day, but it broke down frequently, even catching fire a time or two. Adam and Aric realized they needed something more reliable, so they started renting time on Andrea Spella's roasting machine.

The transition to the larger roaster created some anxiety for McGovern. "Three days before we opened Sterling, I was out at Andrea's roastery, basically with no idea what I was doing," he said. "I'd never used his roaster to roast before. I'd only used our one-kilo roaster. I didn't have enough time to roast the coffee we needed for the first couple days on the one-kilo, so I was like, 'Okay, I'll just use the big one.' I had no idea. I was in a fucking panic. I realized that a lot of people coming to the shop were expecting us to do the best job, right away. The pressure was pretty intense. We didn't sleep at all the two weeks before we opened." McGovern did figure out how to make the roaster work, and the café opened on time.

When Sterling first opened, it presented ten different single-origin espressos a month and offered several different drip coffees as well. The diversity of coffees stood out, especially for a small roaster. (Sterling has since scaled back its offerings, focusing more on the quality of each roast instead of quantity.)

Sterling's style was another characteristic that made the café unique. Miller and McGovern added decorative wallpaper and antique fixtures to the space, making it resemble something you would expect to see in an established café on Paris's Champs-Élysées, not in laid-back Portland. Sterling's baristas contribute to the theme by wearing vintage fashion, from bowties to big band–era dresses. "Dressing up was just our way of saying we were taking it seriously," explained McGovern. "We'd built this beautiful space, and we wanted it to be a jewel box. We knew we could make it as fancy as we wanted because it's this little fifty-square-foot stand, so it would still be affordable. The overall focus was to make sure that the people working matched the decor. We've made an effort to make people's impression of Sterling be of a place that is more precious than you would expect if you knew it was a stand, if you knew it was in an alcove next to Trader Joe's on a really loud street."

In mid-2012, Sterling left its cart behind and moved around the corner into a shared space with M Bar, a trendy but tiny bar on Northwest 21st Avenue. Miller and McGovern remodeled the space to mimic Sterling's previous aesthetic. Sterling's baristas serve coffee in the mornings and afternoons, and M Bar's bartenders take over in the evenings. Though small, the indoor space gives Sterling's customers a place to sit and drink their coffees without having to face the wet Portland winter weather.

About the same time they moved the shop, Miller and McGovern also set up a roastery in Portland's Old Town neighborhood. They bought a Giesen roasting machine that will allow Sterling to expand its roasting capacity when necessary. McGovern said that the company's successful growth would have been impossible without his staff. He praised his staff for being a great team. "Every single one of them is trying to maintain everybody's expectation of this," he said. "They're all personally invested — some are literally invested."

Going forward, McGovern wants Sterling to cater to both serious coffee enthusiasts and people who are more interested in an enjoyable atmosphere. "Our emphasis is on the whole experience of getting the coffee," he said. "The whole aesthetic of Sterling was built around the idea that if people take the time to come visit us, they're impressed with every part of it, not just the coffee. The look and the service are just as important. It's difficult to get the balance just right, but if we can keep that balance moving forward, we'll be successful."

# 20

## Ann and Collin Schneider
### A Sterling Coffee Family

*An integral part of the Sterling–Coffeehouse Northwest team that Adam McGovern speaks so highly of is the husband-and-wife duo of Ann and Collin Schneider, who manage Sterling's café and Coffeehouse Northwest, respectively. Originally from Newberg, Oregon, the Schneiders met when they were sixteen and have been together for more than a decade. They are the type of couple who can (and frequently do) finish each other's sentences. Both are veteran competitive baristas, and in 2011, they became part owners in Sterling.* —WH

If you walk into Sterling Coffee Roasters or Coffeehouse Northwest on any given day, there is a good chance that one of the faces smiling at you from behind the bar will have the last name Schneider. Ann and Collin Schneider spend a big share of their lives at the two Northwest Portland coffee shops, either working in the cafés or training for competitions. While some might frown upon mixing personal and professional lives, for the Schneiders, combining them is a natural fit. Coffee has been a big part of the couple's relationship for nearly as long as they have been together, going back to their high school years. "A lot of people think we met in coffee," said Ann, "because we've worked together for so long. But we met in high school." She smiled at her husband. "It's worked out well for us." Collin nodded. "We convinced each other it was okay for a high school boyfriend and girlfriend to work together," he said.

In the early 2000s, when Ann and Collin were just starting in coffee, Newberg was a hotbed for enthusiastic baristas. The couple worked alongside Tyler Stevens and Josh Toole (both worked for Barista as of 2013) at a shop called the Coffee Cottage. "We were reading every David Schomer[61] book we could get our hands on, teaching ourselves how to do stuff," said Ann. The more they learned about coffee, the less satisfied they became with what they were serving. "It was so elusive," said Collin, "because at that time, you had no idea what equipment to buy and how that affected the quality of what you were trying to do. Without the right equipment or even the basic skill set, it is frustrating." The couple moved to Portland in 2009, after Collin was hired to work at Coffeehouse Northwest. Ann worked at Coava for a stint before later moving to Sterling.

## Competing Together

Since the move to Portland, Ann and Collin have competed in both regional and national barista competitions. For Ann, competing came naturally. "My dad and brother are baseball coaches for a living," she said, "so whenever I heard that there's a competition for what you do for a living, I wanted to do it." Additionally, Ann saw the competition as a way to promote Sterling. "One of the biggest things was that I really wanted to represent where I'm working and show why it's a wonderful place to work," she said. "If you really believe in what you're serving, you want people to know about it. I wanted to make sure Sterling was represented."

Preparation for competition is intense, especially in the month leading up to the event. "A lot of people can go in whenever and practice whenever and not plan anything," said Ann, "but we had to set up a schedule." The couple has a young son, and they enlisted the help of four or five different couples to take care of him during the month. "We called them and told them we'd pay them in beer and Netflix if they would come over after Adalai goes to sleep so we can go practice," said Collin. The friends would arrive about eight p.m., when Ann and Collin would head back to the café to practice for three hours. Their son never even knew they were gone, but the schedule was exhausting. "It's hard to think about gearing up for the competition again because you just don't

---

61. David Schomer, founder of Espresso Vivace in Seattle, is famous for his meticulous investigations into the science behind espresso. His books on espresso and barista technique have served as guides for an entire generation of baristas.

have a life," said Ann. Still, she thought the sacrifice was worth it.

The couple minimized any rivalry between them. Collin described the competition between him and Ann as the healthy kind. "At the end of the day," he said, "we're on the same team, and I just really want her to do her best." Ann concurred. "I feel the same way, of course," she said. "The nice thing is, with the double set of score sheets, you can learn a lot from what each other is doing. We did really different routines each time, and we had really different approaches. He scored a lot better than me at regionals, and we learned a lot from that. I maybe scored higher than him at USBC [United States Barista Championship]."

"She didn't maybe score higher — she definitely did," interjected Collin, laughing.

"We push each other," said Ann. "If anything, it's healthy." The two plan to use their combined experiences as they prepare for future competitions.

## Specialty Coffee

Both agreed that Portland's coffee culture demands a high level of quality. "The first thing you need is accountability," said Collin. "Having peers to keep you held to the meter you measure your quality by is paramount. If we didn't have competition, even as friendly as that competition is in Portland, if we didn't have that meter, we would never progress or try to better ourselves."

Ann defined specialty coffee as "putting your best foot forward with the best things you have — buying the best equipment, buying the best coffee, training your baristas, making sure they're consistent. If it measures up, then that's specialty coffee." Sterling's baristas add to the specialty coffee experience with their fashion. They dress in styles that evoke the glamour of the Roaring Twenties. "The reason we do the fashion and everything is because we decorated the space like it is," explained Ann. "The wallpaper is imported. The wood bar is the most expensive thing in the shop. If we dressed normal, it would look awful in that space with how we present ourselves as a business. We always say we're dressing to meet Sterling, to fill the space out. That's why we present ourselves the way we do."

Making customers feel comfortable in their cafés is a priority for the Schneiders. Ann used the example of her parents to explain how she treats newcomers to the shop. "My parents are in their midfifties, and if my mom comes in and wants a soy macchiato and wants to put Stevia in it, I don't want her to feel bad for that," Ann said. "I want to offer her something that's going to be a quality she could not get or would be told no somewhere else, you know?"

Given the opportunity, the coffee will speak for itself. "The biggest thing we recommend to people is to order what you always get and just let us make it our way," said Ann. "If someone gets a latte at Starbucks, we'll make them a latte. If they get a caramel latte, we'll make them a caramel latte, but we're presenting them with the best options possible. We don't want to alienate people for liking what they like. We just want to give them a better option."

The Schneiders lauded Portland's knowledgeable coffee drinkers for their discerning tastes. "It's a pretty unique climate," explained Collin. "All of our clientele is surprisingly already well-informed, which makes it easy because they're able to recognize good coffee." Sterling rotates frequently through its different coffees, and customers accept that the coffees they have one day might not be around for long. "I don't know if you'd be able to pull that off everywhere," said Ann of the dynamic coffee menu, "but in Portland you can because so many places do that and people look forward to it. As long as the quality of everything else stays up to par, the change in taste isn't that big of a deal. They still know it's going to be good."

## The Future of Sterling

Despite its small size, Sterling has big plans for the future. The Schneiders would like to see Sterling expand to New York and maybe even Europe someday, though they agreed that would be a long time in the future. "The nice thing about our shop is that we could open up in London and it wouldn't be weird because of how we present ourselves," said Ann. In 2012, Sterling launched a fashion line in conjunction with Pino, a local fashion firm. "We don't want to be seen as just a coffee company," added Collin. "We want Sterling to be associated with a little more than that — with quality, comfort, and familiarity, above all."

**Ann and Collin Schneider**

Working in coffee is a career path for both Schneiders, and has been for some time. "We're in it for the long run. It's what we've always wanted to do," Ann said. "Even when we were sixteen, we were planning layouts of our shops someday. At the time we knew nothing about coffee. We just knew we liked it." She continued, "I don't know what path that's going to take with Sterling, but we're very content with where we're at right now."

## Ristretto Roasters
### Great Coffee and Beautiful Spaces

*Founded in 2005, Ristretto Roasters was one of the first companies to challenge Stumptown's dominance of the Portland specialty coffee market. Incidentally, there is a link between Ristretto and my interest in specialty coffee. Back in 2010, I came across an article in* Mix Magazine *that talked about how to make great coffee at home. Reading the article planted a thought in my mind that eventually grew and convinced me to ask Brandon Arends what made Portland coffee special. The* Mix *article was written by Nancy Rommelmann, whose husband, Din Johnson, owns and runs Ristretto. Nearly two and a half years after our first "introduction," I finally sat down with Rommelmann and Johnson to talk about Ristretto's trajectory and place within Portland's coffee scene.[62]*

*We met at Ristretto's third café, on Nicolai Street in Northwest Portland. The café sits between the fashion district dubbed Trendy-Third Avenue and the Northwest industrial area. Located in a corner of the Schoolhouse Electric building (which, in one of its many previous incarnations, was the headquarters of Coffee Bean International), Ristretto Nicolai features imposingly dignified wood pillars and beams that add strength and grace to the café. If you were to carve out a café from a turn-of-the-century factory, the Nicolai café is what you would hope to end up with. Yet, with no houses or apartments nearby, the café's location seems out of place. How could the café be successful in such a spot? That was one of my first questions to ask Din and Nancy.* — WH

Din Johnson grew up in Portland but left in the late 1980s to live in San Francisco. There, he met Nancy Rommelmann, a journalist

---

62. Though both are involved in the company, Rommelmann emphasized that Ristretto's story was mostly her husband's.

who was living in Los Angeles. In those days, neither city's coffee impressed him very much. "Even San Francisco didn't have that great of a coffee scene when I was there," said Johnson. "If you wanted a cappuccino or something, you went to North Beach [the Italian neighborhood], but that was kind of it." After the couple married, Johnson moved to Los Angeles. While he did not really enjoy living in Los Angeles, Johnson said he owes the city and its terrible coffee a debt. "I have to thank LA. It got me roasting my own coffee," he said. Wanting something better, Johnson set up a roaster in the basement of the couple's home. Johnson became engrossed in his new hobby and was soon roasting four nights a week.

In the early 2000s, Johnson felt pulled to return to his Northwest roots. "I had to get out of there," he said. "I couldn't stand LA, so we started visiting up here." Johnson and Rommelmann bought a house in North Portland, just off Williams Avenue.

Before the move, Din planned to open his own construction and contracting business in Portland, just as he had in California. However, while going through the training to get his Oregon contractor's license, he realized he was sick of construction. "I was sitting through the dry contractors' course with these horrifically boring books," he said. "After day three of eight hours of that, I went home and threw the books in the recycling." Johnson knew he had to reinvent himself. "I thought hard about what I liked to do," he said. "Coffee, right? So I started working on a business plan."

Johnson purchased a Probat L12 roaster and got to work on the business. He considered roasting coffee in the garage but quickly changed his mind. "I was like, 'Nah, no way. My neighbors would freak out,'" he said. Johnson also contemplated doing only wholesale, but the business plan quickly evolved to include retail. "How else are you going get people to try your coffee?" he said. "Cold call them with coffee that you roasted in your garage?"

As Din was working on the business plan, Stumptown was cementing its dominance in the specialty cafés of Portland. The city had embraced Stumptown's coffee as its own. The Southeast Portland roaster opened the Annex in 2005, the company's fourth location. "They were everybody's beloved local coffee roaster when we first started," said Johnson. Stumptown was so popular that Johnson's friends wondered how he would ever make a living roasting coffee in Portland. "We told people we were going to open a roastery and coffee shop, and they thought we were nuts," recalled Johnson. "They were like, 'Stumptown, how are you going to compete with them?'"

Rommelmann also heard the doubters. "People would say to me, 'Why is Din doing that?'" she said. "We asked them why, and they said, 'Because there already is a coffee roaster.' They were very surprised and dismayed and almost like, 'Hey, that's really a bad idea.'"

Johnson pushed ahead with his plan. "I just wanted to do what I wanted to do," he said. Din was confident the Portland market could support more roasters, and he used the wine industry as a comparison. "It's like if we had one person in Oregon making wine, you know? It's ridiculous." Johnson leased a six-hundred-square-foot space in the Beaumont neighborhood and transformed it into a café space. Johnson did much of the remodeling work himself, and the shop opened in 2005. Although the business started out slowly, Johnson was happy. "It was pretty lean and tough, for sure," he said. "Living on credit cards — it takes a lot — plus, Beaumont is not a high-traffic area. We just toughed it out, and eventually people would migrate over there and check it out. I didn't care if we were broke. It's better than working somewhere you hate, right?"

## Expansion

As the Beaumont shop began to prosper, Johnson kept his eyes open for opportunities to expand the business. In 2007, the owner of the Hub Building on North Williams approached Johnson and asked if he would open a café in it. At the time, the neighborhood was far from trendy, but Johnson signed up anyway. "It was three blocks from our house, and I loved the neighborhood, so we were like, 'Let's do it,'" he said.

The expansion was once again met with skepticism. "People thought we were a little nuts opening there too," said Johnson. "It was like, 'You're opening where?' It was a ghost town, and guys were selling crack on the corner." The Williams shop opened its doors in September 2008, just as the US stock market (and broader economy) crashed. A couple months later, Portland had one of the biggest winter storms in its history. The city was buried with snow for several weeks, keeping many residents at home. Both events kept business at the new café slow for a long time, and Johnson noted that the tiny shop in Beaumont kept outselling the much larger Williams café for almost a year after its opening.

Eventually, the economy picked back up, and the neighborhood around Williams became the next trendy place to live in Portland. People came to the area to try the new shops and restaurants sprouting up, and they found the café. Today, it can be a challenge to find a seat in the sleek, modern café that has become Ristretto's flagship store. With the arrival of a New Seasons supermarket in the neighborhood in 2013, the area should continue to grow. "It's really worked out. Everyone is happy for us," said Rommelmann.

## Expansion, Again

"This one," Johnson said, sweeping his hand to indicate the Nicolai café where we were meeting, "is in another neighborhood that's developing. Maybe we are a little bit nuts," he said, laughing. "In the long run, I like it. I wanted to go somewhere it's not developed yet. This neighborhood reminds me of where all the breweries in the Pearl are now."

He certainly succeeded in scouting a place before it's developed when he picked the location for his third café. The first time you try to find Ristretto Roasters Nicolai Street café, you wonder what the owners were thinking when they decided to put a café where it is. You arrive, and all you see are railroad tracks, factories, and a large electric substation across the street. Apart from putting a café in the middle of the freeway, you would be hard-pressed to find a place with less random foot traffic than Ristretto's third café. "I like being in places where no one else is," Johnson said.

The story behind Ristretto's venture into Northwest Portland echoes that of the Williams café. Once again, it was the owner of the building who approached Johnson to expand. Brian Faherty, who owns Schoolhouse Electric, asked Johnson to consider putting a café in one corner of the building's first floor. "Brian had tried to get us to do other projects in other places, and we weren't ready," said Johnson. "But when I saw this space, it had just been gutted out, and it was really raw. This one I wanted to do. This space was so awesome."

Johnson hired Accelerated Development, the development division of Portland's Bamboo Revolution, to build the café space. The firm used reclaimed and recycled materials to create a modern industrial-chic feel for the café.

Rommelmann is enamored of the new café's ambience. "Every time I come in here, I'm like, 'Wow!' I feel really lucky to be in this building," she said. Business was not yet booming at the Nicolai café in 2013, but it was steady, and the shop is well-positioned for any expansion of the Northwest residential neighborhood.

## Success in Business

As Ristretto has grown, Johnson has moved into a management role with the company. Ristretto has twenty-seven employees and roasts slightly more than ten thousand pounds of green coffee each month for its three cafés and other wholesale accounts. The company moved its roastery out of the Beaumont store and into a new building just north of the Rose Quarter in 2010.

Overseeing the growing business does not leave enough time for Johnson to spend hours roasting coffee like he once did, but he is still closely involved with the coffee. Din is in charge of sourcing and also has the task of developing direct-trade relationships with coffee farmers, something relatively new for Ristretto. The company buys coffee directly from a friend of Johnson's in Nicaragua who grows coffee, and Din is currently working on developing relationships with some growers in Colombia. "The challenge is to get somebody...who has your same kind of mentality," he said. To bring the coffees to the United States, Ristretto partners with Caravela, an importer who specializes in working with small farmers in Central and South America. Ristretto also pairs with a roaster on the East Coast to purchase container loads of coffee, a buying method that gives the roasters more purchasing power.

Johnson said that Ristretto pays a premium for working with small farmers, but it is worth it. "We're paying $0.35 on each pound to have somebody bring the coffee in for us, which allows us to pay the growers twice as much as they were getting before."

The direct-trade relationship also gives Ristretto more influence over how the coffee is produced. "It gives us a little control, where we can say, 'Okay, let's be a little more careful on this part of the processing,' or something like that. It's worth it, and it's motivating for the growers," said Johnson. "Their lives are instantly improved."

Once the coffees arrive, Johnson takes the lead in developing the roast profiles for each of them. He acknowledged the trends in specialty coffee toward lighter roasts but said his roasting philosophy is a little darker than that of some of his competitors. "It seems like there was a trend where people go as light as they possibly can, which is sometimes too much, and people can't drink it because it's underroasted," he said. "You have to develop some sugar in the coffee. We're trying to get a happy medium in the roast and bring out sweetness in the coffee. I'm not trying to get the same profile on everything, but I want it a little sweeter, a little less aggressive."

Johnson said he would prefer it if everyone only drank their coffee black, without any adulterations, but he learned early on that he would have to be flexible. He recalled the first day the Beaumont store opened. Somewhat of a purist, Johnson had decided to not sell any syrups. No decaf either. "The first order — ever," Johnson said, laughing and shaking his head, "was a decaf vanilla latte. I was like, 'Oh, what am I doing here? But you've got to cave a little bit. You've got to be a little flexible and give people what they want." Johnson quickly added both decaf and vanilla to the menu.

Another nod to the realities of running a business is offering coffee blends. Ristretto has two. "People really like something that is consistent, especially if you're going to wholesale something," said Johnson. "We like it when [wholesale accounts] do single-origin espresso too, but I think it's important to have something that's consistent." In its own cafés, Ristretto offers at least one single-origin espresso alongside a blend.

## Employee Involvement

Both Johnson and Rommelmann gave their employees credit for the growth of the business. "This company is doing really cool things because of the fantastic people who work for us," said Rommelmann. Ristretto's employees do not sign noncompete clauses before they start working, a common practice in the coffee industry, so they're free to expand their career in coffee. In fact, Johnson and Rommelmann have even gone so far as to help Ristretto's production manager, Karen D'Apice, set up her own coffee business, with plans to someday build her own roastery and café.

"We're totally supportive of that," said Johnson. "We tell her, 'Learn as much as you can learn here, and teach us some things.'"

Rommelmann agreed. "Her success is only good for us. We both feel this way very strongly," she said. "One thing Din has always said is that you can grow your own job with Ristretto."

Johnson expects employees to contribute to Ristretto's growth. "We tell people, 'We want your ideas. You're going to create and sustain your own job,'" said Johnson. The couple looks for employees with enthusiasm and ambition. To attract talent, Ristretto pays its employees competitively. Starting pay for baristas is $10.25 per hour plus tips, and many of Ristretto's employees receive health insurance benefits, a rarity at small roasters.

## A Lasting Effect on Portland

Ristretto's entry into the Portland specialty coffee industry marked a new phase in the city's coffee story. Ristretto demonstrated that new roasters could be successful in a town already devoted to Stumptown coffee. After Johnson opened Ristretto in 2005, other roasters followed his lead, creating an array of different options for Portland's coffee crowd. With nearly fifty coffee roasters as of November 2013, Portland is experiencing an industry explosion. "Every week or two, there's somebody," said Johnson. "It's nuts, but I think it's going to be like the craft beer thing. It's going to explode, then find its level. It's got to, right? You can't have a roaster for every person living here."

Despite the crowded marketplace, Johnson and Rommelmann both thought Portland was a great place to be a coffee roaster. "Portland is still affordable enough that you can do these kinds of things," said Johnson. "For me, I wouldn't have been able to do it in California, which is why we moved back to Portland."

### Ristretto on a Rainy Day

When baristas radiate enthusiasm for the coffees they sell, they make the whole experience of visiting a café better. My first visit to Ristretto Roasters was an example of how one barista's insight and passion for coffee can be contagious.

November had arrived in Portland, bringing cold, gray, damp, miserable weather. Grayness, however, is just an excuse to drink more coffee, so on a rainy afternoon, I took the yellow MAX line to the Overlook Park stop in North Portland. From there I walked up Failing Street, crossed over I-5, and meandered through the trendy Mississippi Avenue neighborhood. After walking about fifteen minutes, I reached Ristretto Roasters' Williams Avenue café. When I walked in the door, the aroma in the café immediately signaled to me that Ristretto is a place focused on serving high quality coffee.

Walking up to the bar, I saw on the menu board that they had two espressos available — the Beaumont Blend and an unnamed single origin. I asked the barista which single origin she had on grind. Her eyes lit up, and she exclaimed, "Panama!"

I'd been in lots of places where the baristas are excited about coffee, but I had never seen a barista with quite as much enthusiasm as she had.

"Is that something special?" I asked, secretly hoping she would break out singing Van Halen's famous anthem.

"We just switched over to it," she said, smiling. It was clear that she was enthused about the coffee, as only a fellow coffee nerd could be. "[The other barista] says it tastes like carrots," she said, almost giggling with delight. Carrots!

Up to that point, I had been planning to try the Panama. But carrots (especially cooked) are not my favorite vegetable. I passed for the time being, knowing I would have to talk myself into trying that one.

"Carrots, huh?" I said. "That sounds…interesting. I think I'll take the blend."

"Yeah, carrot flavor does sound kind of strange. Maybe I'll bring you one later," she said.

I sat down at a nearby table and looked around while the barista prepared my espresso. The café had a high ceiling with exposed wooden beams and two skylights that helped brighten up the space in spite of the gray sky. Just past the end of the coffee bar, a glass fence-like structure separated the bar from a large common table at the back of the café. The dark wooden tables and chairs matched the bar, and two couches sat up front next to a large roll-up glass door.

Shortly thereafter, the barista served my espresso alongside a heavy shot glass filled with sparkling water. I sipped it slowly, searching for the "ripe berry" notes that Ristretto's website said could be found in the Beaumont Blend. The shot was full bodied, with an underlying sweetness that lingered on the tip of my tongue. It was very smooth, and I finished it without adding any sugar. It left a pleasant aftertaste.

Had I left the café after drinking the one espresso, I would have been pleased. However, my day got better when, unable to keep it to herself, the barista brought over the Panama espresso a few minutes later.

The Panama was savory and spicy. It tingled on my tongue. The combination of flavors reminded me of salsa — Old El Paso Mild Thick 'n Chunky Salsa, to be more precise (something I ate quite a bit of growing up). Farther down in the cup, I noticed some other characteristics. The espresso was buttery, but it had a much lighter body than the Beaumont Blend. It had a slight drying effect on the middle of my tongue and upper mouth, and the edges of my tongue detected some tanginess. The flavor and feel were very different from the blend.

At first, I did not detect any carrot notes. I was a little disappointed — not because I was excited about tasting carrots but because I had a hard time imagining what carrot flavor would be like in a coffee.

I returned to my notebook and started writing. After a couple of minutes of writing, I was lost in deep thought when I noticed a strange taste in my mouth — carrots! The barista had been right. Maybe I had been trying too hard to find the flavors before. Who would have thought that a coffee could taste like carrots?

When I finally left the café a couple hours later, the rain was falling steadily. I didn't let it bother me, though. My candid conversation with Ristretto's enthusiastic barista and my two tasty espressos had lightened my mood, if not the weather.

## 22

# Andrea Spella and the Humanity of Espresso

*One of the most prominent characteristics of Portland's coffee roasters and cafés is their willingness to experiment with new ideas. Portland coffee is leading the country with innovations like multiroaster cafés (Barista), limited menu offerings (Coava), and lighter-roasted coffees (Heart). But it's not just the new concepts that make Portland's coffee scene stand out. Andrea Spella, owner of Spella Caffè, appreciates the value of tradition. His goal is to create a more traditional Italian coffee experience, one that reveres the history and artisanship of espresso.* — WH

At the age of forty-seven, Andrea Spella's graying temples and encyclopedic espresso knowledge give him a professorial air. Spella was born in Providence, Rhode Island, but he traces his early coffee interest to Chicago, where he grew up over his grandparents' bakery. Spella said his Italian heritage, in which the food culture and espresso are closely linked, played an important role. "We were drinking espresso and coffee as far back as I can remember," he told me when we met in a small conference room a few floors above his downtown Portland café. "Coffee was a natural part of my life. Food, wine, and coffee were all the same way — there were no age restrictions or expectations around the house."

The social nature of coffee was attractive to young Andrea. "A big part of it was not the quality of the coffee or the espresso itself — it was more about the community," he said. "I associated coffee with coming home after school each day and being with my nonna, and her telling me to go down to the bakery to pick what I wanted to eat, and we'd have coffee and a snack together. That was always really important to me, that sense of community and bringing people together." Spella thought he would someday take over the family's bakery, but when he was a teenager, his mother sold the business and moved the family to Albuquerque. The transition was tough, but it taught Spella some lessons he kept for life. "It helped make me who I am today — very versatile with [meeting people from] different walks of life," he said.

When Andrea's mother remarried, the family moved to Milwaukee. Spella was not taken with his new surroundings. "I kept trying to escape because I didn't want to stay in the Midwest," he said. Spella did escape eventually, leaving the region to work in the fine dining industry in different cities around the United States.

## Breaking into Coffee in Colorado

Andrea found the high-end food and wine world interesting, but he was not completely satisfied. One day, while contemplating his life's direction, he had a revelation. "As soon as I asked myself," he said, snapping his fingers, "I realized coffee was a natural fit." With a clear vision, he got going. "I moved to Boulder, Colorado, and just put it out to the universe, asking for the greatest experience of my life," he said. "I wanted to apprentice with a great person, I wanted to roast, I wanted to manage a café, and I wanted to be a barista."

Spella's cosmic petition was answered by Allegro Coffee, a Boulder-based roaster. He began apprenticing under Kevin Knox, an industry legend who was once the green buyer and roaster for Starbucks. "It was a perfect fit," Spella said. "Allegro's philosophies on roasting — the level and the amount of time of the roast and how they treat each coffee individually, rather than dialing in one roast and throwing everything in the roaster — fit with my palate and what I learned in food and wine." In addition to roasting with Knox, Spella also studied with Paul Songer, a Specialty Coffee Association of America (SCAA) award winner, technical adviser, quality control specialist, and head judge for Cup of Excellence. Spella managed Songer's café, Caffè Sole, which acted as Allegro's showcase café. Between his work at Allegro and at Caffè Sole, Spella learned how to be a barista, how to train baristas, and how to maintain equipment. He also gained experience roasting, cupping, and doing quality control.

## Andrea Spella and the Humanity of Espresso

When Whole Foods bought out Allegro in 1997, Spella left the company, preferring to work for a smaller business. Over the next few years, he worked at different cafés in and around Boulder and Denver. "I would usually get hired on as manager or lead barista and then kind of take over a lot of responsibilities for the owners," he said. "I'd say, 'Let me take care of it for you. Let me bring up your quality; let me do the hiring for you. I'll even develop your espresso blends and your coffees.'"

### On to Portland

In 1998, Andrea left Colorado and returned to Milwaukee to spend time with his father, who was suffering from cancer. The stop was temporary because he had his heart set on moving west. "For many years, I knew I wanted to make Portland my home," he said. "I came out and visited and fell in love instantly." In 2001, Andrea found a job at Portland Roasting, filling many roles at the growing company. "I came to them fully trained and helped them build their brand," he said. Andrea started Portland Roasting's training program. He would travel to cafés, train café owners and baristas, do quality control, and make deliveries. "After I left, they created three positions to do what I did," he said. "It was a lot of work."

After a few years with Portland Roasting, Spella knew it was time to step out on his own, a feeling that had taken years to develop. "I had to be able to sink roots and know I was comfortable in my own skin, ready to live somewhere permanently," he said. "That was the only way I was going to start my own business. I had accrued enough experience, I'd moved around enough, and now it was the time to put my name on something."

Spella planned to start either an upscale Italian café or a more local place with a roaster in front of the shop, but he did not find exactly the space he wanted. When a food cart came up for sale at the corner of Southwest 9th Avenue and Alder Street, Spella contemplated his options. "I thought, 'Well, I'll be in the heart of downtown,'" he said. "'I'll get my name out there right away. It could be a first step, and then I can grow my business from there.'" Though not ideal, the visible corner location and low start-up costs convinced him to purchase the cart.

From the beginning, Spella wanted to make it clear to customers that he was not operating in the same manner as other area coffee kiosks. "They give coffee a bad reputation because they're making twenty-ounce, tutti-frutti flavor, one-shot drinks," he said. "For some people, I'm sure they were thinking, 'Coffee from a cart — ugh.'" To overcome the negative preconceptions about the cart's quality, Spella hung the Italian flag outside the window, set up European tables and chairs outside, and played classical music in the background.

Spella also felt it was important to roast his own coffee. "I wouldn't have opened something with my name on it if I weren't roasting my own coffee," he explained. He was confident his ideas would be well received by Portland's discerning coffee drinkers. "I realized the brand and the ideas and the recipes I wanted to do had such a classical sensibility about them that I'd be able to do what I wanted pretty much anywhere."

## Espresso Steeped in Italian Traditions

When you talk with Andrea, you sense his passion for coffee. But if you really want to bring out his enthusiasm, ask him about espresso. "The premise of everything I do is the espresso blend," he said. "I wanted a somewhat classic Italian espresso profile." Spella had different goals than many of his colleagues in the industry. "American roasters tend to develop their roast profile and the blend to fit with the milk, whereas I come from a different angle, where espresso should be complete on its own without anything added to it. Then you can add something to it."

A lot of thought went into the espresso recipe. "Even in Italy, there are different levels of quality," he said. "If you're in a town, you've got a regional roaster and he's roasting several blends. Within two blocks there might be four or five cafés, and each one has a blend. They don't want to have the same blend as the café across the street."

The different blends target different kinds of customers. "There might be a certain café where the prices are a little less, and it's more for the workers at the Fiat plant, versus a more touristy café where you want something more exquisite, more perfumed and aromatic," Spella said. "The first might have some Robusta in it — it's got a kick and you put some sugar in it, and boom, you're out the door and you've got vitality and energy, ready to carry on with the day. The more exquisite one is about lingering with it and appreciating it. I wanted to do more of the appreciated, exquisite style — more ethereal, elegant. Not quaffable but just a beautiful, elegant experience."

Spella began investigating beans from Brazil. Why Brazil? When the Italians first started brewing espresso at the beginning of the twentieth century, Brazilian beans were their beans of choice. "The Italians dabbled with other coffees that they could bring in through other channels," Spella said, "but they always went back to Brazil. They realized that with such high atmospheric pressures forcing water through the coffee, to get a lot of sweetness, a lot of body, and lots of crema, the Brazil works best out of all the coffees. So I thought, 'Okay, I've got to use a Brazil.'"

He was unconcerned about Brazil's reputation for producing average quality beans. "Farming practices in Brazil are much better than a hundred years ago, and I had a feeling that there were coffees from Brazil that weren't just inexpensive blending coffees, that were actually exquisite coffees," he said. "I searched diligently to find these, and I actually found them. When I roasted them to the profile I thought would respect the bean and give it just a little bit of my own touch, I came to realize you could do single-origin Brazil and it would pretty much have everything you would want to represent an Italian espresso."

According to tradition, it takes more than Brazilian beans to make Italian espresso blends unique. "A lot of Italian roasters use anywhere from twelve to eighteen different beans, all blended together," Spella explained. "One has a little of this characteristic, another has a little of that, but most of them are fillers and blenders added to bring down the cost of the whole roast." Having such a wide mix of beans in the blend acts as an insurance against running out of some coffees. "If they run out of one of the beans, in the end cup you're really not going to miss it, since each one is only about 3 to 5 percent of the blend.

"I found such an amazing bean," he continued. "I wanted to add a little something to it, but it doesn't need a lot." He considered going with just one single bean, but that would have introduced variation from year to year. "Part of me wanted to revere the change and say that each year the espresso is going to be different," he said. "But part of me was like, 'I need some type of stability for my customer base,' to know they can come into our café or buy our wholesale beans and they will have the same or a similar experience."

Spella put his own signature on the blend too. "I wanted to add a little something that's my touch to it, so I've come up with recipes that are no more than three components — ever," he said. "Some years they're one, usually they're two, and recently they're three, but that's the greatest number of components I'll put in a blend. I won't go five, six, twelve — whatever." Spella saw no need to reduce the cost of his raw product. "I'm not serving a product for customers who need that cheapening of the blend," he said.

Having done his research, Spella's blend came together in a very short time. "Honestly, having such a strong food and wine background and growing up in the industry, it pushed me forward and accelerated the development process, so it basically took two or three roasting sessions, and I nailed it in an afternoon." All the years of studying and preparation made the difference, he said. "I knew the components I wanted, and I bought the best quality beans, and it just worked out perfectly for me." Spella roasts his beans on a five-kilo roaster and does about half the roasting himself. His longtime barista, Tasha, does the rest. Chiara, another longtime employee, is also learning how to roast. Together, they usually roast between six and seven hundred pounds of coffee each week. Teaching his baristas to roast is all part of Spella's long-term plan. He has no plans to have kids and wants to eventually pass the business on to his baristas.

### Revering the Craft

Everything about Spella Caffè is dedicated to the artisanship, or craft, of producing great espresso and a great café experience. The café has a Rancilio lever-operated espresso machine that requires baristas to pull on a lever to apply pressure to the hot water passing through the grounds.[63] Pulling shots this way is a physical act — it requires the barista to put more of her energy into producing the shot, to become more intimately involved with the coffee. It adds a dose of humanity to the coffee. "It's a labor of love," Spella said. "It has a lot more physicality to it. You can't just…push a button and go get someone a pastry or something."

The style Spella tries to embody in his café is similar to the principles of the slow food movement. "We take a little extra time and care and reverence to produce the product," said Spella. "That was my point too — getting back to the origin of espresso. It was an Italian invention. The machine was made to make a coffee quickly and fresh in the moment for whoever wanted it at the time. I respect that very much and want people to see that."

While Spella Caffè's use of the lever machine is uncommon in the United States, the technique is common in Italy, especially in the southern part of the country. "If you visit Naples, 90 to 95 percent of the machines the baristas are using are piston machines," Spella said. "They revere it. There's this flair and artistry, and it goes along with the culture in Naples that's so different from the rest of Italy." Spella was quick to point out, though, that his espresso is nowhere near as dark as what is typical in Naples. "Our espresso would equate more to a Bologna-Roman style roast profile," he said.

## Training Baristas

To ensure his baristas can pull great shots of espresso, Spella does extensive training with them, especially if they lack previous experience. New employees spend their first three months at Spella Caffè working as a cashier and as a barista assistant. They call drinks and set up the milk and cups for the barista. This allows them to learn the menu and work with customers. "You've already tasted every drink on the menu. You've worked with every customer and every special detail, and then we hit the machine."

---

63. Earlier lever-operated machines, predecessors to the one at Spella's shop, gave rise to the phrase pulling shots, meaning "brewing espresso." The term is still common today, even though these days, baristas at most cafés do little actual pulling.

Because the lever machine is more challenging to learn than a semiautomatic machine, Spella focuses on pulling espresso long before ever teaching anything about milk. A barista trainee may spend two months learning to pull shots and then an additional couple months learning to steam milk. After that, baristas work on incorporating the milk with the espresso. "It's a long training process, but it's worth the effort," Spella emphasized.

In addition to taking care of the coffee, Spella emphasizes the importance of creating a welcoming environment. The social side of coffee is at least as important as the coffee itself, he said. "A big part of what I do today with coffee is the community we create in our café, the welcomeness that's there, and how strangers become instant friends — how they take away a memorable experience and always come back whenever they return to Portland, or the once a year when they get across the river," he said, commenting on how loyal some residents are to their particular neighborhoods. "You know how Southeast Portlanders are," he said. "It's almost like it's another country over there."

## Brick and Mortar, Finally

Spella's cart opened in 2005 and was lauded for its style. "All of a sudden, food carts became very fashionable and all the food writers in the country were flocking here to write about them," Spella recalled. "That really helped me out." The cart's location was good but, lacking insulation, the aluminum cart was vulnerable to changes in the weather. "On a sunny day, the aluminum shell turned into a solar oven," said Andrea. "We would totally bake, and it would get up to 115 to 120 degrees inside, and we'd have to close for business because it was unsafe," he said. "All the refrigerators and freezers were compromised; all the beans were sweating. The machine was overheating. It was just not a good situation."

In 2009, Spella moved into its current 5th Avenue location, a spot he had been interested in for some time. "The funny thing is," he said, "this and another location downtown were two spots I'd been looking at since I moved here twelve years ago and thought would be perfect little Italian cafés. So my dream came true in getting this space." The new space was not much bigger than the cart, but it was much more protected from the elements and had a permanent feel.

For a time, Spella operated both locations simultaneously, but running two shops was too stressful, so he decided to close the cart. Andrea thought his customers would move to the new location with him. It was, after all, only a couple blocks from where the cart was.

What happened, however, surprised Andrea. "We lost all our business, save for about five people buying beans on a weekly basis," he said. "Those were the five people we saved, out of hundreds." Spella sounded downcast when he said this, as if he had been betrayed by the community he believed he had built. The reality was a stark lesson. "In downtown Portland," he said, "it's more about convenience and what's within a block or so. Three blocks away, where the cart is, there's about eight or nine cafés where people can go. Regardless of what the quality is — good, bad, or indifferent — it's more about the convenience."

## Wholesaling for Survival

Spella and his team had to build a new clientele almost from scratch. They also had to deal with a depressed economy. "I moved into the building, and a few weeks after I signed the lease, the owners went bankrupt," he said. "A lot of people left the building, and there were no services here. I thought the tenants would be the foundation of our business."

Struggling, Spella turned to wholesaling. "Originally, I didn't think I'd do so much wholesale," he said. "I thought I would roast for the café and maybe a couple exclusive restaurants." With the crash in the economy and his landlord's bankruptcy, that plan went out the window. "It was a matter of survival, gaining more wholesale accounts, and being very frugal," he said. "But we made it — just barely. If it weren't for the wholesale, we would have been out of business." Spella estimated that today, 60 percent of the coffee the company roasts each week goes to his wholesale accounts.

The company has come back strong from its challenges. The office building above the café has been filling up with tenants, and the wholesale side of the business has reached a point where Spella is no longer accepting any more wholesale accounts. "Now I'm going to help them grow their business, still continue to grow the café's business, and ride it out from here—just enjoy it," he said.

I asked Andrea if he ever wished he had a larger café space. He was torn. "Yes and no," he answered. "These two hundred square feet we have downstairs are perfect for what we do and for the neighborhood. It's a bus mall, and people are coming and going. We're not rushing people out the door, but there is a continuous flow of people coming and going and giving us business." If he does open another café, Spella has little desire to return to the cart environment. "People ask on a weekly basis if we would ever consider opening another cart," said Andrea. "Probably not. I like being inside and having air conditioning. I like not having to deal with frozen water pipes in the winter and not being able to open because of that."

## Bright, Single-Origin Espressos—Not Here

Hearing Spella talk about Italian espresso tradition, it was no surprise he had some strong opinions about the trend toward super light-roasted, single-origin espressos. "First and foremost, I respect what these people are doing and how they are moving forward and challenging themselves and their customers and the industry," he said, referring to his contemporaries. "That's always got to happen—every life, every generation, someone needs to come along and say, 'I want to do it differently, and I think we can.' And then maybe you can learn. Maybe something good comes out, or maybe not, but at least someone tried."

Putting lightly roasted, single-origin coffees through an espresso machine emphasizes the brightness and tartness of the coffees, making them too hard-hitting for many people. "It's very interesting, and I think it's a great study," Spella said. "For roasters and baristas, what better way to get to know coffees than to do those things? But my personal take is that the majority of people don't enjoy drinking coffee that way. It's too bright, it's too in-your-face, and they want more of a coffee experience that I equate with a slightly darker roast or more developed roast."

### Andrea Spella and the Humanity of Espresso

## Putting Down New Italian Roots

Despite his appreciation for Italian espresso, Spella did not think Portland cafés should serve coffees imported from Italy. "It's not respecting the Italian tradition of preparing something fresh in the moment with whatever quality you have and making the best of it," he said. The imported beans sit in warehouses for several weeks or months before they are ever used, significantly degrading the quality of the espresso. "Baristas pop open the nitrogen-pressurized can, and the first few shots of that day are exquisite, but then the next day, it totally flatlines, and it is harsh and acerbic. That's just such a bummer. And it's so expensive too."

Nonetheless, Spella is not opposed to roasting his own coffee in Italy. "My long-term goal is to actually have a little café in Italy," he said. "It will be on the Amalfi Coast, probably in Salerno. It's a beautiful part of the world." Salerno is less touristy than some other towns on the famous coast, but it is cosmopolitan enough to support a high-end coffee shop. "The eventual goal is to go into partnership with someone to help me run it." Spella plans to keep his base in Portland, traveling back and forth between the two locations every few months. Eventually, he would like to have a cultural exchange, in which his Portland baristas travel to Italy and vice versa to share the coffees and cultures of the different locales. The cultural exchanges would be a fitting addition to a company built around the Italian traditions of espresso and, just as importantly, bringing people together to drink it.

## The Sensuality of Great Coffee

It is no mystery why people love to drink coffee. The café experience touches all of the five senses, deeply.

### *Sights*

We are attracted to beautiful things, and coffee is no exception. A great café encounter begins with an opening glance. Upon entering a shop, our eyes inform us of the quality of the coffee that is to come.

Seated at a corner table, we observe the café around us. A skilled barista works efficiently behind the bar, her hands moving deftly between machine, milk, and cup. She gently sways the milk pitcher as she pours its contents into the espresso, casting delicate sepia-toned rosettes on the surface of a latte. Velvety foam rests on top of a cappuccino, blanketing the drink like a down comforter on a cold winter morning. The thick, brown crema on the surface of an espresso glistens under the warm lights of the café.

At the pour-over bar, steady-handed baristas pour delicate, even streams of water in smooth spiral patterns, coaxing out the complex flavors contained in the mahogany-colored grounds. At one end of the bar, a vacuum pot sits on top of the counter, a throwback to an earlier time in this modern setting. Brought to life by a brilliant orange infrared lamp, tiny bubbles cling to the side of the pot as the water heats up, glowing in the neon light. When the temperature breaks the boiling point, the pot transforms into a cauldron of angry lava, bubbling and bursting on the surface. The vacuum pot mesmerizes all who gaze upon it, and curious customers cannot help but stare in awe.

### *Smells*

Coffee has a bouquet of fragrances that attract people to it, and a good café delights your olfactory sense with the smell of freshly ground coffee. The aroma is sweet and fruity, smoky and earthy. Each time the barista grinds a new batch of beans for the brewer, a wave of aroma wafts across the café. The smell envelops you, enticing your taste buds in anticipation of the first sip of a freshly brewed cup.

### *Sounds*

Beans rasp loudly as they fall from brown paper bags into the grinder's hopper. The grinder whirs aggressively, growling out the fresh coffee into the basket below it. A loud thud reverberates through the café as the barista knocks spent grounds out of the portafilter. Steam bursts from the wand into the milk with a thump, then hisses and whooshes as it whips the milk into a cloud of frenzied bubbles.

Nearby, a miniature metal spoon scrapes the side of a ceramic cup, clinking softly as it mixes sugar into an espresso. In some cafés, the din of a bulky black roaster dominates the auditory spectrum, and customers must raise their voices to be heard by the people across the table from them. Lovers longing to whisper secrets or engage in quiet conversation content themselves with communicating through their eyes and expressions. Coffee beans pop and crackle as they flow out of the roaster's interior, each bean still burning inside. They calm quickly as cool, fresh air pulled by powerful fans is drawn across them.

### *Touch*
Your hands gently cradle a cup that is too hot to hold securely. The crema of an expertly pulled shot of espresso is silky smooth, lightly coating your mouth with a delicate film of flavor that keeps the memory of the coffee on the tip of your tongue. When you lift a cappuccino to your mouth, your lips note the warm smoothness of the ceramic mug, followed by the billowy softness of the milk. It is like burying your face in the soft, warm crook of a lover's neck. The flavors of a full-bodied French press coffee swell inside your mouth, continuing to expand long after you have finished drinking it.

### *Tastes*
The climax of the coffee experience is the moment when the coffee finally reaches your palate. Single-origin coffees can be refreshingly simple, with notes of stone fruits or berries or citrus. Blends are more complex, defined by the regions from which they came. Certain coffees are earthy, like leaves

that cover the ground in the fall. Other coffees are chocolaty and luscious. Some remind you of nothing more than coffee, but the flavor brings back something from your past, perhaps time spent with an old friend. Great coffee, whether it is brewed, poured, or combined with milk, delights the taste buds, sends them into ecstasy.

*Sensory* and *sensual* — both words describe the ideal café experience. Coffee satisfies the craving that began when you walked into the café, or perhaps when you rolled out of bed with coffee on your mind. It stimulates your senses and, sometimes, your soul.

# Water Avenue Coffee
## The Synergy of Three Portland Coffee Veterans

*When you walk into Water Avenue Coffee, it is clear that a great deal of thought went into designing the café. The shop is spacious, with a hefty wooden bar made of reclaimed Oregon fir wrapping around the shop from front to back. Painted gray walls give the café a mellow, understated ambience. Sturdy cement floors remind you of the building's industrial past. Behind the coffee bar, the roaster cranks out batches of roasted coffee, whirring and crackling as it transforms pale green beans into fragrant brown gems.*

*Water Avenue has been open only since 2010, but the three owners' coffee experience goes back much further. Bruce Milletto is a Specialty Coffee Association of America (SCAA) Coffee Luminary, well known for a lifetime of work shaping the specialty coffee industry. He founded Bellissimo Coffee Advisers in 1991 and partnered with his son, Matt, to open the American Barista & Coffee School (ABC) in 2004. Matt grew up around the coffee industry and has worked in coffee steadily for more than a decade. Since 2004, he has been teaching and training at the barista school, where he serves as vice president. Matt also founded Barista Exchange, a networking site for the coffee industry that has more than fourteen thousand members. Brandon Smyth, Water Avenue's third owner, has been working in coffee for more than a decade and a half. A former roaster for Stumptown, Smyth is the coffee buyer and head roaster for Water Avenue. He also teaches a roasting class at ABC. Matt and Brandon carved out a few minutes in their schedules to share a few stories with me.*[64] — WH

Water Avenue Coffee's origins can be traced back to Corvallis, Oregon, in the late 1990s. At the time, Matt Milletto was studying

---

64. After I first wrote about Water Avenue for Caffeinated PDX, Matt Milletto asked me to write an edited version to use on the company website, so some parts of this chapter are similar to the story found there.

photography at Oregon State, a rarity at the land-grant university better known for its agricultural research than its liberal arts programs. "I was one of maybe five people going there to study photography," he said, chuckling. Between classes, he worked at a coffee shop called Interzone close to campus.

About the same time, Smyth quit his job in high tech to work at Interzone. Switching to coffee was a big change, but the coffee industry was something that had interested him for years. "There weren't a lot of jobs in Corvallis when I was growing up," Smyth recalled. "Especially when you're younger, being a barista was the cool job to have. That's what drew me to it. I was lucky to get a job at the café."

While at Interzone, Matt and Brandon experimented with various brew methods. "The owner was a super cool guy. We had a lot of freedom," recalled Milletto. "We were doing really fun stuff, like pour-overs and working with a lever espresso machine." Working together set the stage for future collaboration, but that would happen a few years down the road. Both Matt and Brandon had other immediate plans. Milletto left Interzone to spend his last year of school in Macerata, Italy, a small college town in the province of Le Marche.[65] In Macerata, he studied art and photography, but coffee was never far from his mind. When he came back to the United States, Milletto managed a coffee bar in Eugene, and a couple years later, he moved to Portland to teach and train full time at ABC.

Smyth also took a detour before coming to Portland. He left Corvallis and moved to the Bay Area, where he worked at the on-site café for Royal Coffee, a green coffee importer based in Emeryville, California. Working for Royal gave Brandon his first exposure to the diverse profiles of regional coffee varietals. The job was interesting, and Smyth learned a lot, but he missed the Pacific Northwest. "I soon realized that I had left the greatest state in the union," he said. "Portland was always the city I wanted to live in." Before long, Smyth was making plans to return.

---

65. Coincidentally, Macerata is the same town my wife and I lived in during the fall of 2001. It's a small world.

## Water Avenue Coffee

When he came back to Portland, Smyth worked at Stumptown, where he found his life's calling. "When I met the roasters and saw the machines, I knew that's what I wanted to do," he said. "Working there is quite a learning experience — there's lots to do, lots of roasting going on. They have hundreds of coffees from all over the world. It's a great place to learn." Lacking any previous roasting experience, Smyth began his time at Stumptown filling bags with coffee and driving the delivery vans, eventually working his way up into a roaster position. "I've never learned more working anywhere else or met better people," he said.

In 2009, Bruce, Matt, and Brandon were hanging out over beers, talking coffee and looking at vintage roasters online, when they got an idea. Why not go ahead and order one? Given their collective coffee knowledge and experience, the three knew they could put something unique together. Seizing the spark of inspiration, they ordered a French-built 1974 Samiac roasting machine from a company in Switzerland and set about designing a new coffee company.

While they were waiting for the roaster to arrive, which took much longer than they'd anticipated, Water Avenue set up shop at Smyth's house to take care of the wholesale accounts they had already signed up. "I had a small roaster in my garage," Smyth said. "I spent many, many hours in there roasting a couple pounds at a time." When the new café opened in June 2010 near the corner of Southeast Taylor Street and Water Avenue, the trio fired up the Samiac and began experimenting with coffees on a larger scale.

To bring the best out of the green coffees he purchases, Smyth roasts the beans slowly at low temperatures, a method that is often called Scandinavian style. Slow roasting the beans creates more complex sugars, giving the beans a deeper flavor profile. Although it might take a little more time, the difference in the coffee quality is distinct. "One of the reasons Starbucks' coffee tastes burned or bitter is because they roast it so quickly," he said. "The fast roasting process does not let the longer-chain sugars form. We roast it at lower temperatures, making the coffee taste better. I guess you could say I'm a Scandinavian at heart."

While some Portland coffee roasters have done away with espresso blends, opting to serve only single origins, Water Avenue continues to offer its El Toro espresso blend year-round along with a rotating single-origin espresso. "The advantage to having a blend is that you can offer it all year, and it will follow the same flavor profile," explained Milletto. "If you were to just offer single origins all the time, your coffees would be constantly changing. Wholesale accounts don't like that." By offering the blend, Water Avenue can please a wider variety of customers, including those who like the seasonal variation of different coffees as well as those who prefer a more consistent set of flavors.

## Quality Starts at the Source

Like many third-wave roasters, Water Avenue is trying to shorten the supply chain between coffee farmers and the customer through direct-trade relationships. "There are a couple major ways to go about sourcing," said Smyth. "The first is to work with importers here in the United States who bring coffee in from all over, and let them work with farmers. The other way is to directly buy your coffee off the farm, which is absolutely the best way to do it for everybody. We can get higher quality coffee. We get exactly what we want. When I was in El Salvador, for example, I got to process the coffee that we're getting in two weeks."

Direct trade saves money too. "It's cost effective when you do [direct trade] because your coffee prices come down," said Smyth. "The farmers get a good price from us, and we don't have to pay an importer, which is usually about $1.50 a pound. What you can do is give $0.75 more per pound to the farmer."

In addition to being able to pay growers more, Smyth said that working with them has other benefits. "In the short time I've known one of the farmers I work with, we've developed a really strong relationship where we communicate almost every day," he said. "We're planning for next year's crop, trying to figure out what varietal and what kind of process would be the best."

Portland's reputation as a coffee capital has helped Water Avenue build relationships with the farmers. "A lot of farmers are looking at Portland in particular as a litmus test for the rest of the US," said Smyth. "They want to know what we want specifically because they know we're on the cutting edge. So if they're able to produce what we want, they're going to be able to sell well. It's a cool situation to be in."

Brandon is excited about some of the new things growers are doing at origin. "All the farmers are doing really cool experiments with varietals, trying to grow different things," he said. "The Mokka we have is an Indonesian coffee, and it's being grown in Colombia. It's really clean and clear. The Panama Esmeralda that's so famous is the same idea."

## Portland's Unique Coffee Scene

In addition to being pleased by how things have gone with Water Avenue, Milletto and Smyth also spoke highly of Portland's unique coffee culture. "I travel quite a bit to different cities, and it's often on business, so I'm touring a lot of coffee bars," Milletto said. "I think Portland is genuinely passionate about quality. We definitely have led a path for quality on espresso drinks and microroasters."

Smyth gave credit to his past employer for helping develop Portland's coffee culture. "In Portland," he said, "you have a more educated community, and a lot of that has to do with Stumptown. They did a great job of explaining how that works. Our challenges to convey [why third-wave coffee is different from what came before it] aren't as big as if we were in a different city, like if we were in the Midwest or on the East Coast."

Milletto said that one of the keys to building a great coffee culture is to provide an experience that resonates with the local population. "I don't want to say that people are trying to emulate or copy us, but I've been to other cities where it looks like people have tried to start a coffee bar based on an experience they have in Portland, and it's tough to do. I think in every city, you need to know your city before anything. What works here in Portland works for a lot of us, but if you're in Nashville or Atlanta, you really need to be genuine in your offerings and educate your customers."

Smyth agreed. "Education takes a long time," he said. "People have to come in and you talk to them. Little by little, they come to understand what coffee is all about. I have a friend who just started a roastery in Miami who came from here.[66] He said it is really hard for him to get people interested in small-batch coffee roasting. But here in Portland, it's a little different. People are more curious about where their products come from."

Milletto predicted the specialty coffee scene would continue to spread as roasters, cafés, and baristas educate customers about quality coffee. "We have a past client in Boston called the Thinking Cup, and the owner is an ABC graduate," Milletto said. "In cities like Boston, you get one or two great shops, and now people not only have an example to follow, but the customer base is becoming more interested in switching from a Dunkin' Donuts to a specialty coffee retailer." Matt does not worry about having too much competition within the industry, at least not yet. "I've been to NYC and LA to see what's going on there," he said, "and there's a lot of really great shops opening with people doing great things. These bigger cities are not even close to the saturation point of too many coffee shops. It's exciting to see."

## Water Avenue's Future

While there may be a lot of untapped growth potential outside Portland, neither Smyth nor Milletto are in a hurry to provide the coffee for that growth. Water Avenue does not sell much coffee outside Portland, for several reasons. "The big hurdle we have is shipping," Smyth said. "Our coffee is based on being fresh. It's hard to mail."

Supporting the company's wholesale accounts is also an important consideration. "We really try to offer a high level of support and training, making sure everyone is brewing our coffee at its best," said Milletto. "We have a lot of people requesting our coffee, but as a main roaster for a coffee shop, I don't think it makes sense to ship coffee more than one day away. I think going with a local option is often best." That said, they aren't opposed to sending some of their coffee long distance, at least once in a while. "Guest spots at coffee bars in New York — we love that kind of stuff," said Milletto.

---

66. Joel Pollock, of Panther Roasters

## Water Avenue Coffee

The owners are taking a long-term view of success for their company. "A big focus of ours is our employees," said Milletto, "growing their coffee skills and education, and professionally as well. We have some employees that help out in the school. We encourage them to compete. I don't think we created Water Avenue to immediately be a profit center. It's something that is rewarding and sustainable for us too."

Milletto and Smyth want their employees to get the experience of traveling to origin. "We're trying to implement a program where we send as many employees to origin as possible," Milletto said. "Two top employees are going to go each year, based on performance. Bruce, Brandon, and I go to origin as much as we can, but we're realistic too. We need to do what's best for the business. Hopefully someday we can take more trips."

As the business continues to grow, Smyth looks forward to bringing new coffees to Portland. "We'll have some pretty wild experimental coffee and some really straightforward delicious coffee," he said. "Things are changing really quickly, and the coffee is going to get better and better, especially in Latin America. I'd really like for us to be the ones to showcase that."

Water Avenue is just where Smyth and Milletto want to be. "It's the culmination for all of our passions for coffee and our expertise of being coffee professionals," Milletto said. "It's allowed us to really do something from our hearts. We want to be known as a unique and genuine microroaster that started in Portland, in the heart of the most competitive market, that people appreciate for the right reasons."

### Two Days at Coffee School

Many coffee people have told me that being a barista at a specialty coffee shop is difficult. Whenever they said that, I was always skeptical. How hard could it be?

To find out, I took a two-day barista course at the American Barista & Coffee School. The class, led by Tom Pikaart and Sara Ziniewicz, was designed to give students a hands-on introduction to pulling espresso shots, steaming milk, pouring latte art, and maintaining equipment. Eight students took the class, held at the school's headquarters on Water Avenue. Some of the students had their own cafés while others worked for roasters, supporting wholesale accounts. Most had at least some prior coffee knowledge or training.

In his opening remarks, Pikaart made it clear that the purpose of the course was not to perfect our technique. Rather, it was to teach us how to approach learning the craft of being a barista. No one can become an espresso expert in two days, he told us, but you can learn what you need to know to get started. If you have the right mind-set, competence will follow. These were the five things he said we needed to focus on:

- Cleanliness
- Self-betterment
- Passion
- Self-discipline
- Consistency
- Dialing, Pulling, Steaming, Pouring

After an introduction to the principles and procedures of making espresso, we moved over to the machines and got to work. One of the coolest things about ABC is the number of different grinders and espresso machines students can try during the class. Our group spread itself out between four different espresso machines, and there were three or four additional machines we did not use.

The first activity was to dial in the grinders. Knowing how to do this is a critical skill for a barista. Every day, as conditions (temperature, humidity, and so on) in the café change, baristas must make small adjustments to the grind so the espresso tastes good. If the grind is too fine, the water passes through the grounds too slowly, overextracting the coffee and bringing out excessive bitterness. If the grind is too coarse, the water will pass through too quickly, resulting in underextracted and sour espresso. To adjust the grinders, we turned a collar at the base of the grinder's bean hopper, narrowing or widening the space between the grinder's burrs.

Once we had the grinders where we wanted them, it was time to make some espresso. The first time I pulled a shot, I moved comically slowly, as I had to stop and think about each step in the process. As we pulled more and more shots, my technique became more fluid. I would like to think my espressos got better over time too.

After lunch, we moved on to milk. Steaming milk was less intimidating. Having steamed a lot of milk as a Starbucks barista, I had some idea of what to watch and listen for. It was fairly easy to adapt the techniques Tom and Sara taught us to what I already knew.

Pouring latte art, on the other hand, was completely new. Latte art, a common sight in Portland cafés, does not necessarily make the drink better, but it does indicate how serious the baristas in a café take their craft. I found that pouring beautiful latte art is not easy, especially when you are starting out. The biggest challenge was to remember to pour more aggressively as the cup filled up, exactly the opposite of what we do when we pour liquids in any other setting.[67]

Through practice, these skills improve, and a good barista soon does all the little things right without thinking of them. One of our exercises the second day was to teach a partner how to make a caffè latte. We had to write down, from memory, all the steps, and our partner was supposed to follow them exactly, no matter how many things we left out. I had thirty steps on my list, and I still forgot a couple. The lesson helped me understand why some café owners train their employees for a month before allowing them to

---

67. Unless you are like my three-year-old son, who pours milk as fast as possible, no matter how full the cup is.

make drinks for customers. It takes time to make all these steps automatic.

Another takeaway from the class was how important cleanliness is to the quality of the products. Both Tom and Sara emphasized how important it is to clean the machine regularly and thoroughly. Roasted coffee is full of oils that can creep into the hidden nooks and crannies in grinders and espresso machines. These oils degrade as they are in contact with the air, and they produce some funky flavors and odors if left long enough. For practice, we pulled our espresso machine apart and cleaned all the parts that come into contact with the coffee.

One thing that surprised me about the course was its emphasis on using our five senses to monitor the quality of our drinks. I had expected we would rely more on scales, stopwatches, and thermometers, and while Pikaart advocated using these devices to check a barista's consistency, he said we also need to be able to use our senses. Measuring everything, every time, is too time-consuming to use in a café setting, and with practice and attention to detail, a barista can learn to be very accurate and consistent using just the five senses.

### *Lesson Learned*

After taking the class, I now understand why people say being a barista is hard. With so many minute details that factor into making great drinks, you need to practice for a long time to become good. It takes time to master the skills of the craft. "Being a professional is an attitude. It is not a skill set," Pikaart told us as he closed out the class. We might not start out as experts, but we will get there if we keep learning.

A good lesson not just for being a barista, but for life as well.

# 24

# Chris Brady
Hitting the Right (Flavor) Notes at Extracto

*For a forty-three-year-old man who has run his own business for eight years, Chris Brady's hair is surprisingly thick and dark. His bright-blue eyes give off a youthful energy, though a few creases creeping in around the edges let you know he's been working hard. When I caught up with Brady at his Northeast Portland café and roastery, he and his head roaster, Neal Mead, were busy working on a batch of coffee. As a sweet and toasty aroma, reminding me of caramel popcorn, filled the room, Brady commenced with a short lesson on roasting. Then we sat down and talked about his story.* — WH

Chris Brady welcomed me to Extracto Coffee Roasters and immediately began telling me about the coffee he was about to roast, a natural-processed[68] Ethiopia Sidamo. Brady, who owns the café and roastery with his wife, Celeste, spoke with zeal about the flavors that came from the coffee. "It's super, like blueberry pie, strawberry — really great," he said. "I love naturals. They're like the cheesecake of coffee for me. It's like having a piece of dessert." Some roasters shy away from naturals because of their unique taste or because the quality levels are considered by some to be too variable, but Brady dismissed those concerns. "I think naturals have gotten better and better with time," he said. "For a long time, they were really funky and people weren't paying much attention, but they got better and better, and now I think they're phenomenal. Even green it smells like it." He opened up a bag of green beans sitting nearby and let me smell. A bright, rich fruitiness and a hint of winey fermentation drifted out of the burlap sack.

---

68. For a short primer on coffee-processing methods, see Where Coffee Comes From, in the Appendix.

## Roasting Theory

We returned to the roaster, where Neal had dropped the Sidamo into the roasting chamber. Brady pulled out a sample of the rapidly changing beans. They were already a light cinnamon color and very fragrant. First crack (a point during the roasting process when the coffee beans expand rapidly and split, causing a crackling noise similar to popcorn) was coming soon, Brady told me. Following the first crack, exothermic reactions inside the beans would cause a big bump in temperatures. He could hardly hold back his enthusiasm. "To me, roasting coffee is about the best job," Brady said. "You'll never smell coffee like it is when it is roasted. In the first ten seconds, [when] you pick it up off the tray and snap the bean, it's the most rewarding experience you'll find."

According to Brady, three numbers are especially critical when roasting coffee. The first is the base temperature, or the temperature of the drum when the roaster drops the coffee into it. The second is the temperature at which the first crack takes place. The second crack completes the trio, and although many of Extracto's coffees never reach the second crack (roasting that long would make the coffee too dark), knowing where it is helps guide Brady's development of the roast profile for each coffee. "If you looked at these beans under a microscope, it's growing little mountains," he said, referring to the molecules inside the cells. "As these mountains get bigger and bigger, they're letting out $CO_2$. As you get to second crack, the whole thing erupts and you get volcanoes. The inside of the beans — all the lipids and fats go to the outside. When you see a coffee bean with a little bead of sweat on it, it's hit second crack. If you don't, you're before second crack."

Brady called himself a more medium roaster than most. He will roast up to second crack, depending on the coffee. "To me, it's about the cooking process and caramelizing sugars," he said. "I'm trying to get the sweetest, clearest picture of this coffee that I can. This is a great fruity coffee. I don't kill the fruit and roast it too long or too dark because suddenly you kill the very thing that makes it galactic."

Maintaining the precise temperatures is critical to having the coffees turn out how he wants them. "My roaster, if I do everything right, it will stay to within three-tenths of a degree within a certain second on a certain minute," Brady said. In addition to temperature, the timing is also critical. "Depending on how fast or slow you're going, for that bean, there's a moment in time that makes a galactic cup of coffee," he said.

Each roaster's idea of what makes good coffee is unique, said Brady. "I roast and make coffee super specifically for what I do. I use all the bits of information I have learned and what I see as the history of coffee. I have the history of modern espresso in my head, and I have who did what and why they did it — scientifically, so I can tell my people how that machine works so they can get it down, so I can have them not be the variable. I want the grinder and my roaster to be the only variables." The proof of the quality of the roast is in the cup. "For me it's all about flavor," he said.

When Neal dropped the roasted beans onto the cooling table, Brady pulled a couple beans from the tray and held them under his nose. He broke a freshly roasted bean under his nose and inhaled, encouraging me to do the same. "That's about as fragrant as the coffee will ever be," he said. The variation of the beans on the cooling tray was striking. The Ethiopian beans were various shapes, sizes, and colors. Brady explained that Ethiopian coffees rarely are separated by varietal, each of which is slightly different. Also, the coffees come from a mill instead of a single farm, which means that a wide variety of coffees from different farmers make it into the same finished product, adding to the diversity. "If we kept roasting them darker, we could probably get them to look all the same, but you would lose the fruit," said Brady. The lighter you roast, he said, the more variation you see.

Chris also pointed out several quakers on the table. Quakers are green coffee beans that come from cherries that did not fully develop before they were picked. On the tray, they stood out for their light color, and Brady seemed unconcerned by their presence. "I like a little chaos," he said.

## From Alaska to Oregon

With the batch complete, Chris and I moved over to a table in the café to talk about his history. Brady started working in the coffee industry during his high school days in Juneau, Alaska, where he was a barista at the Orpheum, an old theater and café that was a popular teen hangout. In addition to learning how to pull shots on a lever espresso machine, Brady met his future wife, Celeste, at the shop. "Her parents actually call it the orphanage," Chris said, smiling. After high school, Brady moved to Portland in 1988 to pursue a musical career. He was the bassist and lead vocalist for the rock band Pond. Brady played with Pond for ten years, touring the United States and Europe, and making "a ton of records." He also played in another band — Audio Learning Center, on Vagrant Records.

When he wasn't touring or recording, Brady worked at Portland-area cafés. He spent five years at Three Lions' Café, where he put together the company's espresso program. Brady later worked for Torrefazione Italia, an Italian-style café chain based in Seattle. At Torrefazione, Brady worked with Jeremy Tooker[69] and Eileen Hassi, who later founded Ritual Coffee in San Francisco. "Jeremy Tooker is a really great guy and knew a lot about coffee and taught me a lot about coffee." Tooker's enthusiasm was contagious. "I just got the bug," Brady said. "I started researching it. I went online, reading Coffeed, Coffee Geek, reading a ton, buying [David] Schomer's books, studying Schomer. Anything I could do, any inkling of information I could find, I collected."

Brady said he also learned a lot from the people running Torrefazione. "Those guys were really good at customer service," he said. "Whether you really knew somebody or didn't know them, if somebody came in twice, you knew their drink." Starbucks ended up buying Torrefazione in 2003, acquiring Seattle's Best Coffee in the same transaction. After the purchase, it became clear that Starbucks had no desire to keep Torrefazione open, so Brady left.

At that point in his life, Chris was unsure what to do next. He considered studying electronics, but a friend in the industry told him he would have to move to Texas or Washington, DC, to get a job. Having no desire to leave Portland, Brady decided instead to

---

69. Portland coffee trivia: Tooker, who left Ritual to open Four Barrel in 2008, had his first coffee job at Java Man, a Portland-area café chain.

start his own café, opening the doors in 2006. "Running your own business is harder than I ever thought it would be, but it's super rewarding," Brady said. "My wife calls it our third child, and the Prescott café is our fourth child. In a lot of ways, they demand a lot more time than our regular children. In that way, it's laborious, but it's awesome. I don't know what else I'd do."

Despite the challenges, being an entrepreneur gives Brady a certain level of independence. "I want to do work that I am excited about," he said. "I don't want to do jobs that I hate. I never wanted to go to school and get a job, just to get my week off at the end of the year."

As the boss, Brady must use his authority judiciously. "I'm sure a lot of people think I'm a grumpy pirate because I call things as I see them," he said. "For people who are loyal to me, I'm super loyal. And for people who aren't loyal to me, I don't have time for them. I only have so much time in my day, and I do the best for my employees and my children and my customers, and I will bend over backward to do whatever for everybody." Looking around at the full café, Brady estimated he knew 80 percent of the people there. "I feel super privileged to serve them," he said.

**Very Hands-On**

Some business owners prefer to start a business and then let their employees take care of the details. Not Brady. "I want to stay passionate about it and excited about it, and I want to know about it. I think that's where I'm different. I want to be the company. Sometimes I see other people, and they want to own the company. They want to be like, 'Hey, I own a thing.'" Brady takes a different approach. "I want to know how the espresso machine works," he said. "I fix my own espresso machine. I deliver all my coffee. I install other people's espresso machines. Neal and I roast all the coffee. I train everybody to make espresso. For me, I want to be the master of all that."

When Extracto first opened, it sold Stumptown coffee. Two years later, Brady started roasting his own. "I knew I would roast at some point," he said. "I wanted more transparency." The economics were a big factor too. "At a certain point, I looked up, and

I was taxed, and I wasn't making any money. I was like, 'Okay, I'm giving $50,000 a year to a roaster. I think I can probably keep that.'" Chris bought a 1951 Probat and set it up at the back of his café, having never roasted before. "I thought, 'I know a lot about espresso. I'll figure it out,'" Brady recalled. "So I figured it out. I made a lot of mistakes, and these people went through a lot of bad coffee in the first six months. I knew what my espresso machine was capable of and that Fetco [brewer] was capable of, and I kept doing it until I figured out the parameters and got better and better at it. Now I think I'm pretty good."

Brady said he learned a lot from other roasters, even though the roasting community is not always open with information. "Nobody talks openly about roasting. Unless somebody shows you how to do it, you've got to figure it out. Unfortunately, a lot of people who have been taught end up competing against the guy they learned from. It's very Star Wars, where the Jedi…takes on his master." Having passed his own Jedi training, Brady keeps most of his secrets to himself, even with his friends in the industry. "Joel [Domreis] from Courier is one of the sweetest guys you've ever met," Brady said. "I love him and would drive five hundred miles for that guy. We don't talk about roasting."

The only person Brady does talk with about roasting is his head roaster, Neal Mead. "If I was suddenly falling off a building and needed somebody to push a button to catch me, Neal would be the guy to do it," said Brady of Mead, who has been with Extracto since 2009. "It takes a lot of trust and a lot of belief in somebody to really [teach them about roasting]. When I go out and he's roasting, this place could catch on fire, and he's the one guy I know who could handle it. He's a superstar, and he's a hard worker. "

Together, Brady and Mead roast around one thousand pounds of coffee each week, a number Brady said could be significantly higher if he chose. "I'm trying hard to not grow too fast," he said. "I'm trying to control growth in an organic way, to keep my company happy, to take care of the people who give me a lot of their time."

Celeste, Chris's wife, is one of the people who puts in a lot of time. Her involvement has been integral in the success of the business. "She does all the jobs I don't want to do," said Chris. Celeste takes care of details like scheduling, payroll, and paying the bills. "She also tells me if she thinks my coffee sucks," said Chris. "She has a great palate. She'll go, 'Your coffee's getting a little dark,' or 'Oh, I think that's a little thin.' I take her seriously. We've been drinking coffee for twenty-two years together."

## Coffees Geared for Customers

Brady puts a great deal of effort into getting his espresso blend just right. The results should speak for themselves, he said, no matter how people treat it. "I want people to taste it. It's not bitter. It's got some fruit and chocolate in it. It's great on its own. It's great in an Americano. It's really good with milk. It cuts through milk. It's easy to use. It's not just for espresso. It's great for French press or pour-over, Fetco, or AeroPress, or Turkish, or whatever. You want something that somebody can take home and they can make it." A long list of attributes, perhaps, but Brady emphasized how important versatility is. Coffee that is easier to brew makes customers happy. "Most people, when they go home, have no idea how to make coffee, right? They throw it in a Bunn and go, 'Looks good!' and they hit the button. You want to up their chances of that tasting awesome.

"My thing is, once you hand someone a coffee, they should do whatever the fuck they want to do with it," Brady said. "You should never have to say, 'Oh, you should stir that,' or 'You should drink that right now.' If people want to pour it in the trash and lick the side of the cup, it should taste good."

## Few Worries about Competition

Brady does not lose any sleep over the proliferation of roasters and cafés in Portland. "It was kind of a bummer when Caffé Vita popped up four blocks away, but whatever," he said, smirking. "It hasn't hurt my business at all. Everybody drinks coffee."

So far, there is plenty of space for everyone in the city. "There's awesome people around who are working really hard, and I want them to do well. I think there's enough coffee drinkers around, we can do really well. Coava's doing a great job, and Joel [Domreis, from Courier] is such a sweetheart. He has saved me so many times,

# Caffeinated PDX

I can't even tell you. Jeremy [Adams] at Cellar Door is a really nice guy. Andrea Spella, great guy. Everybody's doing their thing, and I wish them all the best. At the same time, I'm doing my thing—I don't want them to bug me." Occasionally, Brady travels around Portland visiting cafés and trying other coffees. He said he finds a wide variance in the quality levels. "I went to Coava the other day and had a Kenya that was really good," he said. "That day I had a couple other coffees, and all of them were pretty bad. But it was like, 'Okay, I'm not running their companies. I'm running my company.'"

## Long-Term Plans

Extracto's growth has been steady, and Brady plans to keep it that way. "I want it to grow gradually so I can control it," he said. "If I wanted to do five times as much tomorrow, I'd make a couple phone calls and start doing a lot more grocery. I could sell a lot more coffee." Growth opportunities are everywhere, if Brady chooses to pursue them. "I had some Chinese businessmen come in and say, 'Wow, we love your place. We want to open a bunch in China,'" Brady said. "I'm like, 'Well, it sounds really expensive.' They're like, 'Money's not an object.' That's not really what I'm about. I said if they want to learn how to roast, you can hire me as a consultant and pay me a portion and call it something else. It's interesting, but for me it's not about making money. It's about really giving myself something to do and having fun with this. Beyond that, I don't care."

For the most part, coffee has been an enjoyable endeavor (which might explain Brady's lack of gray hair), and Brady said he has no plans to get out. "I want to have fun with life. I never want it to be something I don't want to do, because I've had tons of shitty jobs over the years." He laughed. "I was an industrial temp. I used to make music for a living, and I'd come home and try to get a job for a week. I've worked at Valvoline, Stone Mill Foods; I've worked at the Vitamin Factory; I've dug ditches and worked in cemeteries. So roasting coffee and shoveling green is pretty sweet, I'd say. Sitting there and smelling amazing coffees and hanging out and talking to people who are fanatical about coffee—I love it."

# 25

## Wille Yli-Luoma
### Carving New Trails at Heart Roasters

*When you meet Wille Yli-Luoma,[70] owner of Heart Roasters, you can see the echoes of his professional snowboarding career. He moves like an athlete, with a compact, spring-like physique tailored for barreling down mountains and flying off twenty-foot jumps. His smile comes quickly then disappears behind a mask of focused intensity as he starts talking about coffee. "I have the kind of personality that when I go into something, I go in 100 percent, and that's my focus," Yli-Luoma told me when we sat down together at his East Burnside Avenue café. Wille's selectivity when purchasing green coffees and his dedication to a light roasting style have allowed Heart to carve out a unique place in a crowded industry.* — WH

Portland's coffee roasters came from many backgrounds, but few come from as far away as Yli-Luoma, who grew up in Finland. He first came to Portland when he was sixteen to snowboard at Mount Hood for a month. Coming to the United States for work was not the teenaged snowboarder's favorite thing to do, but Yli-Luoma found Portland to his liking. "Portland was the only place where I felt there was something more, some connection, or some kind of cultural feel," he said. Several years later, Wille was living in Sweden when the dollar dropped in value. He was being paid in dollars, so he applied for a work visa and moved to Portland in order to get the most out of his paychecks.

Before he moved to the States, Wille had been around coffee a lot, but he himself was not a connoisseur. "My family drinks so much coffee," he told me. "I would make them coffee like five times a day. I never drank it, but I always made it." That changed

---

70. Pronounced VEE-leh lil-WOA-ma. To hear it pronounced as Wille does, visit http://www.youtube.com/watch?v=XUzx6q22kCs.

as he spent more time in Portland, where he started visiting local cafés. Stumptown in particular left an impression. "They were showcasing a lot of different varietals that I'd never seen before, and it really sparked my interest a lot," he said.

Not content to just consume the local coffees, Yli-Luoma began refining his brewing skills. "I started buying a lot of different roasters' coffees, and I was pulling shots on my home espresso machine," he said. "Then I got a little nicer home espresso machine, and then I went from that to a two-group Synesso in my kitchen." His grinder technology followed a similar progression as he planned for a future in coffee. "At this point, I already had an idea I would open a coffee shop, but it became almost an obsession, playing around with coffee," Wille said. "It wasn't like I was drinking coffee all the time. I was tasting it, but I was more interested in what was happening, who was roasting what, and how it worked in an espresso machine. I wanted to learn more."

The next logical step after brewing was to learn about roasting. Yli-Luoma bought a small home roaster to practice with, and he also purchased a bigger machine for his future roastery. He traveled to Denmark and Sweden to talk with top roasters and visit their roasting facilities.

## Opening the Café

For his first location, Yli-Luoma chose a spot on East Burnside Avenue, an area that seemed in need of a good café. "I had friends that lived in the neighborhood, and I always felt like there was no good coffee here," Wille said. "I was always like, 'Where do you go for coffee?' You go downtown, there's places to go. You go to North Portland, there's a couple places to go. You go to Southeast, and there's places to go. I felt like this was kind of a dead zone, and there was nothing really good here. To me, that seemed like a good sign."

Wille collaborated with friends to design the café in a style he called a "mixture of minimal, midcentury, and early industrial combined." When the shop opened, it received accolades for its clean, modern look. To raise interest in the roasting process, Yli-Luoma had placed the gleaming black-and-silver Probat roaster in the front of the shop. A curved table nearby invites people to sit next to the roaster for a front-row view of operations. "I didn't want to hide anything from people," he said. "I wanted to have a conversation with people about what we were doing — have them really see the whole process." A sign hanging near the roaster asking people to not disturb the roaster while working reduces interruptions.

## Sourcing

Many things stand out about Heart's coffees, one of which is the effort Yli-Luoma puts into sourcing them. "I'm comfortable saying we pay the most for green coffee in Portland," he said. "The lots we have selected, in order to keep them, we have to pay a premium. I'm okay with it, but it definitely makes us pay more. Then we end up getting better quality." Wille travels to origin himself to taste coffees and negotiate directly with the farmers and cooperatives. He then works with importers to bring the coffee to Portland.

The closer he gets to origin, the better. "The main thing about buying so-called direct is that you get to pick your lots before anyone else," Wille said. "I get to pick the coffees that we want to roast and represent. So I'm not picking off an importer's menu."

Yli-Luoma had just returned from a trip to Kenya, where he was able to secure some exclusive coffees. "I got to taste coffees that are now sold to me, and no one else is going to get to taste them or have a chance at getting them," he said. "They're coming from the farm, they get milled, and I get to taste a sample. If I approve it and accept it, it goes straight into vacuum packs and no one else can buy it. That helps get our quality up much higher." Yli-Luoma said he enjoys meeting the producers and the people who work at the co-ops where the coffees are processed. He regularly takes them bags of roasted coffee so they can see what Heart does with the coffees it purchases. "They get excited," he said. "The more they get that, the more motivation it gives them to make their farms better and more successful."

Competition for the best coffees is tough and is only going to become fiercer as time goes on. "There are a couple importers out there trying to snag some of the good lots," Yli-Luoma explained.

"They get exclusive rights to certain farms. Right now, I see coffee becoming very challenging at source — it's going to be a fight to get the best coffees. It's a little uncomfortable, but it's just the way it is."

One advantage Heart has over the large roasters is its size. Larger roasters need to purchase bigger quantities of coffees to serve their customers, and many growers just do not produce enough good coffee to fill that need. "So what are [larger roasters] going to do?" Yli-Luoma said. "Go around and buy from fifty farms and only buy the top tier? You can't do that. Versus a smaller size like us, we can be fine by buying from two or three farms and just buying the higher quality. This is where I think being a smaller roaster is actually kind of an advantage."

Yli-Luoma plans to maintain the quality of his green coffees by building relationships with specific growers who share his desire to produce a good product. Doing so will take time but will ultimately be worth the effort. "I already have a relationship from one of last year's farms in Guatemala," he said. "This year, there were other roasters trying to buy their coffee, and he's like, 'No, I'm committed to this guy in Portland. I'm saving the coffee for him until he tastes it.'" Wille had purchased the farmer's entire microlot the year before, so the farmer gave Heart the first opportunity to buy the next year's crop.

Yli-Luoma looks for coffees that have been selectively picked at the peak of ripeness, which means the beans have a higher sugar content. The cherries must be processed well to remove defects and avoid off flavors getting into the coffee. Nearly all of Heart's coffees are washed-process coffees.

## No Naturals

One thing customers will almost certainly never see on Heart's menu is a natural-processed coffee. The flavors that can get into the beans as they sit on the drying patio do not sit well with Yli-Luoma's palate. "The naturals I've tasted, I have this gag reaction when I cup it," he said. "It's really, really offensive to me, so that's one of the reasons we won't have naturals."

The processing degrades the purity of the final product, he said. "It's something that gets into the bean from the outside. It's an off flavor, almost like tainting." Wille shared a story about a sourcing trip to Ethiopia, where he tasted a washed coffee that left him unimpressed, surprising his traveling companions. "It was so close to tasting like a natural to me," he said. "All these people were raving about it, and I gave it a super-low score. They're like, 'What?' and I'm like, 'This is disgusting. It's so dirty. It's like a natural coffee.' They were shocked, but it just didn't sit well with me."

Seasonality also plays a role in which coffees make it into Heart's lineup. Each region has its harvest season, when the coffees are at their peak ripeness. Yli-Luoma insists that his coffees are fresh and that they do not sit in a warehouse until the next harvest comes around. "We don't have any Guatemala or El Salvador on our shelf right now [the end of February]," he said, "and if anyone has it in Portland, that's a first sign to me of a poor reflection of quality because you're serving a product that's out of season, and it doesn't hold up."[71] Yli-Luoma sees diversifying by geographical region as a good strategy to avoid selling coffee grown the prior season. "Trying to work with Colombia and Brazil and Rwanda would offset that time, and those coffees would be in season, versus when the Guatemala, Ethiopia, and Kenya would be in season," he said.

## Roasting Style

Heart is known for offering the lightest roasts in Portland and possibly in the entire United States. Oliver Strand, writing for the *New York Times*, called it "advanced coffee." Yli-Luoma said he was influenced by his visits to roasters in Denmark, who also roast very lightly.[72] "When I had their coffee, it was so refreshing, and I was like, 'Wow, this is so clean. I'm not tasting smoke; I'm not tasting ash. I'm tasting coffee, like it's a fruit.' I'm like, 'Wow, this is amazing! This is what I want my coffee to taste like.'"

Yli-Luoma takes a similar approach. "Our goal is to showcase that coffee at its fullest, whatever coffee we're buying," he said. "In

---

71. According to Yli-Luoma, this is less critical with Ethiopian coffees, which have a longer shelf life than those from Central America.

72. Finland's coffee culture may have predisposed him toward lighter roasts too. Finnish coffee has the reputation for being some of the lightest-roasted coffee in the world.

order to do that and get every nuance out of it, you have to roast really light. As soon as you roast darker with the coffee, you are blunting a percentage of that coffee." Although Heart is known as a light roaster, Yli-Luoma is ambivalent about the label because some roasters have given light roasting a bad reputation. "People are roasting coffee, and it tastes grassy or it tastes sour," he said. Good quality green coffee roasted well should never be sour, he said, as long as it is prepared correctly.

For Yli-Luoma, even the term *light roasting* is somewhat misleading. "I don't even look at it as light roasted anymore," he said. "I don't think of it that way. I look at it as the proper way of roasting. We roast coffees to their full potential to get everything we can out of them. I'm getting more narrow-minded about it, where I don't feel like coffee has so many different roasting profiles. I try to look at what works best." Heart's staff uses Extract Mojos[73] to read extraction percentages when they cup coffees and brew them. "When you brew coffee, and when the coffee extracts really well and it's still light roasted, then you're doing something right."

Close observation and analysis are a big part of what happens at Heart. "Everything is thought through," Yli-Luoma said. "There's no like, 'This is some random magic.' There's a lot of work behind it. Every bag has a batch number. Every batch is logged in the computer. Every bag is cupped by the roaster and myself. We know what we sell." Being able to track each coffee is a critical piece of quality control. If a coffee tastes particularly good, for example, Yli-Luoma can go back to check the roast log to see what happened during the batch to gain a better understanding of the variables that affect the final product. The scientific approach ultimately leads to better quality.

## Effort in the Brew Too

After putting in all the work to source and roast the coffee, Wille is just as careful with brewing. "Brewed coffee is actually what I

---

[73]. An Extract Mojo is a refractometer, modified for coffee by Vince Fedele, that measures the percentage of total dissolved solids (TDS) in a brewed coffee. Using the TDS and the ratio of dry coffee grounds to brewed coffee (by mass), a person can calculate the extraction percentage of the coffee.

pride myself the most on," he said. "I would say it's probably the hands-down best you can get in this town, and not just because it's my shop." He explained that Heart's coffee is always fresh — baristas brew coffee every twenty minutes — and all brew parameters and extraction percentages are closely monitored with precision instruments. "The chances of you getting a well-brewed cup of coffee here on a regular basis are high," Wille said.

Yli-Luoma thinks Heart's coffee is actually more appreciated around the United States than it is in Portland itself, and he might be right. Portland's large concentration of roasters and cafés can make it hard to stand out, though Yli-Luoma still believes Heart is one of a kind. "I truly don't feel like I'm in the category of the quality of roasters in Portland," he said. "I think we're doing something completely different than any other roaster is doing." Comparisons with competitors do not sit well with him. "I get upset sometimes when people start comparing me to other roasters here in town because we're not doing the same thing," he said.

To make sure Heart's coffees meet his standards, Yli-Luoma cups every day, checking profiles to see what can be improved. "It's really easy to become jaded when you taste the same coffees all the time," he said. "If I've traveled and I come home, I can taste very clearly if I don't think something is all right. I then make sure everything is adjusted back to track."

Wille said that if one of his coffees is just a little bit off, he will pull it from the shelves. "I'll put it on a second-quality shelf that gets sold to some of our wholesale accounts' kitchen staff. They're not allowed to sell the coffee to anyone, but they get the coffee at our cost." Heart's dedication to controlling quality this strictly makes it unique, said Yli-Luoma. "I don't think there's any roaster around who does that. I think most people would just throw it in with the next batch and move on."

The care that goes into producing Heart's coffees is higher than other roasters', he said, because of the raw product and the care that goes into it. "How do you explain that to the public without sounding snobby?" he asked. The differences between coffee companies might be hard to see for someone without really knowing what is going on with the coffee. "There's a distinct difference, but to the public person, it's a coffee shop; it's a roastery." Yli-Luoma is confident that his and his staff's efforts will be recognized. "Over time, people will see, and that's what's happening. People are starting to ask for our product around the world."

In conversation, people within the industry regularly compliment Heart's coffees. "There's a thing that goes on with Heart coffee that I really appreciate," said Ryan Willbur, marketing coordinator for La Marzocco USA (who previously worked for Lava Java, Stumptown, and Intelligentsia), when I asked him what coffees he had been drinking lately. "Truth be told, I think these guys are roasting the best coffee in the country right now. If I could only have one coffee roaster in my kitchen for the rest of my life to brew my own coffee, it would be Heart."

With praise like that, it is no wonder that Heart is a rising name in specialty coffee. Wille Yli-Luoma's insistence on sourcing current crop and washed coffees, roasting them to emphasize the flavors in the beans instead of the roast, and precisely monitoring his café's brewing parameters makes Heart stand out, even in an industry full of people trying to do their own thing. Heart has already built a loyal customer base in Portland, and with a growing reputation outside of Portland, the future looks bright for the snowboarder turned coffee roaster.[74]

---

74. Heart announced plans to open a new café in downtown Portland's West End during 2013.

## Sarah Allen
Supporting Baristas Worldwide at *Barista Magazine*

*In addition to being a hub for specialty roasters and cafés, Portland acts as a center of information for coffee professionals. Three of the most important publications in the industry — Fresh Cup, Roast, and Barista Magazine — all call the Rose City home. Barista Magazine, owned and operated by Sarah Allen and her husband and business partner, Ken Olson, has become one of the most widely read publications in the specialty coffee industry. With more than ten thousand subscribers in seventy-six countries, Barista Magazine's influence stretches around the world, from Moscow to Johannesburg. Sarah, the magazine's editor, met me on a breezy January day at Case Study Coffee on Northeast Sandy Boulevard to talk about her magazine, the barista community, and Portland's influence on the industry. — WH*

Sarah Allen grew up in Berkeley, California, where she was conditioned from a young age to be a coffee drinker. "My first coffee memories were my parents taking me to the original Peet's," she told me. "My parents were big Berkeley hippies, and they would go to the original shop on Walnut and Vine and plop me and my sister down on bags of green coffee while they talked to their friends." A few years later, Allen developed a coffee tradition of her own, cutting class with her friends to grab coffee at Peet's. After high school, Allen attended UC Davis, where she studied English and wrote for the campus newspaper. When she returned home for visits, Sarah would pick up large bags of coffee from Peet's, bring them back to school, and store them in her freezer. "All my friends thought I was crazy about coffee then, but it was only because of Peet's," she said.

Immediately after college, the *Oakland Tribune* hired Allen as a full-time editorial assistant. A year later, she was promoted to music critic, and she spent the next three years writing about music and film for the paper. "It was awesome, but it was super temporary because I'm reviewing concerts," she said. "I do it, and then it's over the next day. Or I'm interviewing Elton John, and I'm one of twenty reporters he talks to that day. It didn't feel important at all."

Ready for a change, Sarah enrolled in the University of Oregon's graduate journalism program with the intention of working for the *Oregonian*. "The *Oregonian*, back before newspapers were slammed so badly, was one of the newspapers people went to work for for the rest of their career," she said. After graduating with her master's degree in 2000, she got a job writing for the paper's Living section. A year later, with revenues flagging, the paper had to cut the budget, and Allen was sent to the paper's bureau in Tigard. Working in the suburbs was not what she had envisioned. "I was hating my life," she said. "It was the most soul-deadening thing."

Around that time, Sarah met Ken Olson, her future husband and business partner, who was also struggling to find satisfaction in his work as a writer. To get a fresh start, they both quit their jobs and went camping for two months. Upon their return to Portland, Sarah landed a position as assistant editor at *Fresh Cup*.

## Founding *Barista Magazine*

Within a short time, Sarah quickly moved up and became the publication's editor. "Coffee reminded me of all the good parts of the music industry when I was a music writer," she said. "It's like these crazy, passionate super-geeks, and they all tend to be really intelligent and curious and fun and weird." Allen wrote *Fresh Cup*'s first-ever article on baristas, "Calling the Shots: Will American Baristi Ever Earn the Respect They Deserve?" in June 2003. "At that time, the barista community was just starting," she said. "The Barista Guild had just had its first meeting. Barista competitions were just beginning. I thought it was so interesting."

Allen had studied subcultures while she was in grad school, and although working at *Fresh Cup* allowed her to write about coffee's subculture, she realized what she really wanted to focus on was the barista subculture. Sensing an opportunity, Sarah left

*Fresh Cup* with the intention to start a magazine about baristas. The move was met with some skepticism. "When we started *Barista Magazine*, people told us we were totally nuts, that baristas were temporary service workers who didn't give a crap," she said.

Not everyone thought the couple was crazy, however. Stumptown's Duane Sorenson encouraged the couple to go for it. "Duane was the first person we told we were starting *Barista Magazine*," Allen said. "He was one of the only people who was like, 'That's such a great idea.' He said, 'This community needs it.'"

Before starting the magazine, Allen wanted some street cred, so she spent a year working with Stephen Vick at Zoka in Seattle, helping him train baristas for competition. At *Fresh Cup*, Allen had judged several barista competitions, and she used her experience to coach Zoka's baristas. "Steven and I were the training team," she said. "He did all the tech stuff, and I did all the performance stuff." Few companies put much effort into baristas in those days, and Zoka quickly gained a reputation for producing great baristas.

After Allen's year at Zoka, she and Olson prepared to launch the magazine. They set up an office in their house, wrote articles and took photographs, hired a designer to put it all together, and released their first issue in April 2005. Sarah acts as editor, and Ken, who also has a master's in journalism, is the publisher. The magazine has grown steadily ever since, attracting a readership of entrepreneurs from around the world. "*Barista Magazine* is called *Barista Magazine*, but our readership is all café owners," she said. "They're people who say, 'Hi, I'm Steph, and I'm a barista, and I also own my own café.' The thing they distinguish themselves by is being a barista. That is a huge thing in the industry."

## Coffee as a Worldwide Phenomenon

One of the reasons *Barista Magazine* is so widely circulated is that its articles cover six continents. "The global nature of coffee is one of the reasons why I gravitated toward coffee," Allen said. She and Ken solicit articles from people working abroad, but they also travel the globe themselves, covering events, attending trade shows, and writing about anything coffee-related. In addition to covering North America, Allen has traveled to Europe, Africa, Central and

## Caffeinated PDX

South America, and Asia. If there were a specialty coffee scene in Antarctica, *Barista Magazine* would probably cover that too.

Just prior to our conversation, Sarah and Ken had been to Ethiopia, traveling with some friends who own a roaster in Johannesburg, South Africa. In the Ethiopian countryside, Allen got to drink coffee as fresh as she had ever experienced. "We're out in the middle of nowhere, and every single little village has a coffee stand," she said. "It's like their shop, and it's basically a tarp and some plastic lawn chairs, and the woman who makes coffee probably picked it from a tree that's as close as that espresso machine over there [about fifteen feet]. Then she roasts it in a pan and grinds it, and it's so delicious. It's really good coffee. That was really amazing."

Russia was another country that left a strong impression. "Russia is awesome and weird and wild," she said. "You can't go there by yourself because it's a terrifying place. And a bottle of water costs $14." Specialty coffee in Russia is growing in fits and starts. "Starbucks tried there and totally bombed," Sarah said. "They didn't launch themselves the right way, so it never succeeded. But there's two specialty roasters in Moscow — Coffee Mania and Koffein — that are really popular."

Allen has been to origin countries several times, and she said she sees the impact that specialty coffee is having on developing countries. "In Central America, the systems are in place." Farmers have more resources than ever before to improve their livelihood. "The farmers know about it. They've seen it happen. They've seen buyers come in and say, 'If you improve your washing station, you're going to improve your prices.' That happened. They did get higher prices, and now they're moving on to the next steps."

All over the coffee world, things are happening quickly. Sarah covered an event in Paris in the fall of 2012. "Paris is really exciting," she said. "It's kind of like where New York was five years ago. It's super interesting because it has this huge history of coffee culture. I think of it like San Francisco, in a way. It's the romance of the city and the coffeehouse culture, and now all these specialty people are coming in — these young guys starting to do microroasting, in a city like Paris that's so expensive. That was really interesting to see. I think Paris is going to change hugely in the next year."

## Sarah Allen

Not every change in the industry has been positive. Allen was unequivocal when I asked if McDonald's entry into the specialty coffee market is helping or hurting the industry. "Hurting," she said, without hesitation. "I've thought about it a lot. If you see a McDonald's billboard with latte art on it, isn't that good? No, it's not, because it will also say, 'Why spend $4 on a cup of coffee when we're doing it this way?' It's like half the message. You're teaching people that coffee should be something special, but you're also reinforcing to them it should be cheap. And the whole reason for the specialty coffee industry is that at the end of the day, we're all doing this for the good of the planet, right? We're doing this for better wages for people in developing countries and for sustainability."

### Portland's Place in the Coffee Industry

Allen said that while other cities are quickly improving their coffee scenes, Portland has shown a willingness to lead. "It's pretty well known around the country that Portland is not just down the street from Seattle, where everything started with coffee," she said. "Portland people are restless at all times, always willing to try new things. I think it partially happens because we still have all these liberal, well-educated people coming to Portland, but it's a lot cheaper place to live, so you can open a café a lot more easily than you can in San Francisco, for example."

Allen acknowledged Portland had room for improvement. "When SCAA [the 2012 SCAA Event, the organization's annual gathering] was happening here last year," she said, "I remember so many people saying, 'We're so excited to come to Portland 'cause, like, every café you have is specialty, right?' I was like, 'No, we're a city like any other place, and we probably have a higher percentage of places that are specialty, but there's still a lot of bad coffee places around.'"

One of the ways Portland stands out is for its cooperation within the community. Allen gave the example of how Coava and Water Avenue, although they are competitors, ultimately are on the same side. "They're both specialty roasters, and the bad guy is the one saying they are unnecessary," she explained. "It's important for those companies in the same city to band together because then Portland becomes a destination place for coffee. It didn't happen just because of Stumptown. It happened because of all these people."

She brought up Coffee Roasters United (CRU), the partnership between Sterling, Case Study, and the Red E, among others, as an example of how the Portland community works together. "I think it's cool what Case Study is doing, and the group they're working with [CRU]," Allen said. "That is a really cool community kind of thing — something that was destined to happen in Portland."

Allen thought the explosion of new roasters was overdue, if anything. "The whole reason it took so long is that Stumptown was so good, so people didn't really feel a need for anything else," she said. "But then it happened, and it just diversifies the market." If each new roaster can find a core customer group, it has a better chance to survive. "In Portland, I feel like people are fiercely loyal," Sarah said. "The original Stumptown people are fiercely loyal. I think people were excited to be the first loyal customers to Coava and will stay fiercely loyal."

The intense competition forces new roasters to provide a quality product. "If I'm going to spend $20 for a pound of coffee that's a really special coffee, I want to know it's coming from someone who really knows how to roast it," she said. "Roasting isn't something everyone can do. It makes sense there would be a top group of them. I don't know who's buying the coffee from the smaller roasters. I think it's great they're doing it, but I also don't think it feels very sustainable."

According to Allen, Portland's influence on the industry grew with the arrival of another Barista — the café, not the magazine. When Billy Wilson opened his first Barista location, people realized they liked having more than one roaster's coffee available on a daily basis. "That's one of the biggest things that has happened in the last few years — the multiple-roaster concept, which Billy totally started," said Allen. "No one else could have started it because Billy had a name and if anyone else would have tried it, their roaster would have said, 'Screw you. You can use another roaster.' So that totally changed things."

## Opportunities for Baristas to Make Better Careers

Although baristas get more respect than they used to, there are still people who believe opportunities for baristas are limited. Allen disagrees. "Maybe this sounds harsh, but I don't buy that." Opportunities abound, for people willing to take a risk. Allen speaks from experience — founding *Barista Magazine* allowed her to turn two of her interests, writing and coffee, into a career. "You can make it work in any industry if you want to," she said.

She continued, "If you push enough, you can find those opportunities. I really do think so. So many baristas have done it." Baristas routinely switch companies in search of new opportunities. "If that person's not giving you the opening, apply to be an apprentice roaster. This industry is incredibly forgiving to people who might not have conventional attributes, like a college degree," she added. "Lots of cafés like hiring people who don't have a lot of barista skills because they like raw talent." Allen said the coffee industry is like the music industry. "In music, anyone will be accepted if they can play guitar really well," she said. "Here, anyone will be accepted if they can pour really great coffee."

## *Barista Magazine*'s Legacy

Baristas have come a long way in the past eight years. "I feel like we've worked arm-in-arm with the Barista Guild, and everybody is moving this thing forward." Allen said *Barista Magazine* has inspired many people to stay in the industry. "I feel like we've done a good job with the magazine when someone comes up to me and says, 'I used to be a barista, and I liked coffee, but I didn't really see any future in it. Then I read your magazine, and I thought that this is really something serious, and I can make a career out of it.'" She mentioned that Tracy Allen, a consultant who also writes a business column for *Barista*, is now the second vice president of SCAA, which means he will likely be the president in 2015. He would be the first SCAA president to come from a barista background, a far cry from when baristas were just an afterthought in the industry.

Sarah was pleased with *Barista Magazine*'s legacy. "I'm really, really proud of the fact that *Barista Magazine* has championed baristas for so long," said Allen. "I'm really so proud every time a barista comes up to me and says, 'Your magazine made me feel like what I was doing was relevant.' Because it totally is. That makes me feel really good."

### Barista Skills

Baristas perform many roles. They are expected to be scientists, artists, chefs, pharmacists, therapists, dishwashers, and actors. First and foremost, baristas need to know how to make good espresso. Italian tradition says that the espresso quality is determined by the four Ms: *miscela* (blend of coffee beans), *macinazione* (grind), *macchina* (espresso machine), and *mano* (the skilled hand of the barista). Of the four, the barista's skill is the most difficult to monitor in a café setting. A shop owner can buy good beans, a reliable grinder, and a technologically advanced espresso machine, but without the barista's skill to bring them all together, it will always be hard to consistently serve quality beverages.

A good barista is full of tacit knowledge — the unquantifiable understanding a person gains only through experience that resides deep within the barista. A barista can watch the espresso as it flows out of the portafilter and know immediately if that espresso is going to taste good (or bad). She can listen to the sound of the steam wand in the milk and know what the texture of the cappuccino will be. She remembers what her regular customers order and mentally starts preparing their drinks as soon as they walk into the café. A great barista will have that drink prepared at the same time the customer orders it so that neither the customer nor the drink has to wait for each other.

The barista takes the data available to her and applies it to the coffee-making process. What does an extraction time of twenty-two seconds mean? Nothing, unless you know that particular espresso normally pulls at twenty-five seconds and that the sun came out an hour ago, lowering the humidity in the air and making the beans move through the grinder more quickly, increasing the particle size and causing the ratio of grinds to water to be off during the extraction. A quality barista notices this and adjusts the grinder accordingly.

Baristas need a certain grace under pressure. During the morning rush, drink orders come fast and furious as customers line up in front of the register. People want their drinks in a hurry — some of them are double-parked or are already late for work. This crush of people pushes up against the laws of physics and chemistry that govern how quickly great coffee can be made or how quickly foam can be steamed to just the right texture.

### *Go See for Yourself*
To experience what a great barista can create, put this book down (better yet, take it with you) and go find the best café in your neighborhood. When you arrive at the café, ask the barista what's on grind. Many cafés will have one or two different espressos (some have more, but that is rare, even in Portland). The barista will be able to tell you a little about each of them and describe some of the flavors in them. If you are not a regular espresso connoisseur, ask the barista for a recommendation. After ordering, watch closely how the barista measures out the coffee into the portafilter, how she carefully levels the grounds in the basket and tamps them before wiping the rim of the basket and inserting it into the group head. A good barista moves with purpose and precision, not wasting motion or energy.

If straight espresso is not your style, order a cappuccino and note the sound of the steam wand as the barista gently steams the milk. The hiss should be a bit rough at first, like paper tearing, then become more of a soft roar as the barista submerges the tip of the steam wand farther into the milk. Note how she carefully times the steaming process so the milk is ready at the same time as the shot of espresso. Observe the delicate swaying of her hand and wrist as she gently fills the cup with white and brown swirls of milk and crema, finishing the pour with a sweep of the hand across the top, tying the swirls together into a heart, rosette, or tulip.

You might also try a pour-over of one of the coffees on the menu, prepared freshly just for you. Once again, take note of the precision of the barista's movements and measurements. She brings out a scale, gently sets the brewer on top, and adds the grounds to the vessel, noting the mass. From a long-necked kettle, she pours delicate streams of water, starting in the center of the grounds and spiraling outward in ever-larger motions, ensuring the most even extraction possible. As the coffee expands and blooms, she slowly adds more water until the mixture reaches the desired mass. At the proper moment, the barista pulls the filter from the brewer, pours the coffee into a cup, and hands it over for your enjoyment.

The barista might "just" be making coffee, but she is doing it the best she can because she cares about her craft and your experience. She is the final link that brings the farmer, the processor, the roaster, and the customer together every day.

## 27

# Nossa Familia
## Keeping It in the Family

*With hands semifrozen from a brisk morning bike ride, I knocked on the door at Nossa Familia's headquarters, having come to learn about Portland's own Brazilian coffee company. Nossa Familia, which means "our family" in Portuguese, is a fitting name for the company founded by Augusto Carvalho Dias Carneiro. For more than one hundred years, the Carvalho Dias family has been raising coffee on its farms (*fazendas*) in Brazil, and through Nossa Familia, some of this coffee is now making its way to Portland and beyond. Thus, there are two intertwining narratives that form the Nossa Familia story: the history of the family's connection to coffee and the story of Nossa Familia itself. Augusto and Sarah Bailen Smith, Nossa Familia's marketing manager (the "coffeevangelist"), sat down with me to share both.[75]* — WH

Augusto Carvalho Dias Carneiro[76] grew up in the city of Rio de Janeiro, but each year, he would escape the city for a few months to visit his family's ancestral farm in the Sul de Minas region. In 1890, Augusto's great-grandfather and three older brothers had moved to the area to be near the sulfurous healing waters that flowed from springs along an ancient volcano. They settled close to the city of Poços de Caldas, about 160 miles north of São Paulo, and soon after, Augusto's great-grandfather planted his first coffee trees. The rich volcanic soils and the high altitude provided just the right environment for the coffee to flourish. "We were very lucky they settled there," said Augusto. Over the years, the farm prospered and was passed down through the generations. Today,

---

75. Bailen Smith left the company in July 2013.

76. It is typical in Brazil for people to have several last names. For brevity purposes, I will use Carneiro when referring to Augusto.

the Carvalho Dias family operates three different farms in proximity to one another: Fazenda Santa Alina, Fazenda Recreio, and Fazenda Cachoeira. Visiting the farms was a chance for Augusto to get a taste of life in the countryside and also to connect with his extended family.

In high school, Augusto planned to study engineering and play tennis at an American college, but he did not have a strong preference for a particular place. The University of Portland responded to his application, so Augusto moved to Portland, sight unseen. "I sent letters to over 120 schools," he said. "I wanted to play tennis and go to school, and I just ended up here." Arriving on campus in the fall of 1996, the university's soccer-crazy culture made him feel right at home. The Portland area's numerous opportunities for biking and the residents' love of coffee also made the city a good fit.

After graduating from UP, Augusto got a job as an engineer, but he quickly realized engineering was not his passion. He missed Brazil and was looking for a reason to travel there more frequently. Starting a coffee company was one way to make that happen. On a trip to see his family in 2004, he spoke with one of his cousins about importing coffee from the family's farms to Portland. The cousin liked the idea, so he sent Augusto back to Portland with seventy pounds of coffee roasted on the farm in Brazil. Augusto brought the coffee back and shared it with family and friends. It was a hit, and Augusto, along with one of his college friends, decided to start a company.[77] Each partner put in $400 to bring the first shipment to Portland via FedEx.

At the time, coffee was much cheaper and the Brazilian *real* was much weaker than the US dollar, so shipping the coffee up in small quantities was profitable. Still, Augusto knew that bringing the coffee to Portland that way could not be the long-term business model. Nossa Familia's wholesale customers began to ask for different types of packaging, various lead times, and an assortment of freshness levels, so they had to come up with another way to supply the coffee to Portland.

---

77. The friend is no longer invested in the company.

Augusto's cousins had invested in a lot of infrastructure at the farm, including a storage warehouse, a sorting facility, a processing facility, and a cupping lab. They also had their own export company, so knowing which coffees to bring in would not be a problem. However, Nossa Familia still needed a place for the beans to be stored and roasted once they arrived in Portland. Augusto approached David Kobos and Brian Dibble, Kobos's owners, to see if they might be interested in roasting for Nossa Familia. They were, and for the next several years, Nossa Familia would import the green beans, and Kobos would store and roast them. "Partnering with Kobos was good for us," Augusto said. "We combined my family's coffee knowledge with their roasting knowledge."

While the relationship with Kobos was fruitful for both companies, it was a short-term solution for Nossa Familia. In 2012, Nossa Familia opened a new facility in the Pearl District, allowing the company to store and roast its own coffees. The company purchased an American-made Loring Kestrel roaster. According to Bailen Smith, one of the best features of this roaster is its efficiency. Most roasting machines have an afterburner in the exhaust system that removes the flakes of parchment that are released from the beans during roasting. While the afterburner cleans up the discharge, it also sends a lot of heat waste out into the atmosphere and significantly raises energy costs. The Loring, by contrast, sends the exhaust back through the drum heater, conserving the heat inside the drum while removing the chaff from the exhaust. The closed-loop system uses much less energy than a typical roaster. "We roasted twelve thousand pounds of coffee in a month, and the energy bill was less than $400," she said.

The new location also made it easier to manage seasonal coffees and share microlots with customers. Since the move, the company has begun to bring coffees in from select family farms in other countries, creating an extended *familia*. In 2013, Nossa Familia set up a walk-in espresso bar in one corner of the warehouse to offer its coffees and other treats for passersby in the Pearl.

## A Long-Term Perspective

With traditions going back more than a century, it is no surprise the family maintains a long-term view for its fazendas. "My family has always done things with the idea that we want to keep the farms running for more than a hundred years," Augusto explained. Fazenda Cachoeira is certified by Utz Kapeh, a Dutch organization that requires coffee companies to adhere to strict social and environmental criteria to receive the certification. For most of the year, Fazenda Cachoeira produces its own electricity, using a turbine the family installed in the 1950s on the property's waterfalls (*cachoeira* is the Portuguese word for "waterfall"). Permanent housing on the farm is provided for the families who work there. "When you do something for this long, by nature you have to be sustainable," Augusto added.

The farms also invest in technology to help improve the quality of their coffees. In the past, all Brazilian coffee was lumped together before being sold on world markets as a commodity, resulting in a lot of average coffee coming out of the country. When the government loosened the export restrictions in the 1990s, it created an opportunity for farmers to showcase their individual coffees. Augusto's cousin Gabriel took advantage of the new freedom and began submitting his coffee to competitions and building connections with world-class baristas. The world noticed that Brazilian coffee could be very good, and Fazenda Cachoeira coffee has been a part of some of the world's best competition blends. In 2004, coffee from Fazenda Recreio won the Cup of Excellence.

## Sharing Brazilian Culture with Americans

For people who want to see firsthand how coffee is grown and processed, Nossa Familia has started the tradition of taking groups of customers to visit Brazil every year. The trip coincides with the beginning of the coffee harvest, and travelers help pick coffee cherries from the trees and watch as they are processed into green beans. Bailen Smith, who went on the 2011 trip, recalled picking some unique coffees: "We were able to harvest coffee from these hundred-year-old coffee trees [Fazenda Santa Alina has a centennial grove, where none of the plants have been taken out since they were planted in 1907], and you could take a cherry off the plant, toss it in your mouth. When you bit into it, it tasted like honey — super sweet, but it doesn't have the depth of fruit that a typical cherry would."

## Nossa Familia

The first trip, in 2008, was just a group of friends biking around the countryside. Most of the people brought their tents and camped out at night under the stars. The weather cooperated — most of the time. "One day a huge storm came in, and we were in the house, and you could see the tents being folded flat by the wind. Everything got soaked," Augusto recalled.

Unplanned weather events notwithstanding, the trip was a success, so they decided to do it again the next year. The first tours were focused on biking, with lots of planned activities. The group covered many miles on their bikes, riding around the rolling hills of the Brazilian countryside. On subsequent trips, the groups spent less time biking and more time doing other things. "You can go biking everywhere," Augusto explained, "so the goal became just to experience the culture and everything there is to see." Fazenda Cachoeira is located about eight miles outside Poços de Caldas, a town of about two hundred thousand people, so in addition to experiencing life in the country, participants also get a glimpse of life in the city. "We do the cultural thing as well," said Augusto, who still leads the trip himself. "There is a lively arts and crafts market in the city, and you can visit several restaurants. You're not just sitting around in the middle of nowhere."

When I asked what he thinks is the best part of the tours, Augusto responded that it is "not so much the coffee, but the family. It's something you can't sell." Augusto's grandparents still live on the farm, and one evening they invite the tour's guests into their house for dinner. It is an opportunity to share stories, culture, and great Brazilian food.

Bailen Smith shared what stood out to her. "For me, what I came back with — not having been in the coffee industry for a long time — was that I had no concept of what it took to get a green bean to the United States," she said. "It did not occur to me the effort, the level of care, all of the processes it took to get there. We were talking about the beans being dried to the correct humidity, but the coffee also has to sit and rest for sixty to ninety days before it can be shipped. There's the storage and all the equipment and above all, the people."

She also mentioned the impression the family made. "The best part was meeting Tuca [Augusto's cousin who manages of one of the farms], who said, 'I'm not a grower of coffee; I'm a leader of people.' I really forget that's what it's about. You can have a product at the end of the day, but if you don't take care of the people, it's not worth it. That made a huge impact."

Coffee has a way of bringing people together, and Nossa Familia was founded on the idea that coffee could provide a bridge between Portland and Brazil. In Nossa Familia's case, the coffee brings cultures and family together. After speaking with Augusto and Sarah, it was clear that above all, family is the focus of Nossa Familia. One of the sayings at Nossa Familia is that instead of fair trade, the company engages in family trade. For generations, the Carvalho Dias family's coffee heritage has been cultivated by people who care about sustainability and high quality coffee. In these values, Portlanders and Brazilians have something in common.

## Cellar Door Coffee Roasters
### Neighborhood Coffee and a Whole Lot of Niceness

*Located on Southeast 11th Avenue between Hawthorne and Division, Cellar Door Coffee has been satisfying the caffeine cravings of nearby Ladd's Addition residents for more than half a decade. Jeremy Adams and Andrea Pastor, the owners, founded the company in 2007, roasting small batches of coffee in their garage and selling it at farmers markets. As their direct-to-customer business increased, they opened a retail café, a place that feels like the neighborhood's living room. Around the city, Cellar Door's owners have a reputation for environmental stewardship and for being great people.* — WH

Andrea Pastor grew up in Michigan and later studied English and psychology at the University of Chicago. In 2004, she met Jeremy Adams, now her husband and business partner, in Santa Cruz, where they worked together on an organic farm. The couple spent six months of what they called "intensive living" on the farm, learning about organic agriculture. Both enjoyed their time but did not think they could make a living at farming, so they moved to Portland (where Andrea's brother had gone to college) with the intention of starting a coffee roaster. Coffee would provide the living that farming could not.

Not everyone thought Pastor and Adams should get into the coffee business. "We told people we were thinking about starting a roasting company, and they were like, 'Why? Why would you ever go up against Stumptown?'" recalled Pastor, sitting in the front seating area of her café. "And we'd say, 'We're not even going to think about it that way. We're just going to do our own thing.'" The couple bought a three-kilo roaster and began studying how to roast coffee, using Sweet Maria's website as a primary reference. "We were getting a little nerdy about it and trying a bunch of different things," said Pastor. The couple went to Coffee

## Caffeinated PDX

Fest and visited several roasters, seeking advice. Often, the advice was not forthcoming. "The thing about roasters is they don't ever want to tell you anything," Pastor told me. "It's not like the beer community, which seems to be a lot more open with its recipes and ideas. A lot of the coffee roasters we talked to ended up being, 'Why are you even going to bother? You don't know what you're doing. You have to be trained by some master roaster.'"

Undaunted, Pastor and Adams set up the roaster in their basement and soon began roasting for other people. They sold coffee subscriptions and delivered beans by bike. When the Montevilla Farmers Market opened in the July 2007, Cellar Door sold brewed coffee and beans from a booth. The coffee quickly became popular for market visitors, and sales grew.

Growing sales pushed Cellar Door out of the couple's basement and into its current location in February 2008. Adams and Pastor began selling at another farmers market the following summer. "We were doing two farmers markets and running the shop," recalled Pastor. "Jeremy was pretty much running the shop by himself, I was roasting coffee at home, and we had a two-year-old. It was insane." Stretched to their limits, Pastor and Adams hired their first employees.

### Where Everybody Knows Your Name

Pastor called Cellar Door's business philosophy "mom and pop-ish." Portland is their home and will be for a long time. "We've made a decision to dig in here," Pastor said. "I don't think Jeremy or I have any grand ambitions of taking over the coffee universe. We're a very small company." To add to the neighborhood feel, Cellar Door has added small conveniences, such as a tab board. "There are people who come in three times a day," Pastor said. "Baristas have to immediately know everybody's name because people come in and say, 'Put it on my tab.' That can be kind of difficult [for new employees], but it also means people feel like they're at home." Above all, the goal for Cellar Door is to be accessible to everybody. "We didn't want to have a 'cool' coffee shop that felt know-it-all-y or sterile," she said. "We wanted a place that we'd want to hang out in, even though we don't really get to hang out."

## Cellar Door Coffee Roasters

Incorporating family was also part of the plan from the beginning. "When we were talking about starting a business, we wanted the family to be able to be involved," Andrea said. "My parents work with us. My mom helps me bag the coffee, and my dad does our accounting. Our daughter, who has grown up here, runs around like she owns the place."

## DIY Specialists

Today, Cellar Door's main roaster is a twelve-kilo Diedrich roaster tucked into a corner of the basement. Walking down the narrow staircase that leads to the basement is difficult enough if you are not carrying anything more than a camera. Trying to squeeze a roaster down the stairs and into the basement would be like trying to stuff an NFL lineman into a Mini Cooper, a difficult prospect by any measure. What makes the roaster's location more remarkable is that Adams and Pastor had to move it in themselves. They tried to hire someone, but no one would do it. "The roaster weighs about eight hundred pounds, and it's top-heavy, so it's not a simple move," said Adams when I caught up with him. "We called piano movers, and they didn't want to try. I called gun safe movers, thinking they would be interested. They're used to moving top-heavy objects. They were interested until they heard how much it cost. They'd say: 'It's worth $25,000? I'm not touching it.'"

Their options exhausted, the couple moved the roaster themselves, with a little help from their friends. "The neighborhood pitched in to help us," said Adams. "Someone let us use some straps. One of the neighbors helped with his forklift. It was a challenge, but we just did it. Hopefully, we'll never have to move it again."

The roaster move is an example of the couple's do-it-yourself ethos. Adams is a tinkerer who has many projects spread around the café. He built a custom pour-over stand for the coffee bar, installed a more accurate temperature control on the espresso machine, built a special lift for moving coffee bags into the basement, and also designed and built a special smoke remover for the roaster's exhaust system that uses less energy than a typical afterburner. Occasionally, customers will find a half-finished project sitting on one of the back tables, evidence that Adams has had his toolbox out again.

Pastor estimated she does about 90 percent of the roasting. Cellar Door currently roasts up to three hundred pounds a week — less than some roasters, according to Pastor, but more than they need for the shop. "We definitely have room to grow," she said. Adams is capable of roasting, but he prefers to be upstairs with the café. "Jeremy is kind of the people person, so he's up here in the café," said Pastor. "He's built a really nice community, just by being himself." One of Cellar Door's longtime baristas, Thomas Suprenant, fills in on the roaster when needed.

Cellar Door's owners deemed 2013 a busy year. They opened a restaurant above the café called 2nd Story with Erin McBride, a friend of both Pastor and Adams from the organic farm in Santa Cruz. McBride was the pastry chef at Portland's famous Higgins restaurant for several years, and she now does all the baking for Cellar Door.[78] "It's brought together all the things we wanted to do but couldn't because the manpower wasn't there," said Pastor. "Now we get to control the quality of the ingredients and the variety of things we sell to complement the coffee."

Portland can be a tough town to stand out in among coffee companies. "It's hard — there are so many roasters in town," Pastor said. "It's like, how do you even get shelf space sometimes?" Still, the competition did not intimidate her. "I don't see it being a huge negative because our business is built around the people who are in the neighborhood and who really like us and want to come in. We don't plan on opening five shops and trying to dominate Portland."

## Leaning Left and Not Afraid to Say It

Unlike many business owners, Pastor and Adams are not afraid to take a stand on political issues. In 2011, Adams was mentioned in the *Oregonian* for supplying Occupy Portland with coffee. Pastor told me the support was a natural fit. "I think, politically, that's just

---

78. In July 2013, McBride announced she was closing the restaurant but would continue to do the baking for Cellar Door.

where Jeremy and I lean," she said. "We support a lot of groups with donations of coffee. We'd gone down to Occupy a bunch of times. Jeremy spent a lot more time down there than I did. He even helped set up the bicycle-powered generator."

But isn't it risky to take a political stance as a business owner? Yes, but, "if anything, having your own business makes you notice certain things even more acutely," explained Pastor. "When you're a small business and you realize you can't get a loan, even though you have a perfect financial record, and then some big company will come in and get a practically interest-free loan and be able to develop millions of dollars' worth of property, and you're like, 'I just want $10,000 so I can expand my small business,' it really puts a fine point on the situation."

Adams and Pastor bring a progressive philosophy to sourcing their coffees too. "It's kind of important to us — when we can — to do fair trade organic, or at least organic," said Pastor. "For a while, especially when the prices spiked, Sumatras were completely prohibitive to get fair trade organic. But when we can, that's a pretty important criteria for us."

Cellar Door is committed to using renewable energy. The business participates in Portland General Electric's Green Power Oregon program, and the low-energy smoke-removal system Adams built adds to the overall goal of being more environmentally friendly.

## Specialty Coffee

For Pastor, one of the things that defines specialty coffee is an awareness about how the coffee makes it from farm to cup. "It's an attention to detail, actually caring about the coffee," she said. "Even though the price is based on the commodity market, we don't treat it like it's a commodity; we treat it like it's an actual specific product that has a value from the origin."

Another characteristic that stands out in specialty coffee is having the courage to try different coffees roasted different ways. Even in coffee-enlightened Portland, not everyone is accustomed to drinking light-roasted coffees. Roasters have to set their own roast profiles and not just listen to what their customers are asking for. "If we did that," said Pastor, "we would only ever serve French roast because that's what people come in asking for, even to this day. We try to tell them, 'We don't roast our coffee that dark, but if you like that kind of flavor, you might like the Sumatra, or you might like something a little bit earthier.' We try to steer them to something that's not just charred."

Pastor cited the challenge of trying to change customers' perceptions. "We really benefit from the fact that Stumptown did so much education on that side a decade before anyone else was pushing that," Pastor said. "But we still get people in every day asking for a twenty-ounce macchiato, so we're still working on how to talk to people about it, to get them to appreciate that coffee's not just something to wake you up in the morning."

Even when you have the best intentions, the message doesn't always get across. "Jeremy is the nicest guy ever, and I can't imagine how anyone would ever find him imposing," Andrea said. "Just two days ago, some guy walked in looking for a cup of coffee, and Jeremy said, 'Oh, yeah, there's some in the airpot. We've got some French press coffee. Feel free to fill up your cup.' And the guy was like, 'I just need a regular cup of coffee. Do you have any brewed decaf? I need decaf.' And we were like, 'Well, we could make you a decaf Americano,' and just the fact that Jeremy used the words *French press* and *Americano* made this man shut down and run out of the shop, saying, 'I just wanted a cup of coffee!'"

### Future of the Industry

Looking at the future of specialty coffee, Pastor was worried about the changing climate. As the climate warms, coffee will have to be cultivated at higher altitudes. Moving up the mountain reduces the amount of land available for cultivation. Carried to an extreme, there won't be any more space for growing coffee. "I'm not entirely sure what the future holds for specialty coffee. Apparently, Starbucks is moving out of coffee because they foresee that fifty years from now there won't be good coffee," Andrea said. "In Ethiopia now, there are literally places that can't grow specialty coffee now that could ten years ago."

As the climate changes, this may put more pressure on the food supply in developing countries. "Jeremy and I always joke that what we really want is for farmers to stop growing coffee so they can concentrate on growing their own food. I don't know what it means for us as an industry."

Pastor is not worried about the next ten years so much. She hopes that people pay more attention to where their coffee comes from and how the people who grow the coffee are treated. People are definitely more aware than they were a decade ago. "It's been an evolution of consciousness," she said. "When I was in college, nobody knew what fair trade coffee was, and today, in Portland at least, most people have an idea."

## 29

## Oblique Coffee
### The Chandlers' Labor of Love

*Portland attracts coffee talent from all over the country, but many of the city's roasters in town are homegrown. One of these is John Chandler, who, along with his wife, Heather, owns Oblique Coffee Roasters on Southeast Stark Street. Chandler and I sat down together for coffee in his café, which also doubles as his second living room, since the couple lives on the second floor of their remodeled 1891 Victorian-era building.* — WH

A lifelong Portland resident, John Chandler has deep roots in the area. He was born in Northwest Portland, grew up in Tigard, and studied literature at the University of Oregon in Eugene in the early 1990s. Like many college students, Chandler started drinking cheap coffee to survive late-night study sessions, before Starbucks convinced him the beverage could be more than just a caffeine boost. "Starbucks was a positive experience for me, where it wasn't just Folgers — gross, gross coffee that was literally toxic sludge because it had been on a burner for over an hour and a half," he said.

After graduation, Chandler worked on a commercial fishing boat out of ports in Oregon, Washington, and Alaska, returning to Portland during the offseason to fill in as the self-termed "warehouse guy" at his father's electrical construction business. John's fishing career came to an end when he was injured on the job. The injury limited his mobility for a couple years, so he went to work full time for his father and became an electrical estimator. Chandler rose up through the ranks, becoming a project manager and a project engineer, before moving to the high-tech industry, where he worked for eleven years for different Intel contractors.

## Caffeinated PDX

### Renovating the Landauer Mercantile

In 2006, John was returning to Portland from a business trip to Phoenix when he decided it was time to start a new career. "Ever since I was in college," he said, "I wanted to have a bookstore where I could live upstairs and have a store on the main floor." Chandler did some calculations and concluded that running a bookstore would not be profitable. Instead, he decided to start a coffee roaster, as soon as he found the right space.

Browsing online, Chandler found the historic Landauer Mercantile, a Victorian structure built in 1891, at a very attractive price. The listing said the building "needed a lot of work" — a glaring understatement when you see pictures prior to the remodel.[79] At the time, it was leaning nearly two feet to the right, with a seventy-foot-tall elm tree growing aggressively out of the basement. Most buildings in that condition would be quickly torn down, but the Chandlers saw an opportunity to build their dream.

The couple closed on the mercantile in March 2006 and spent three years renovating it. The project required them to take everything out of the building, jack it up, and put in a new foundation. They removed the elm tree, saving much of the lumber for later woodworking projects. John and Heather did all the lath and plaster demolition inside the café, hung insulation, built the counters and cabinetry, varnished, and painted. The project cost more than half a million dollars, which the Chandlers financed primarily through a construction loan.

Oblique Coffee opened in 2010, and business has steadily grown since. John said he found that moving from consulting on large business-to-business projects into the service industry was a stark adjustment. While most of Oblique's online reviews were positive, those that were not got under his skin. The large construction loan hanging over the business made him sensitive to any bad publicity. "At first, when we were scrambling, just trying to hold on, it really bothered me, I think because it was financially critical," he said. "The bills were so big. I was chomping at the bit to pay that

---

79. All of the renovation work is chronicled in detail on Chandler's personal website: http://jmchandler.com/.

down." Today, after multiple years of steady growth, Chandler is no longer as concerned about the occasional bad review. "Ninety-nine percent of the customers are great," he said. "It's that less than 1 percent that's not so cool, but that's okay. Those are actually good odds. When you look at the law of averages, it's really not that big a deal." He paused. "Until they come in again, and then I'll be thinking, 'Oh, it's not you again!'"

## Recognition for Renovation

The couple's work on the Landauer has paid off for the Chandlers in many ways. The renovation project created goodwill in the neighborhood and also received citywide recognition. The Architectural Heritage Center invited the Chandlers as honored guests to the organization's annual fundraising auction. In addition, Oblique received *Willamette Week*'s Best Labor of Love for 2009 award. Chandler said the recognition felt good after all the hard work the couple put in resurrecting the building.

The Landauer also gained a few minutes of fame as the setting for multiple sketches on the Independent Film Channel's TV series *Portlandia*. Chandler responded to a casting call on Craigslist, inviting the producers to use the building. He did not receive an immediate response, but when the show's crew was filming at the Lone Fir Cemetery down the street, a location scout came by the shop and liked what he saw. Less than a week later, the cast was filming at the shop. In the sixth episode of season one, both John and Heather can be seen in the background as Fred Armisen and Carrie Brownstein talk with the mayor (Kyle MacLachlan) about starting a professional baseball team in Portland.

## Wholesale Strategy

While Oblique's retail business has grown steadily, the Chandlers have decided to focus more on wholesale strategy, partly because of the shop's location. The café is tucked away on Stark Street, about halfway between Laurelhurst Park and Lone Fir Cemetery. While neighborhood residents have made Oblique a regular stop, the shop is a place few people casually stumble onto. "Nobody really knows about us because we are in a no-man's land," said

Chandler. Oblique sells coffee through New Seasons and was just about to finalize an agreement with Whole Foods at the time of our conversation. Several cafés and restaurants around Portland now serve Oblique coffee.

In a city where there's so much good coffee, how does a roaster stand out? Chandler described his strategy. "We focus on nice people," he said. "I don't know how else to say it. We focus on finding nice people that just want good coffee and a good value. We're pretty simple people; we like really good coffee; we've got a better price point than most people."

Just under three years from opening the business, Chandler is ready to hire more people. Oblique has a couple employees working shifts at the coffee bar and will soon hire another to help with roasting and packaging so Chandler can focus more on sales and management. Looking at the long term, John did not plan to open more retail locations, preferring to sell beans instead of beverages. "Retail is great," he said, "but wholesale is where we want to focus our efforts. Retail has its limits. You can only get to a certain point. Then you need to open up other retail locations."

Chandler is unquestionably competitive — he is trying to grow his wholesale business, sometimes at the expense of other Portland roasters — and his competitiveness keeps him searching for ways to stand out. "I'm the kind of person that, where everyone else likes to zig, I like to zag," Chandler said. "I typically watch what other people do and then do what they're not doing. Not to be innovative. I just don't want to be a follower. Then again," he continued, noting the irony, "I followed Stumptown into the industry, and it's because I love the coffee so much."

## Expansion Plans

Chandler preferred to not give away too many details about his future plans, but he did say he and Heather were looking to expand Oblique's business outside Portland, most likely internationally. He did not want to keep "fighting with the neighbors" (that is, other Portland roasters) for wholesale business and was looking for other areas to expand into. "Portland is where I'm from, and this will always be in my family, but our business will be expanding to other nations. There's a lot of opportunity outside the US," he said. "The market is so huge, and the world is such a big place. There's so many other places to go and to enjoy coffee."

Chandler hinted that the expansion would someday include a coastal area in Central America. "I want to be able to develop a small-business expansion into a community that's got good surf and good water quality," he said. "And then I can start buying good coffee in that area, roasting it, and selling it to locals at a discount. Ultimately, I want to help grow whatever community we're in. That's our job as human beings. This is not a dress rehearsal for me. I take my life seriously, and we're doing things consciously."

Any international expansion is still a few years out. The couple's first goal is to first pay off the construction loan on the building they already have. "You think globally and act locally. That's what this building is for," Chandler said. The international focus is also a way of protecting the couple's investments. "It just makes sense. In today's international economy, it makes sense to diversify your holdings internationally so if anything does happen in the United States, you've got alternatives."

Although the Chandlers do not have kids right now, their future offspring are included in the plans for Oblique. "We want to do this long term," said John. "It takes time to grow things responsibly. I want to be able to hand this business off to my kids." Being an entrepreneur has been a burden and a blessing. "The challenge for me will be trying to do this seven days a week for the rest of my life. I didn't realize that I was going to throw my weekends away and never get that back until we sell the business. I wouldn't trade it for anything, though. I absolutely love it."

## Case Study
### Coffee as a Culinary Art

*Some people in third-wave coffee are adamant that coffee be drunk by itself or with limited quantities of milk. Rejecting beverages that are little more than sugared milk drinks, these café owners limit the number of syrups and sell smaller drinks than you would find at a second-wave café like Starbucks. The most idealistic of the purists do not even sell traditional flavors such as vanilla or chocolate.*

*This style works well for these café owners and their companies' bottom lines, but others take a more nuanced view of how coffee should be enjoyed. They agree that while coffee is best in its purest form, it can also be combined with other flavors to create something just as pleasurable. At Case Study Coffee, owner Christine Herman-Russell takes a culinary approach. While her cafés start with excellent coffees, they also create some high-end culinary delights centered around the coffee. The key is insisting on quality in everything the café sells.* — WH

Christine Herman-Russell remembers discovering coffee when she was going to high school in the Bay Area. In those days, stopping by a small café on the way home from school and ordering a mocha seemed like the grown-up thing to do. "I pretended to like it," she said. "You know, coffee for a kid can be a bit much. I'm sure it was bad." As she got older, her taste for coffee became more refined, and she began to frequent Peet's.

In 1993, Christine moved to Portland to attend Reed College. She moved up with Wes Russell, now her husband and business partner. In Portland, the couple encountered an entirely different coffee culture than they were used to. "We discovered Stumptown when they opened up in 1999," recalled Christine. "We were living very close, and Wes made that his daily stop, right when they first opened their doors. We developed our appreciation for coffee through them."

## Culinary Artists

After finishing up at Reed, Herman-Russell worked at the Black Rabbit, a McMenamins restaurant in Troutdale, for about a year. She enjoyed working in food service enough that she decided to go to school at Western Culinary Institute. Around that time, Wes and Christine began studying coffee more closely. Wes combined his appreciation for coffee with his technical prowess (he previously had a business refurbishing high-fidelity audio equipment). "We actually bought a [La Marzocco] Linea and started playing around with it," said Christine. "Wes PID'd it,[80] and we had it in our living room. That was a lot of fun." The couple also bought a Gene Café and a Sonofresco, two types of home coffee roasters, and began learning how to roast.

As Christine finished up at Western Culinary Institute, she and Wes planned to start a chain of high-end drive-through coffee kiosks, going as far as purchasing a couple Airstream trailers. "That was going to be our niche," said Christine. However, the concept was never realized. Instead, the couple founded Espresso Arts, an espresso catering service, in 2005. They tried to keep it more high-end than a traditional catering service. "We wanted to do something different, so we had very limited syrups available," she said.

The couple also invested in the latest technology to improve their coffee. "We started with San Marcos that had little heat exchangers," she said, referring to the espresso machines they used at the time. When the La Marzocco GS/3 came out, Espresso Arts immediately purchased two. "We probably had two of the most heavily used GS/3s in the nation," recalled Herman-Russell. "They're amazing little machines."

Although they liked the catering business (which was profitable), a long-term catering job at the Pacific Building in downtown Portland convinced the couple it would be fun to have their own shop. The Pacific's property manager wanted to assuage tenants while the lobby was being remodeled, so he hired Espresso Arts to provide coffee during the remodel. Twice a week for four months,

---

80. To PID an espresso machine means to add a special control to improve water temperature stability.

## Case Study

Wes and Christine set up their espresso stand to serve people on their way to work. "It was amazing," recalled Christine. "We had a French press and a line that was solid for two hours. It was a lot of fun, and you're making everyone's day. They're so happy to see you."

Having a group of regular customers was rewarding both financially and relationally. "We saw regular faces every day, and they were always so happy," she said. "With catering, you have to win someone over who's buying your services who might not even be a coffee drinker but was told to find a coffee cart. Then they go, 'Wow, that was amazing. We'll use you again next year — maybe.'"

### The First Café

In early 2009, the couple began to look for a place to call their own. Their first intention was to find a small space downtown for a step-up espresso bar, but nothing came up. They expanded their search and found a large space on Northeast Sandy Boulevard. The couple figured the large space would be too expensive, so they asked if they could rent half of it. When the landlords offered them a better deal than expected, Wes and Christine took the whole thing. Instead of being a small stand, their first café turned out be one of the largest specialty shops in Portland: Case Study Coffee.

Wes and Christine called their new company Case Study because of the experimental nature of what they were trying to do. "Could we bring that public house, comfortable experience to everyone, including the downtown neighborhood?" she said. "What does it mean to do exactly what you want with coffee and provide an amazing experience for people along the way?"

Answers to those questions came in June 2010, when Case Study officially opened. The café quickly morphed into the environment they were looking for, as people from the neighborhood filled the shop. "It really materialized all on its own, how it behaved. We knew what we wanted it to do, with that big public house feel and the big dining area," said Christine. "We were hoping to create a space where people would not only come to do their work on their laptops but hopefully socialize too. Everyone's now talking about that third place [a space for people to come together that is not work or home, a concept Starbucks promoted] — how do we make it that third place? Sandy became that. We had groups of writers come and hang out and write together. We had people come in and have meetings. It's just a very social atmosphere. That was thrilling to see."

Ricky Sutton, Case Study's barista trainer and self-described "coffee guy" (Sutton has a wide variety of roles at the company), said the space stands out, even in Portland. "One of the things I think is Case Study's most positive attribute in Portland's coffee community is the aesthetic of the shop," he said. "You walk in, and you see something that is atypical. It's different than the standard coffee shop setup. You immediately have to think, 'What's this place doing differently? Why doesn't it look like a fast-food place?'"

Before they opened, Wes and Christine planned to have one barista make every drink — an espresso chef, so to speak. That plan did not last long. "When it's just turn and burn," Christine said, referring to the morning rush, "we had to give up that Intelligentsia idea that one barista is going to make your drink from start to finish. Honestly, people don't care, even though we wanted them to. They just want their drink quickly and made well."

## You Want It, We'll Make It

Instead of fighting against the Starbucks culture, where adding syrups is the norm, Herman-Russell sees it as an opportunity to express her own culinary interests. Christine collaborates with her staff to develop recipes for the syrups. These range from a seasonal pumpkin spice syrup to a bourbon caramel syrup made with real bourbon whiskey. All of the syrups are prepared in-house — a commitment to quality that goes along with the artisanal nature of specialty coffee.

Christine said that offering a few different options makes sense. "Coming from espresso catering, you have to cater to all shades of folk," she said. "You need to have the passion to talk to everyone about coffee on their level. Don't talk down to people; give them the best version of what they want. We make an amazing caramel macchiato. We're not going to tell customers they shouldn't drink it."

# Case Study

In addition to offering house-made syrups, Case Study roasts its own coffee. Christine does most of the roasting herself, which allows her to set the taste preferences. She personally enjoys bright, fruity coffees, but she also makes sure to have something for customers who just want something that tastes like coffee and chocolate. Case Study's roast profiles are in the middle of the spectrum. "People think we roast a light and a dark, which is what our bags say," she said. "The 'dark' roast is for espresso and the 'light' roast is for brewed coffee, but they're all shades of medium." Christine wants the coffee to stand for itself. "What I like to do is taste a coffee. I don't want to taste any roast. Yes, you'll taste some roast in the espresso, but as little as possible, so you're not masking the flavors inherent in the coffee. I'll always take it up to that point."

## Specialty Coffee Is…

Herman-Russell defines *specialty coffee* as "trying your best to do the highest quality and to do right — by the products you're using, by the space you have, by the customers you have, and by the relationships you have with your vendors." Paying fair prices, buying quality green beans, and roasting them well are also important. "It's just trying to strive for excellence and fairness with everyone involved in the process, from the coffee growers to the consumers," she said.

Technology plays an important role in meeting the café's quality goals. "Wes and Christine care a lot about having the best equipment that the world has to offer, so you don't have to fight to get it to make great product," said Sutton. "The road is paved for you, and it's smooth sailing. You just pull excellent shot after excellent shot, and it happens naturally."

One trend Christine sees coming in specialty coffee is improving the hospitality aspect. "I think the next phase in the waves of specialty coffee is the coffeehouse experience," she said. "You're already seeing it a lot, and I'm thankful for the barista competitions for bringing the industry toward the actual experience of the consumer."

## Buying Coffees Cooperatively

The crowded Portland coffee scene does not worry Christine. Instead of trying to compete with each other, she said, each of the high-end shops ought to focus on a bigger target. "I think our biggest issue is Starbucks, and that should be what everyone is focusing on," Christine said. "However, I don't want to believe we're in competition with anyone. We're not trying to step on anyone's toes. There's enough to go around, so long as we're working toward educating people on buying a better quality product."

One way local roasters can compete with companies like Starbucks is by working together. Case Study is a member of Coffee Roasters United (CRU). CRU is a collaboration between five Portland coffee roasters that pool their resources to buy high quality coffees. Christine credited Sterling's Adam McGovern for coming up with the idea. "It's wonderful," she said. "Some of the larger independents can buy pallets of coffee at a time. They're still paying great prices for their coffee to their farmers, but they don't have to deal with a middleman, so they're getting some amazing coffees at still pretty decent prices." CRU works with importers to find microlots that are within a certain range of bags that the five cafés can purchase together. If the coffee is one that all CRU members want to buy, they can purchase the entire lot together. "No one else in town will have the microlot," said Christine, "so we get access to some amazing up-and-coming farmers, and because we're buying the entire lot, we can get somewhat of a price break on it."

As of late 2012, CRU had purchased three different coffees together. "It's still in its fledgling stage," Christine said. "Finding the time to collaborate has been difficult, but we're working on the next one." The group is considering adding a few more members so they can increase its purchasing power to buy twenty-five to thirty bags at one time.

## Downtown

Case Study's culinary offerings upgrade second-wave ideas to third-wave quality, and the formula seems to resonate well with customers. In November 2012, Case Study opened a second shop, at the corner of Southwest 10th Avenue and Yamhill Street in downtown Portland. Wes and Christine expected the café to start slowly, like the Sandy café did. However, with an established

## Case Study

reputation and one of the busiest corners in the city, one month after opening, the new shop was already receiving four times the business Christine and Wes had planned for. Like its predecessor, the new Case Study is a large space with abundant seating. Despite its size, the café fills up regularly with customers, something that obviously pleases its owners. "People come in here and sit down and use it as a public space. It's really fun. It's great that people caught on to our vibe of what we wanted it to be," Christine said, looking around the busy shop. "I couldn't be more thrilled."

## 31

## Speedboat Coffee
### The Niemyers Prepare to Take Portland Coffee Outside the City Limits

*Portland attracts people for all kinds of reasons — quality of life, affordability, and outdoor recreation opportunities are often mentioned when you ask people why they live here. Making lots of money rarely enters into the conversation. Portland has a relatively young, highly educated population sometimes derided for its lack of ambition. According to the television show* Portlandia, *Portland is the place "where young people go to retire."*

*Despite its laid-back reputation, Portland does attract people who like to work. Two such people are Don and Carissa Niemyer, who own Speedboat Coffee in Southeast Portland. In addition to running their café, both aficionados participate as judges at Specialty Coffee Association of America (SCAA) barista competitions. They both judged at regionals and nationals during the 2012 and 2013 seasons, and Carissa was selected to judge the 2013 Northwest Regional Barista Competition (NWRBC) final. — WH*

Originally from small-town Oklahoma, Don Niemyer moved to Fort Collins, Colorado, when he was thirty years old and started working at Starbucks. The job laid the foundation for his coffee future, though his knowledge was far from complete. "I knew what a typical person at Starbucks knows about coffees," he said. "In those days, we were still using those old-school manual Lineas, so I actually knew how to make coffee — dosing and everything — but I knew nothing of proper steaming of milk. But in the late nineties and early two thousands, nobody else did either. Very few people were as deep into coffee as most people in Portland are."

On a trip to Dallas, Don met his future wife at a local café. "Carissa was on a shift one night in the coffee shop and some of my friends were playing there, so coffee's been central to our relationship, literally from the first second," Don said. Seven months and two days after they met, the couple got married. Carissa moved up to Fort Collins and worked at another independent café. At that point, she did not care much about quality. "We'd pull shots," she said, "and whatever came out, you'd put in the cup. I remember sitting there forever being like, 'Come on, hurry up, get to the line [in the shot glass]!' and later, somebody else would say, 'Oh! That went fast.' Whatever it was, you'd just put it in the cup." Perhaps unsurprisingly, Carissa only drank tea at her shop.

Eventually, the couple decided to leave Colorado and find a place where neither had long-established friends or family members — an *our* place, so to speak. "Portland, for a lot of reasons, came onto our radar," said Don, "not the least of which was because Portland is *the* city for coffee."

### Westward Ho!

In 2006, with one daughter in tow and another due very soon, the Niemyers moved to Southeast Portland. They chose the Belmont neighborhood specifically because it was near Stumptown's Belmont and Annex cafés. Southeast Portland is where Carissa fell in love with coffee. "I went to the Annex on Don's birthday to a cupping," she said. "We went and I tried some Ethiopian Yirgacheffe. I was like, 'Now *this*, I like.'"

At the time, Don was managing a Verizon retail store by the Gateway Transit Center, but he was not happy. "One day I'm having this conversation with my assistant manager," he recalled. "We were in the back room, wondering what we were doing working for this company and saying we should be doing our own thing." In the middle of the conversation, Don pulled out his smartphone and found a café for sale on Craigslist. He called the number in the listing and learned that the shop was across the street from where he was standing. Without hesitation, he walked over to check it out, finding a "glorified concession stand that served bad coffee from Costco."

Poor quality notwithstanding, the Niemyers bought it a short time later. They purchased a La Marzocco Linea and began serving Stumptown coffee. The café was profitable from the outset, and it gave the couple an opportunity to hone their coffee skills and

## Case Study

prepare for bigger things. "I called it my laboratory," said Don. "This was going to be where we learned about coffee. We knew we wanted to do something that wasn't just a kiosk."

Although the shop was small, it was still a big commitment. Don compared having his own business to becoming a parent for the first time. "I remember having this extremely clear realization when I brought my first daughter home from the hospital, thinking, 'We've been working for nine months, and now we did it!'" he said. "Then, it's like, 'Oh, this is just getting started, and it's never going away! I can't even go to the grocery store now without considering my daughter.' That's what being an entrepreneur is like. This thing [the business] is with you all the time, and you will never get away from it. It's a very present source of joy and thrilling excitement and life-sucking, vampire-like pain at all times."

### Coffee Tycoons, for a Short Time

Bolstered by the success of their first shop, the couple soon purchased Speedboat Coffee, a small shop at Southeast 51st Avenue and Foster Road. Shortly thereafter, they bought another kiosk on the MAX line. "The first shop was making a profit with very little investment," said Don, "and I thought I could do that on these two shops and use the streams of income to support what I jokingly called my real shop — Speedboat. But that never really happened."

The expansion proved to be more of a headache than a benefit. "I do not recommend it, nor would I do it again," said Don about having the third café. "It was bad timing. I did it because it was an opportunity to have another shop for almost no investment." Overwhelmed, the couple sold the second kiosk after six months. Neither Don nor Carissa sounded regretful about the sale. "We purchased our sanity," Carissa said.

With the problem kiosk out of their hands, Don and Carissa focused their energies on the other two cafés, especially Speedboat, which was very different than it is today. The previous owners really liked the idea of having a coffee shop but were not passionate coffee enthusiasts. "They had every flavor of syrup you could imagine," said Don. "They had twenty-four-ounce snickerdoodle mochas, that type of thing."

Carissa looked forward to changing the menu. "We kept it the same for a few weeks after we bought it, just to keep it consistent," she said. "On the day Don gave me the go-ahead, I threw away seventy-five bottles of syrup."

Rebranding the shop was a challenge, especially in the Foster-Powell (FoPo) neighborhood. To an outsider, FoPo is best seen through the windows of a car while traveling at thirty-five miles an hour. The district seems abandoned by the city's leaders, who are more focused on rehabilitating neighborhoods closer to downtown. FoPo lacks the core density of walkable shops, cafés, and restaurants that more welcoming neighborhoods have.

Despite the shortcomings of the neighborhood, the Niemyers have turned the location into a profitable shop, garnering respect from other coffee people. "Don and Carissa are two of my favorite people in the industry," said Matt Brown, who used to work with Speedboat as a Stumptown account manager. "If they weren't down there on Foster, everybody would know who they were and they'd be one of the biggest shops around. They're rock solid. They hire well, they make good drinks, and they have the right heart."

In addition to having their own shop, the Niemyers are certified United States Barista Championship (USBC) judges, which gives them an opportunity to keep their skills sharp and contribute to advancing the specialty coffee industry. Carissa also has her own doula practice, so juggling two kids and two businesses keeps both Niemyers busy.

## Spreading the Movement

Within the next couple years, the Niemyers plan to leave Portland to return to Fort Collins, Colorado, and open a new café. In preparation for the move, the family moved out of their house and into a twenty-one-foot Rialta motor home. They plan to use the RV to tour coffee shops in the West as they make their way to Colorado, and Don is writing a blog about the experience.[81] When the Niemyers reach Colorado, they want to bring some of Portland with them. "For us, one of the things we would be hanging our hat on is that

---

81. Don's blog site: http://rialtacoffeetour.wordpress.com.

## Case Study

we're shop owners from the coffee mecca, bringing that knowledge and a trailer full of those relationships to a new city," Don said.

The Niemyers hope to work with Stumptown instead of finding a roaster in Colorado or roasting coffee themselves. However, Stumptown normally does not sell to cafés so far from one of the company's three roasting facilities because it is difficult to monitor its coffees from afar. "I know there's lots of other good roasters," said Carissa. "It's just that Stumptown has been so good to us. They have such a good business model and do so many things we believe in."

Don and Carissa Niemyer are a living example of how Portland is influencing the rest of the coffee world. The couple came to the city for its coffee, learned all they could about coffee and how to run a business, and will soon take what they have learned elsewhere. Next stop, Fort Collins.

## Marcus Young and Nathanael May
### Two Portland Coffee Leaders Look at the Present (and Future) of Coffee

*Second-wave coffee companies Peet's and Starbucks educated a generation of people about coffee, preparing palates and minds for the new wave of roasters and cafés that followed them. The two coffee giants also trained a lot of today's industry leaders. Marcus Young and Nathanael May are two Portland-area coffee professionals whose stories weave their way through Starbucks and Peet's. May is the coffee education director for Portland Roasting, and Young is now a senior trader and relationship manager at Sustainable Harvest Coffee Importers. At the time of our interview, he was the coffee visionary and green buyer for Central City Coffee, a new roaster under the umbrella of Central City Concern, an agency that provides services to homeless people in Portland.[82] Both are also closely involved with barista competitions, having judged multiple regional and national contests (I have judged with both of them on occasion). One evening, the three of us sat down (over beers, for a change) to talk about the state of the industry, starting with their own coffee stories.* —WH

Marcus Young grew up in Denver, Colorado. He came of age in the mid-1980s, prior to the explosive nationwide growth of Starbucks. For Young, coffee was a social thing that attracted him when he was a teenager. He remembers sitting around at a local Village Inn and drinking "horrible coffee" when he was thirteen years old. In high school, he spent time in independent coffee shops, like Paris on the Platte and St. Mark's. "We'd just go there to hang out," he said. "They were all kind of bohemian. It was our gathering place. It was our version of going to the local tavern."

---

82. Portland Roasting is a partner in Central City Coffee's venture, providing training and consulting services as well as storage and roasting facilities.

## Caffeinated PDX

After graduating from the University of Colorado, Young headed to San Francisco for grad school. He worked at one of the first Starbucks to open in San Francisco, right after the company's noncompete agreement with Peet's expired. "It was great," he remembered. "The first two weeks of training were all about cupping coffee."

Young didn't stay with grad school or Starbucks, but he kept running into coffee. Young founded his own software company, building e-commerce systems for businesses. One of his clients was a coffee roaster who was trying to help coffee farmers in Guatemala. "He didn't have a name for it, but he was running a social enterprise," said Young. "He was involved in his church and wanted to do some good back here too, so he decided to create a private-label coffee company. I had way more fun going to his meetings, where we would cup coffees and evaluate coffees and play around on his roaster. That was far, far more interesting than anything I was doing with software."

Despite coffee's appeal, it did not become Young's career choice until a few years later, when he moved to Portland. After working as an IT manager for a local resort, Young found a job managing a downtown Peet's Coffee. His store showed dramatic sales increases, and Young used his success to move into consulting, green buying, and business development for Batdorf & Bronson, a roaster based in Olympia, Washington. After working there for just over four years, Young left the company in October 2012 to start Central City Coffee.

### May's Coffee Journey

Nathanael May is originally from Southern California, and his first exposure to coffee came through his parents. "Coffee for me was always something my parents did, that I thought was cool and adult." When Nathanael was in high school, he moved to Eugene, where he was surprised by the abundance of coffee in the Northwest. "In California at that point," he said, "coffee was not really a big thing. Starbucks hadn't really expanded into Southern California yet. We got to Eugene, and there were drive-throughs everywhere. My mom was very picky, so we always went to the best drive-through." May did not drink the coffee, but he did develop a taste for hazelnut steamers at his mother's favorite drive-through.

After high school, Nathanael attended Florida College in Tampa. Coffee was not big on campus while he was in school, but six years later, when May returned to work at the college, he found that Starbucks had moved in and transformed the city's coffee scene.

One day, a friend who was an assistant manager at Starbucks invited Nathanael to a tasting. "They were doing French presses of Sumatra and pairing it with foods," May said. "He paired the Sumatra with some sautéed mushrooms, and said, 'Now, taste the coffee, then taste the sautéed mushroom, and taste the coffee again to see what having the earthy taste of the mushroom in your mouth does for the coffee.'" May's perceptions of coffee would never be the same. "I tasted the coffee, the mushroom, and the coffee again, and that second coffee taste — that is the moment in my life I can point to and say my life changed dramatically from there in where my career was going to be. It was like scales had fallen off my eyes, and I realized that there was a depth to coffee I had never known before."

Soon after, May met his future wife and moved back to California. He went to the place he "knew had the very best coffee in the world" — Starbucks — and found a job as a store manager. Eventually, May became disillusioned with Starbucks' drift toward selling food and breakfast sandwiches, and he left to work at Peet's, and then Java City, a roaster in Sacramento. From Java City, May moved to Portland Roasting, where he has been the coffee educator and barista trainer since 2010.

## Coffee's Pull

With both Marcus and Nathanael, coffee's alluring nature drew them in. Once they began to learn about coffee, it was hard to not keep learning. "It's funny because I think you have two different responses to what you see behind the curtain in coffee, the place where the magic happens outside the café," said May. "For me it was visiting the Starbucks roasting plant outside Carson City, Nevada. You either say, 'Wow, this is really cool,' and it doesn't have any effect on you, or you say, 'Wow, this is really cool. I want to do this for the rest of my life.'" For May, the latter was true. "I want to be a part of what's happening here and the connection this has to the rest of the world," he said.

Young echoed that feeling. "I was working for this small business, doing the website. The owner had a roaster and a warehouse, and we'd sit around his dining room table, where his home office was, cupping coffees and telling stories about the producers he knew in Guatemala and how he wanted to give the high school band an opportunity to raise money. It was pretty amazing to see how the separate entities could interact with one another."

"For Marcus and me," Nathanael added, "coffee was not ever something we thought we were going to get into. For most of our generation of coffee professionals, it's been that way. Very few people come to coffee organically out of school thinking that coffee is going to be their thing. I hope that starts to happen." May's wish might come true, especially as more and more people grow up around specialty coffee. "If there was a program for coffee like UC Davis has for wine, that would be rad," said Marcus. "The Coffee Quality Institute could be absorbed by Oregon State University and become the CQI of Oregon State — that would be so cool!"

Coffee is already gaining standing as a valid career choice. When we spoke, May had just returned from the Barista Guild retreat, where he noticed more high school students attending than in previous years. Some had taken days off from school to come work on their coffee skills. "It would be interesting to see if that has trickled down into more areas where young people are starting to see that coffee is the cool thing. And if a program at a university would attract people that wanted to have a degree in coffee agronomy or something like that, it would be awesome."

More than ever before, younger people have taken up the idea that business should be a force for good, not just for making money. "Coffee draws people together," said Young. "Folks who are coffee roasters have experience in the developing world. Maybe not visiting often or even ever, but they're going to know the stories and what's happening there. Coffee draws people who have a sort of curiosity about the world. One thing leads to another, and folks want to do a social good."

Creating social good is easier in the coffee industry than in others. "Coffee is an intoxicatingly direct line to people in other parts of the world who need help," said May. "There's so many social endeavors people can get involved in where the money you send goes off into a general help fund, but when I'm buying coffee directly from a farmer in Guatemala, the money is going right there, and I can see what's happening."

May's employer is leading the way. "The biggest impact Portland Roasting has had on the industry," said May, "has been the direct-trade model they were doing a long time before other places were doing it. They started buying coffee directly in a number of countries in 1999, before a lot of people would buy coffee from farmers."

"At the end of the day," said Marcus, "it's a great thing for everybody. We're all going to get better coffee, producers are going to get more money, and there's more transparency."

## Barista Competitions

One way people are being attracted to the industry is through barista competitions. Both May and Young believed barista competitions have benefited the specialty coffee industry. "Every year that goes by, when I mention barista competitions to noncoffee people, they're less surprised," said Young. "People have heard of them. The competitions have had a huge effect. They are the absolute best way to train baristas, better than any other certifications out there."

The baristas' intense training sessions are pushing the industry forward. "I think that a lot of the standards in the specialty coffee industry, especially around the espresso shots, have been deeply impacted by the cutting-edge research by people training for barista competitions," said May. "The barista competitors are the ones pushing the envelope on a lot of the definitions of things, challenging long-held beliefs."

"I love competitors who are willing to take a risk and a chance," said Young, "to push their concepts forward to challenge the judges." The competitions also bring better exposure to the industry. "Who would have thought ten years ago that we'd have rock star coffee professionals? A lot of more advanced consumers also know their names."

Whether people become rock stars or not, the baristas who do not win are improving and are able to take their newfound knowledge back to their cafés, their customers, and friends. They are excited about coffee, and the enthusiasm is contagious.

## Defining Specialty Coffee

In 2012, when the SCAA surveyed coffee drinkers about what the term *specialty coffee* meant, the answers ranged from high-end coffee roasted by Blue Bottle (a top roaster based in San Francisco, known worldwide for its quality) to the International Delight flavored creamers produced by Nestlé. The survey results pointed out the difficulty of educating customers and how many places people start from in their understanding of coffee. "I think the disconnect is more in the word *specialty*," said Young. "I don't know what *specialty* means. I think people don't know what *specialty* means. It's a flawed term, but at the end of the day, people appreciate quality and recognize the intention behind it."

Above all, specialty coffee is about care and effort to do the best job possible with each coffee grown. "There's a video I use in my training from the mideighties by the precursor to the SCAA," said May. "In the video, the guy starts out drinking his coffee and saying, 'This is one of the finest coffees in the world. It's rich, full-bodied, and distinctive. And the beans that made this delicious cup were grown right here.' He calls it specialty, or gourmet, coffee. He says, 'What makes specialty coffee special? It's all about the extra care taken from seed to cup.'"

May expanded the definition. "The farmer is growing the coffee in a way that is sustainable and produces quality seeds. Roasters roast the beans in a very intentional way so it produces a great cup of coffee, and cafés brew it in an intentional way that honors all of the steps in the process before it. You make specialty-grade coffee not special at all if you roast it poorly or brew it poorly, or you can make nonspecialty-grade coffee feel more special if you roast it and brew it really well."

Young also spoke of a high level of consciousness. "Every step of that supply chain being deliberate," he said. "From the producer to the milling to the transport in a timely fashion, to import, storage, roasting, and then brewing."

## Scaling Specialty Coffee

Specialty coffee is spreading across the country, and one of the main questions in the industry is whether specialty coffee companies can scale to make more of a nationwide impact without losing the qualities that make them special. So far, the industry is off to a promising start. Blue Bottle, Stumptown, Intelligentsia, and others are expanding quickly, showing no signs of slowing down. It is easier than ever to find good coffee. "There are lots of companies out there buying and roasting awfully good coffee on an awfully large scale," said Marcus. He singled out Coffee Bean International (CBI) and its partnership with Target as an example. CBI roasts high-end coffees for Target under the Archer Farms label. "I'm pretty stoked that anywhere in the country, I can walk into a Target and buy a tin of coffee that I know is going to be awesome."

Nathanael was even more enthusiastic. "The fact that you can walk into Target and buy a Cup of Excellence coffee… that's gigantic!" he exclaimed. "That's what, $14 for half a pound? That's ludicrous! Selling a Cup of Excellence coffee that's well-roasted for a reasonable price is great." Many would argue that $28 for a pound of coffee *is* ludicrous, but May's point was valid — there is now more, better quality coffee available in more locations than ever before.

While good quality coffee is more abundant than it used to be, competition for quality green beans has increased as well. Populations that did not traditionally drink coffee, such as those in Korea and China, are drinking much more coffee than they did a decade ago. In coffee-producing countries such as Brazil and Colombia, efforts are also underway to develop a specialty coffee culture to replace some of the instant coffee culture that is predominant in those countries. These changes in consumption patterns have the potential to produce an imbalance between the supply and demand for specialty coffee beans, creating rising prices for roasters around the world. Over the next ten to twenty years, the specialty coffee industry will face a big test of its business model. "This [growth] is great, but it's also scary because it's going to raise the price of coffee," said May.

Despite the uncertainty, no one wants a return to the low prices of the past. "In 2001, coffee was going for about $0.42 per pound," said May. "That's insane! Nobody can live selling coffee for $0.42 a pound! Most of the really big sustainability initiatives you see — fair trade, Rainforest Alliance, Bird Friendly coffee — all that kind of stuff became a bigger focus of the coffee industry as a whole after that crash. People were like, 'Let's never let this happen again.'"

Young had a different worry. "My concern five years ago, as people started putting together all these microlots, was that people were going to be pulling the best coffee out of their container-sized lots and the overall cupping scores of the container lots was going to decrease. But I think that what we've actually found is that the overall coffee quality is increasing."

I asked them about differentiation in the coffee industry by origin and quality level. Could either of them see problems with certain green coffees selling for $100 a pound, like the famed Geisha from Panama Esmeralda has at auctions? "It's hard to see any [problems]," said May, "especially since it's just selling for that much because it's excellent coffee. It's not any weird gimmick."

"It creates buzz," explained Young. "It gets people talking and thinking about coffee as more than some brown stuff. That's just awesome." The buzz about crazy coffee prices attracts press, which in turn makes people more curious about exploring specialty coffee.

## Continuing to Grow the Industry

Specialty coffee is growing quickly, but how does it keep growing? "It comes down to service, largely, and accessibility," said Young. "It's not about teaching people, telling people, training people. It's about demonstrating, so the more opportunities there are for someone to be in [Portland's] Old Town [neighborhood] and stumbling into a great coffeehouse — that's a step." Even Portland, the best coffee city in America, has room for specialty coffee to grow. "Outside the core of Portland, there are huge coffee deserts. I can walk from my house and get a good cup of coffee, but I can't walk from my house and get a cup of coffee I'm legitimately excited about, so I think there's an opportunity for retailers to move into these spaces and demonstrate great coffee," said Young.

Winning customers is a slow process. "It's partly meeting people on their own terms and partly shepherding them a little bit," Young said. "If somebody's ordering a hazelnut mocha, that's great — make it the best hazelnut mocha they've ever had. Then a year down the road, they'll try a mocha, then a latte, and maybe eventually they'll try a beautiful black coffee, which they can then begin buying for brewing at home. That's where suddenly the volume increases exponentially, and companies like Costco will have an incentive to sell excellent coffees."

Both Young and May wanted the specialty coffee industry to be more accessible to everyone, more open and welcoming. Industry people need to temper their desire to share what is happening in coffee with a dose of humility. High-end coffee is sometimes perceived as a haven for coffee snobs, with its exuberant, over-the-top product descriptions that sound as complex as wine labels and its insistence that people drink coffee in a certain way (without syrups, milk, or sugar, in most cases). "We in the specialty coffee industry need to get off our high horse and our need to educate people to what specialty coffee is and just expose them to a lot of great coffee," said May, who thinks the industry can use Starbucks' ubiquity as its model. "Whether people drink Starbucks or not, they know what it is, and there's a perception that Starbucks is high quality coffee. The key, then, is exposure and not education."

May mentioned Portland's craft beer industry as a model to follow. "The beer industry has done a great job of promoting their industry without crapping on people who don't drink craft beer," he said. "If I go to Hair of the Dog to buy a craft beer, then go home and drink a Miller Lite, no one's going to say, 'You suck. How can you enjoy low quality beer?' But the coffee industry — we tend to be all or nothing. You can have specialty coffee, but don't you dare put Coffee-Mate in it."

Beer is not a perfect comparison, however. "Here's the barrier we have in the coffee industry that no other craft industry has," said May. "You can get a craft beer, take it home, and open it up and drink it. You can buy a bottle of wine, take it home, open it up, and drink the wine. You can buy craft cheese, open it up, and eat the cheese. With craft coffee, we sell you a pound of coffee and say, 'Here's the twenty steps you have to follow to make a great cup of coffee.'"

Helping people make better coffee at home will be a key to growing the industry, said Young. "Part of the challenge is that we have to expose people to great coffee but also give them enough education to get them through the final step of brewing."

From their initial entry into the coffee industry through Starbucks and Peet's to their current positions at Portland Roasting and Central City Coffee, both May and Young are leaving a strong impression on Portland's coffee scene. Through their jobs, their participation in barista competitions, and other forums, each is advancing the cause of specialty coffee — to raise the profile of the industry and bring a better and more equitable cup of coffee to more people every day.

## Concluding Thoughts

Coffee is a complex industry, spanning the globe and providing a living for millions of people, from the poorest villages to the richest cities. With nearly two billion cups drunk every day worldwide, coffee is a common human experience, one of the threads that holds society together. Going back to the days of the penny universities of England, where anyone could sit at a table with anyone else for only the price of a cup of coffee, coffee has been a beverage accessible to all classes. Coffee gives the same energy boost to an executive on her way to work in the morning as it does to the janitor about to spend eight hours on a graveyard shift. In all but the extreme cases, even the most expensive coffees are more affordable than other luxury items such as wine. Perhaps that is why Portland, a city that prides itself on its working-class roots, embraces coffee so tightly.

At times, Portland seems like a parody of itself, with its tattoos, hipsters, and general weirdness,[83] but it does have some seriously good coffee. Some wish to dispel the notion that Portland is a coffee mecca with better coffee than anywhere else. After all, other cities — New York, Los Angeles, Chicago, San Francisco, and Seattle, to name a few — have rapidly evolving coffee scenes. Other places may be close, but for my money, Portland is still the best place in the United States to be a coffee drinker. The diversity of styles and proximity between good shops make Portland stand out from its peers. Coffee is more than *just* coffee in the Rose City — it is a fundamental part of the lifestyle.

Building on the traditions of the people who came before them, Portland's coffee entrepreneurs are bringing a fresh perspective

---

83. In July 2013, Portland's Hoyt Arboretum held an event to set the world record for...tree hugging. More than 950 people showed up to (literally) hug trees. You can't make this stuff up.

to this centuries-old industry, raising the quality of coffee and the ethics behind it. Participating in the movement collectively known as third-wave coffee, they put their focus on improving each step in the supply chain, paying more for coffees, roasting them to bring out nuances, and creating new standards for brewing and service.[84] Together, they advance a new way of thinking about coffee.

Critics scold third-wave coffee for being too enamored with itself. More cynical commentators dismiss the focus on coffee farmers, processing techniques, roasting, and brewing methods as a marketing ploy. They reject the notion that a barista is a professional, or they complain when cafés try things like serving their espressos in glass snifters instead of ceramic cups, labeling such practices snobbish and elitist.

For a long time, I wrestled with the idea that third-wave coffee is elitist. Eventually, I came to the conclusion that it is not, at least not intentionally. The third wave is about people giving a damn about what they are selling and trying to do the right thing for everyone, from the small-plot farmer in the mountains of El Salvador to the barista trying to pay off his student loans. Yes, roasters and baristas who are so sure they are the only ones who know how to roast or prepare coffees can be off-putting, but most of their intolerance is innocuous, if not innocent. They have such passion about the coffee, they struggle to understand why others do not see things the same way.

Going forward, the industry has many issues to sort out. The distribution of earnings in the coffee supply chain is still skewed heavily toward the companies that control the green bean trade. Many small farmers lack the resources to improve their coffees and risk being left out of the quality revolution. Urbanization threatens to create worker shortages on coffee farms as young people seek out better lives in the cities. Climate change is shifting where and how coffee grows and could lead to social unrest

---

84. In the early days of the third wave, people became so focused on the coffee that they forgot about their customers. Fortunately, as more roasters and cafés improved their quality, these companies realized service is at least as important as the coffee, and today, most people you interact with at specialty coffee bars are welcoming.

## Concluding Thoughts

in coffee-growing regions. Income rises in developing countries are creating more demand for better coffee, making competition for green beans even fiercer. Many companies, especially cafés, have not yet figured out how to provide benefits to their workers.

Despite these problems, specialty and third-wave coffee are spreading quickly, to the delight of discerning palates around the world. In the future, Portland's best roasters will continue to grow, improving the overall quality of the city's coffee scene for everyone. As the market becomes more crowded, people will move to start companies in places where quality coffee is not so abundant. We see this happening already as Stumptown expands into other cities and other Portland industry people start companies elsewhere. Joel Pollock, a former roaster for Stumptown, and his wife Leticia, who worked at Ristretto, moved to Miami to start Panther Roasters, now considered Miami's best. Jeremy Tooker (originally from Portland) started San Francisco's Ritual Coffee Roasters with Eileen Hassi. When Tooker left to start Four Barrel, also in San Francisco, Duane Sorenson invested in Tooker's new company, as did Jodi Geren, Stumptown's former chief operations officer. Don and Carissa Niemyer, as chronicled in this book, intend to move to Fort Collins, Colorado, to bring a bit of Portland with them. Others will follow their lead.

By taking a look at what has happened in Portland, we gain a better understanding of the changes taking place across the country and beyond, from Spokane to Johannesburg, Melbourne to Boston. Each place will develop differently, but many of the ideals driving the Portland coffee scene forward are fundamental to the movement elsewhere. By supporting cafés and roasters that take care of their people, we are building a more equitable and enjoyable society. This is why third-wave coffee matters. It makes a difference in the lives of the people who work in it.

Searching out cafés specifically for their great coffee is fun, but the real draw to coffee is its communal aspect. People drink coffee to share experiences, to form communities with their friends and with the baristas behind the bar. Whether you are wandering around the early-morning streets of Saronno, Italy, or sitting down in a Stumptown café in Southeast Portland, coffee is a beverage that brings people together. There is a Turkish proverb that says, "The heart desires a friend. Coffee is just an excuse." As much fun as it is to sneak into a café and sit at a back table for hours, it is more fun to take a friend and enjoy your coffee with someone else. When you start exploring your local coffee scene, take someone with you. The experience will be all the richer.

# Acknowledgments

Many, many people contributed to this project, whether they knew it or not. If I happened to miss your name, please forgive me. I am still grateful for your help.

I will start by thanking the people who were kind enough to sit down with me for formal interviews: Katy Boyd Dutt, Michael Boyd, Matt Boyd, Brian Dibble, David Kobos, Jim Roberts, Mark Stell, Skip Colombo, Kevin Fuller, Sarah Allen, Rita Kaminsky, Hanna Neuschwander, Marcus Young, Nathanael May, Don and Carissa Niemyer, Augusto Carvalho Dias Carneiro, Sarah Bailen Smith, Ricky Sutton, Matt Higgins, Matt Brown, Devin Chapman, Sam Purvis, Andrea Pastor, Phuong Tran, Billy Wilson, Christine Herman-Russell, Chris Larson, Andrea Spella, Brandon Arends, John Chandler, Matt Milletto, Brandon Smyth, Adam McGovern, Ann and Collin Schneider, Din Johnson, Nancy Rommelmann, Mindy Farley, Keith Miller, Chris Brady, Marty Lopes, Ryan Cross, Laila Ghambari, Ryan Willbur, Wille Yli-Luoma, and Jana Oppenheimer. Some spoke with me multiple times.

In addition, countless others contributed to my coffee education, through less formal conversations (I wish I had everyone's last name), or through putting me in contact with others: Liam Kenna, Jeremy Robillard, Glenn, and Haley — all from Stumptown Annex — taught me a lot about where coffee comes from. Jeremy Adams, Jenya Campbell, Katie Gilmer, Dane Lorasch, Bernie Diveley, Tom Pikaart, Sara Ziniewicz, Rachel Goldstein (Panama!), Matt Hogan, Jill Purdy, Stephanie Backus, Heather Chandler, Kevin Dibble, Alissa Baron Stranzl, and Brett Felchner included. Plenty more baristas on the West Coast generously shared their coffee knowledge with me when I stopped by their cafés and started asking questions.

Thanks to my old crew at Starbucks on Soldiers Field Road in Boston for making serving coffee such a fun experience and sending me down this road of coffee appreciation: Amy Barksdale, John McCusker, Curt Doten, Elie MacLennan, Colleen, Lannie, Jenny, Revi, Jackie, Brendan, Jeff, Kristen, Jess, Tamir, Danielle, and Julia. I miss you guys.

Thank you to the head judges who guided me as a competition judge: Scott Conary, Heather Ringwood, Miguel Vicuna, Mike Strumpf, Phuong Tran, Marcus Young. Thanks to the other judges for providing a fun and supportive atmosphere.

Thanks to my tech support team, who also helped put together CaffePDX.com: Mathias Sunardi, Jinsu Lee, and Cory Klatik.

A big thanks to all the Portland café owners who let me colonize their tables to write for long periods of time, especially Essam Buker, of Park Avenue Cafe, and Chris Larson, of Coffee Division.

Thanks to Ali McCart, Vinnie Kinsella, and the rest of the team at Indigo, who helped turn a rough project into a finished book.

Finally, to my family — Shayna, Miriam, and Kellen — thank you for putting up with me, as this project nearly drove me crazy at times. I'm sure I would have quit long ago without your support.

— Will Hutchens, November 2013

Appendix

# Where Coffee Comes From

Each time you order an espresso or a mug of brewed coffee, your drink is the conclusion of a long journey. Before it gets to the roaster or café, coffee has gone through a lot of steps to get there, starting out as a small seed in a faraway land. Technically, a coffee bean is the naked seed of a coffee tree, which is really a shrub. Coffee trees grow primarily in the tropical and subtropical regions, and the two most prolific species are Arabica (*Coffea arabica*) and Robusta (*Coffea canephora*). Arabica beans are generally considered to be of higher quality, especially those grown at higher altitudes.

If started from seed, the coffee tree takes about five years to reach full production. The trees flower in the spring, and soon thereafter, small green fruits (cherries), about the size of an olive, form on the branches. As the cherries ripen, they change color. Some varieties turn a deep crimson, others bright yellow or orange. Each tree produces approximately enough cherries in a year to equal a pound of roasted coffee.

Much like a tomato or a peach, coffee tastes best at its peak ripeness, when the sugars are fully developed inside the fruit. Each coffee cherry ripens at a different time on the branch and will not continue to ripen after it is picked. Too many green cherries in the final product will add sourness to the coffee when it is later brewed, so farmers who care about producing high quality coffee selectively pick the coffee by hand or strip-pick it and sort it. Both techniques add to production costs.

Mechanically harvested coffee is becoming more widespread (especially in Brazil), but this is not feasible in most areas. First, the harvesters are expensive, and most farmers do not have enough capital to invest in the machinery. Second, much of the land where coffee is grown is high in the mountains, on steep slopes where it would be impossible to drive any type of machine. Therefore, most coffee is picked by hand and will continue to be picked by hand for years to come.

After the coffee is harvested, it is processed quickly. Workers haul the cherries to a processing station, either on or off the farm, where the seeds are separated from the fruit and prepared for storage as green beans. At the processing center, the coffee is sorted to remove unripe cherries, dirt, leaves, and twigs that may have ended up in the pickers' baskets. Workers separate the cherries by hand or by using a density-based method in which the cherries are dumped into a vat of water. Ripe cherries sink to the bottom, while green and defective cherries float to the top and are skimmed off. After sorting, the next step is to remove the layers of the fruit that envelop the seeds (most cherries contain two seeds). Three primary methods are used, each creating different taste profiles in the finished cup.

## Washed (Wet) Process

The first method is known as wet, or washed, processing. Cherries are sent through a de-pulping machine that mechanically removes the skin and most of the mucilage surrounding the seeds. After being de-pulped, the cherries are transferred to a fermentation tank, where naturally occurring enzymes break down the remaining mucilage. In every processing method, controlling the fermentation of the sugars in the coffee cherries is extremely important, and processors must be very aware of how fermentation is progressing. If left too long, fermentation imparts strange flavors to the seeds, so someone monitors the fermenting coffee at all times of the day. Once fermentation is complete, the seeds are washed in clean water before being set out to dry on raised beds or drying patios.

Many roasters prefer to purchase washed-process coffees because they tend to have the cleanest, most consistent flavor profiles of all the methods. The washed method creates a clean, bright coffee that emphasizes the flavor characteristics inherent in the bean cells. If the mucilage is not removed quickly, the flavors transferred into the beans can be unpredictable.

If a coffee farmer or co-op can afford to use the washed method, they generally do because it provides the processor with the most control over the finished product. The pulp is removed early on, allowing the coffees to dry more quickly than with other methods. This method also produces the most homogenous coffees, with few defects.

The biggest downsides to wet processing are the amount of specialized equipment it takes to implement it as well as the amount of wastewater it creates, which is often discharged into nearby streams. To reduce water pollution, some farmers have introduced a variation on the washed method that relies on machines to completely remove the remaining pulp and mucilage from the seed. Though this mechanical method is better for the health of nearby streams, it also limits the complexity of the flavors in the finished coffee when compared to the standard washed process.

## Natural (Dry) Process

With the natural process, nature is allowed to take its course. Instead of mechanically separating any of the fruit from the seed before drying, the cherries are spread out to dry on raised beds in the sun. Workers at the processing facilities continually turn the long piles of coffee to ensure they dry evenly. When the coffee reaches an acceptable moisture level, the dried fruit pulp and mucilage are mechanically removed from the seeds.

Processing coffee using the natural method has several benefits. First, it is low cost, as far as capital is concerned. Farmers do not need any type of special equipment to separate the skin and fruit pulp from the coffee seeds prior to drying. It does not require large amounts of water during the process, and by extension, does not create large amounts of wastewater that can pollute nearby streams and rivers. The method uses less electricity too.

The second benefit of the natural process is that it can create some very complex-tasting coffees. As the seeds dry in the sun, some of the sugars and other flavor compounds in the fruit pulp are transferred into the seeds. These compounds later come out in the brewed coffee (assuming the roaster did not burn them by overroasting the coffee). Natural coffees are often sweet and syrupy, with flavors like berries, stone fruits, or even sweet silage.

The natural method is simple and low-tech, but it also creates challenges for coffee growers. For the farmers, the natural process method introduces significant amounts of risk to the coffee production process. One of the biggest worries for producers who process their coffee this way is the weather. When the beans are spread out on the drying beds, they are exposed to the weather. With all the fruit on the seed, it takes from eight days to three weeks for the seeds to dry. The longer the coffee is outside, the more chance it has to be rained on. If a rainstorm comes through, it can quickly ruin the harvested coffee. Farmers rarely have any type of insurance for this, so a big rainstorm can be a disaster for the coffee itself as well as the farmer.

In addition to being exposed to the weather, naturally processed coffee can also be very difficult to keep consistent. The fruit pulp on the seed can ferment or even get moldy if it does not dry out quickly. Moldy or overfermented coffee tastes bad. Furthermore, roasters who insist on consistent flavor profiles tend to stay away from naturals.

## Pulped Natural (Semiwashed, or Honey) Process

The pulped natural process is kind of a middle ground between the washed method and the natural method. After the first sorting, the coffee cherries pass through a machine that removes the skins and some of the fruit pulp. The sweet, sticky mass of cherries and seeds is then spread out in beds where they dry in the sun. Once dried, the mucilage is mechanically removed from the seeds.

Pulped natural coffees tend to be a little sweeter and less acidic than wet-processed coffees. By leaving more of the fruit on the seeds, sugars and flavor compounds add complexity to the flavor of the finished coffee. The beans do not need to sit as long on the drying beds as in the standard natural process because the skins and some of the fruit are already gone. The pulped natural process adds complexity without exposing the farmers to as much risk as the natural process does.

## Resting, Milling, and Shipping

All three of the processing methods leave the dried beans covered only with their parchment (the endocarp layer surrounding the seed that becomes paperlike during the processing). Parchment coffee is allowed to rest in warehouses for a month or two, and then it is milled to remove the parchment, sorted again for defective beans, packed, and shipped abroad. To maintain quality, the beans must be stored and shipped in dry conditions. Otherwise, all the efforts that went into producing the coffee can be quickly made worthless by an outbreak of mold or, in some cases, by sharing the shipping container with something that produces an odor the coffee beans absorb. To monitor the quality and prevent surprises, the coffees are cupped at origin and then again when they reach their destination. This ensures the quality is the same as what was expected when the coffee was purchased. Once the coffees are checked for quality and accepted, they pass on to the capable hands of roasters and baristas, like those profiled in this book, who turn a bland raw product (green coffee beans taste like wood) into one of the most widely enjoyed beverages on the planet.

Having a basic understanding of the coffee supply chain helps enthusiastic customers become more engaged with the people making their coffees. More and more roasters are printing detailed information about origin and processing methods on the coffee bags, and understanding what some of the terms mean will help you find more types of coffees you like. If you happen to go to a cupping and the host starts talking about where coffees come from, you can track the conversation more easily. You can also choose to ignore this information, because the best coffee companies focus on performing every step with care, ensuring that all you really need to do is enjoy what is in your cup.

# Barista Jargon

As with most industries, the specialty coffee industry has its own vocabulary. If you are new to specialty coffee, here's a primer on some of the terms you are likely to hear as you learn about the industry.

**AeroPress:** A full-immersion brewing device that resembles a large syringe (without the needle), with which the user plunges hot water across finely ground coffee.
**Americano:** A beverage consisting of espresso diluted with hot water. It gets its name from American travelers to Europe, who, unaccustomed to drinking espresso, asked to have their espresso watered down.
**Barista:** The person in a coffee bar who makes coffee beverages.
**Cappuccino:** Traditionally, a four- to six-ounce beverage made of espresso and textured (foamed) milk.
**Chemex:** A type of pour-over brewer that uses a filter made from the same filter paper found in a chemistry lab. The round filter is folded into the shape of a cone in order to hold the grounds for brewing.
**Cold brew:** Coffee that has been brewed at low temperatures for long periods of time. It is sometimes referred to as Toddy coffee, after the company that popularized the method in the 1960s.
**Crema:** An emulsion of coffee oils and water that sits on top of an espresso after it is pulled. It typically has the appearance of a shiny, reddish-brown foam.
**Cupping:** A method for analyzing the quality and flavor characteristics of coffee. Coffee buyers cup hundreds of coffees before they decide what to buy. Cupping involves smelling the aromas and fragrances of the coffees before slurping it to check the flavor profile. The procedure is relatively standardized around the world.

## Caffeinated PDX

**Direct trade:** Coffee that a roaster purchases directly from a farmer instead of through a broker or distributor.

**Espresso:** A brewing method that forces steam through finely ground coffee under pressure (approximately nine bars) for twenty to thirty seconds. The result is a concentrated coffee beverage with a volume of approximately one to two ounces.

**Four Ms:** Refers to the Italian terms *macinazione* (grind), *miscela* (blend), *macchina* (machine), and *mano* (hand of skilled barista) that all must be well executed to create the best espresso.

**French press:** A device that brews coffee by fully immersing the grounds in water. A plunger-filter separates the grounds from the brewed coffee. Sometimes referred to as simply a press.

**God shot:** A term that refers to an exceptionally good and memorable espresso.

**Go to origin:** Take a trip to visit coffee farms, a desired goal for seemingly everyone working in coffee.

**Knock box:** A small box containing a rubber-coated bumper, which baristas use to free the espresso grounds (puck) from the portafilter after brewing.

**Kill it:** To make great coffee.

**Latte:** The Italian term for "milk"; popularized by Starbucks to mean a beverage of eight to twenty ounces consisting of espresso and steamed milk plus a little bit of foam. More accurately called a caffè latte.

**Macchiato:** A beverage composed of espresso and a dollop of foam. In most third-wave cafés, the macchiato comes as a 1:1 ratio of espresso and steamed milk (similar to the Spanish *cortado*).

**Mocha:** A beverage that contains chocolate, espresso, and textured milk. At some establishments, it comes with whipped cream on top.

**On grind:** The type of coffees a café has in the espresso grinder hoppers available for espresso beverages. Analogous to *on tap*.

**PID:** A temperature-control apparatus that eliminates nearly all variance in water temperature on an espresso machine. The term is an acronym for proportional-integral-derivative controller. PIDs are now considered a standard feature for modern espresso machines.

## Barista Jargon

**Portafilter:** The metal basket that baristas fill with ground coffee before attaching it to the espresso machine to pull a shot. Shorthand for *portable filter*.

**Pour-over:** A manual brewing method in which the barista pours hot water (about 200°F) over coffee grounds, sending brewed coffee through some type of filter, and collects it in a cup or carafe below the filter. Some cafés may have more than one pour-over coffee available, distinguishing them by the type of brewing apparatus used (such as Chemex, V60, Mellita, Kone).

**Puck:** The coffee grounds remaining in a portafilter after they have been used to brew an espresso. The word is derived from grounds' resemblance to a hockey puck.

**Pull a shot:** The act of brewing an espresso. The term is derived from the early espresso machines that required a barista to actually pull a lever to add the pressure required to force the hot water through the coffee grounds.

**Relationship coffee:** Coffee generated from relationships in which the farmers and roasters are working together to improve the quality of the coffee as well as the price the growers are paid. Stumptown Coffee uses the term in place of *direct trade*.

**Ristretto:** A method of pulling an espresso shot at a low volume, resulting in a very thick, viscous shot with highly concentrated flavors.

**Roaster:** Term that can refer to a machine that roasts coffee, a company that sells coffee it roasts, or the person who is in charge of the roasting.

**Roastery:** The location where coffee is roasted. *See also* roaster.

**Shakerato:** A beverage consisting of a shot of espresso, a bit of sugar and ice, shaken together in a beverage shaker. The resulting drink is foamy and lightly sweet. Also called an espresso freddo.

**Shot:** Another term for *espresso*. It can also refer to the amount of espresso that comes out of one side of a double portafilter.

**Siphon:** A brewing device that uses a full-immersion brewing technique. A siphon has two glass carafes, one on top of the other and separated by a filter. When water in the bottom chamber reaches boiling temperature, it flows upward into a second chamber filled with coffee grounds. When brewing is complete, the heat source is removed from the bottom chamber, and the cooling air inside creates a vacuum that pulls the brewed coffee down through the filter.

**Tamp:** The act of compressing the ground coffee in the portafilter before it is locked into the espresso machine. Tamping the espresso assures that the water will pass through the grounds evenly for a full extraction of flavor compounds. The word can also refer to the instrument used to do the tamping.

**Toddy:** A type of cold brew coffee named for the company that popularized the method in the 1960s. *See also* cold brew.

**Vacuum pot:** *See* siphon.

# Index

Able Brewing, 140, 140n
Abruzzi Coffee Roasters, 65
Adams, Jeremy, 267–273
Adrià, Ferran, 119
advertising, early 20th century, 26–27
airpot brewers, 45
Albina Press, 103–12
    Barista Guild parties, 105
    career opportunities, 110–11
    exclusive coffees, 109–10
    Kaminsky at, 145, 149
    McGovern on, 190
    reputation, 39, 104, 105, 111, 130–31
    training process, 106–7
Allegro Coffee, 212–13
Allen, Sarah, 251–58
    on Albina Press, 119
    background, 251–52
    *Barista Magazine*, 252–53, 257–58
    on global coffee scene, 253–54
    on Portland, 255–56
    on Stumptown, 79
Allen, Tracy, 257
alt.coffee, 116
Alterra Coffee Roasters, 145–46
American Barista & Coffee School, 148, 225, 231–34
American Revolution, 25
Americans, cost consciousness, 28n
Arabica coffee beans, 29n, 30
Arbuckle, John, 26
Arbuckles' Ariosa Blend, 26

Archer Farms, 301
Arends, Brandon, 19–22, 93, 167–68, 172, 187
Artigiano, 118
artists, 71
Asia, coffee industry in, 100
Ava Gene's, 81
awards, 46

Backus, Nathanael, 70
Backus, Stephanie, 70
Bailen Smith, Sarah, 261, 263, 265
Bakery Bar, 147–48
Baldwin, Jerry, 27, 33, 54
Bamboo Revolution, 139
Barista Alberta, 123–24
Barista coffee shops, 21, 120–26
barista competitions
    Arends on, 19–20
    benefits for industry, 149–150, 156, 167–68, 285, 299–300
    career advancement, 148
    judging, 168–176
    NASCORE competition, 116–17
    preparing for, 154–55, 196–97
    as a promotional tool, 196
    protocol, 172–76
Barista Guild of America, 33
Barista Guild party (2006), 104–5
*Barista Magazine*, 33, 251–54, 257–58
baristas
    attitude, 105–6, 156–57, 208–11, 234
    career opportunities, 33–34, 98, 257

baristas *(continued)*
   consistency, 106, 149, 234, 258
   skills needed, 258–260
Batlle, Aida, 150, 150n
bicycle deliveries, 65
Black Tiger Blend, 58–59, 59n
Blue Bottle, 81
Blue Bottle café, 25
Bowker, Gordon, 27
Boyd, David, 44, 45
Boyd, Dick, 44
Boyd, Matt, 43, 47
Boyd, Michael, 43, 47
Boyd, Percival Dewe (P. D.), 37, 43–44
Boyd, R. P., 44
Boyd Coffee Company, 43–48
Boyd Importing Tea Company, 44
Brady, Celeste, 238, 240–41
Brady, Chris, 235–242
   background, 237–39
   Extracto Coffee Roasters, 39, 239–242
   on naturals, 235
   on roasting, 236–37
Bravilor, 45
Brazil
   coffee industry in, 163, 215, 261, 264
   Nossa Familia trips, 264–65
*Brews to Bikes* (Heying), 129
Brooks, Brian, 188–89
Brown, Matt, 177–185
   background, 113, 177–78
   at Barista, 181
   at Coava, 183–85
   at Coffeehouse Northwest, 179–181
   on Niemyers, 292
   at Stumptown, 181–84
   Wilson and, 114–15

Cafe Moto, 73
CaffePDX.com, 18n
Caffe Sole, 212
Caffe Trieste, 28n
calibration, 170, 171–72
"Calling the Shots" (Allen), 252
cappuccino, 19, 174
Caravan, 58
Caravela, 205
Carmichael, Todd, 79
Carneiro, Augusto Carvalho Dias, 261–66
Carvalho Dias family, 261, 262
Case Study Coffee, 40, 281, 283–87
Castle Rock, Washington, 113
Cellar Door Coffe Roasters, 267
Central America, coffee industry in, 25, 77, 254
Chandler, Heather, 40, 275–79
Chandler, John, 40, 275–79
Chapman, Devin, 153–160
   awards, 153
   background, 153–54
   competitions, 40, 140, 154–56
   on connecting farmer with customers, 157–59
   on hospitality, 156–57
   Purvis and, 162
   on striving for improvement, 160
Chigounis, Aleco, 90
Civil War, 26
cleanliness, 234
climate, for coffee production, 25
climate change, 272–73, 306–7
Clover brewing machines, 78
Coava, 138–143
   Brown at, 183–85
   Chapman at, 140, 154, 156–57
   competition strategy, 138–39, 162–63
   Purvis on, 167
   reputation, 40, 135, 139–140
   roasting style, 140–41
   sourcing coffee, 141–43
coffee, historical overview, 23–29
*Coffee: A Dark History* (Wild), 24

# Index

Coffee Bean International (CBI), 37, 38n, 56, 95, 96, 301
Coffee Bean Roasters, 55–56
Coffee Cottage, 195–96
CoffeeGeek.com, 115–16
Coffeehouse Northwest, 19, 179–180, 188–192, 195
coffee industry
    competition for business, 131–32, 230, 307
    direct-trade relationships, 35–36, 63, 65, 109, 228–29, 299
    diversity, 184–85
    evolution of, 34
    exclusivity, 104
    multiroaster concept, 39, 113, 120–22, 125, 131–32, 256
    opportunities in, 110–11, 165–66, 253–54, 277, 298–99
    Portland's influence on, 39, 293, 299, 305–6
    supply chain, 35–36
    sustainability, 38, 63, 66–67, 164–65, 273, 299
Coffee Mania, 254
Coffee People, 38, 55–61
Coffee Profiler, 45–46
coffee purists, 281
Coffee Roasters United (CRU), 132, 256, 286
Colombo, Skip
    Brown and, 182
    at Fresh Pot, 85–90
    at Stumptown, 81, 90–92
    Constantinople, Turkey, 24
    cooperatives, 285–86
    copycat cafés, 28
Counter Culture, 29
craft beer industry, 303–4
Crase, Chris, 189
Cross, Ryan, 76–77
Cup of Excellence, 69
cupping, 17, 35n, 67–70

Cupping for the People, 68
Curtis-Fawley, Sarah, 70
customers
    educating, 38–39, 54, 77, 229–230, 272
    knowledge level, 47–48, 198, 272
    price sensitivity, 28n, 50

D'Apice, Karen, 207
dark roasts, 50
decaffeination process, 68
de Clieu, Gabriel, 25
dialing, 232–33
Dibble, Brian, 49–50, 49n
Dibble, Kevin, 49
Diedrich Coffee, 57–58
direct-trade relationships
    benefits, 30, 63, 205–6, 228–29, 246, 299
    exclusive coffees, 109–10
    Farm-Friendly Direct program, 65
    Stumptown, 30, 36, 75, 109
Domiguez, Bud, 52
Domreis, Neal, 240, 241–42
Dutt, Katy Boyd, 43–47

El Injerto, 77
Endicott, Shane, 88–89
equipment
    importance of, 107
    leasing from roaster, 45, 121
    lever machines, 216–18
    for processing, 30, 163
    siphon brewers, 126–27
espresso
    blend consistency, 106, 206, 215, 228
    evaluating, 19, 174
    as focus of competitions, 19, 171
    four Ms, 258
    Italian blends, 214–16
    single-origin, 32, 206, 215, 220, 228
Espresso Arts, 282
*Espresso Coffee: Professional Techniques* (Schomer), 116

espresso machines, 26, 28, 28n, 216–18
espresso pearls, 119
Espresso Royale, 85
Ethiopia, coffee industry in, 24, 30, 254
Ethiopian coffees, 237
ethyl acetate, 68
Europe, popularity of coffee, 24–25
exclusive coffees, 109–10
Extract Mojos, 248, 248n
Extracto Coffee Roasters, 235, 239–242

Faherty, Brian, 204–5
Fair Trade USA, 50
Farley, Mindy, 110–11, 129–134
farmers
    communication with, 141, 142, 164
    direct-trade relationships, 30, 63, 109–10, 205–6, 228–29, 246
    fairness to, 31, 35–36, 63, 306
    innovations in coffee, 229
    quality vs. quantity, 158–59
Farm-Friendly Direct program, 65
Fazenda Cachoeira, 264, 265
Fazenda Santa Alina, 264
Ferguson, Jeff, 55–56
Finca El Injerto, 99
fires, 52–53, 123–24
first crack, 236
flavor
    consistency, 31, 46, 107, 141, 206
    food pairing, 70, 297
    influences on, 22, 127
    seasonal changes, 46, 106, 247
    taste balance, 174
    flavoring syrups, 33, 97, 284
Folger, Jim, 26
Food for Thought Cafe, 21
Fortune, Brent, 118
Foster-Powell (FoPo) neighborhood, 292

Four Barrel, 307
Fowler, Ward, 146
*Fresh Cup*, 252
Fresh Pot, 85–92
Fuller. Kevin, 103–12
    background, 103–4
    Barista Guild party, 105
    exclusive coffees, 109–10
    future plans, 112
    hiring policy, 110–11
    Miller and, 130–31
    on simplicity, 108–9
    on technology, 107
    training employees, 106
    trip to Central America, 77
    Wilson and, 39, 118–19

gangs, 89
Gaturiri, Ethiopia, 30
Gehrke, Keith, 138–39, 140, 161–62
Geisha coffee, 164, 302
Gemaleddin, 24
Geren, Jodi, 307
Ghambari, Laila, 123
Giuliano, Peter, 31, 73n, 121
Gloria Jean's, 57
Godin, Seth, 71
*God in a Cup*, 31
Golden Cup Award, 46, 46n
greenwashing, 63–64
Griswold, David, 38
Grosse, Becky, 122
Grosse, Jamie, 122
Groteboer, Jodi, 111
Guatemala, coffee industry in, 163–64

Hair Bender blend, 14, 76, 83
Hair Bender Salon, 73n
handpicking, 30, 30n
Hartwich, Scott, 86
Hassi, Eileen, 238, 307
Haven Coffee, 76, 76n

# Index

Heart Roasters, 39, 243–250
Herman-Russell, Christine, 281–87
Heying, Charles, 129
Higgins, Matt, 135–143
    at Albina Press, 137–38
    background, 135–36
    Coava, 110, 138–143, 161–62
    coffee studies, 136–37
Hills brothers, 26
history of coffee
    early age, 23–26
    first wave, 26–27
    overview, 23, 34
    second wave, 27–29, 33
    third wave, 16–17, 23, 29–34, 306
Holmberg, Gilbert, 52
Horse Brass Pub, 182
hospitality, 156–57, 180, 285, 303, 306
Houk, Fred, 29
Hutchens, Will (author), background, 9–18
Hydeman, Josh, 111

Il Giornale, 28
instant coffee, 26
Intelligentsia, 29, 79
Interzone, 226
Italy, espresso in, 214–15

Jim & Patty's Coffee, 58–59
Johnson, Din, 201–7
    background, 201–2
    business expansion, 203–5
    employees and, 206–7
    relationship with farmers, 205–6
    Ristretto Roasters, 39, 203–7
Johnson, Mike, 45

Kaldi, 24
Kaminsky, Rita, 145–151
Kelso, Jim, 90
Kelso, Washington, 177
Kirbach, Steve, 90

Knox, Kevin, 212
Kobos, David, 37, 44n, 49–54
Kobos, Susan, 49, 51
Kobos Coffee, 49–54, 263
Koffein, 254
Kolschitsky, Franz, 25
Kone filters, 40, 40n, 139, 140

Laird, John, 136–37
Landauer Mercantile building, 276, 277
Larson, Chris, 74
latte art, 233
Lava Java
    background, 93–95
    Brown at, 178
    commitment to quality, 95, 97, 99–100
    location, 93, 96–97
    switch to Stumptown, 96, 117
    Wilson at, 39, 94–95, 114–15, 117
Lebanese restaurants, 20
Leebrick, Ed, 73, 82
Lempira coffee, 158
lever machines, 216–18
Lighthouse Roasters Fine Coffee, 73, 82–84
Linea Caffe, 151n
Little Red Wagon Store, 51
Lopes, Marty, 122
Loring Kestrel roasters, 263
Lounsbury, Matt, 90

Macerata, Italy, 226, 226n
Maglia Rosa, 98
Mancia, David, 158–59
marketing, early 20th century, 26–27
Maxwell House, 26
May, Nathanael
    background, 295, 296–98
    on social good, 299
    on specialty coffee, 300–304
M Bar, 194

McBride, Erin, 270, 270n
McDonald's, 255
McGovern, Adam, 187–194
   background, 187–88
   Brown and, 179–180
   Coffeehouse Northwest, 39, 180, 188–192
   Sterling kiosk, 193–94
   Wilson and, 120
Mead, Neal, 235, 240
Miller, Aric
   at Coffeehouse Northwest, 189
   Sterling Coffee Roasters, 39, 181, 192–94
Miller, Keith, 129–134
Miller, Trevin, 132
Milletto, Bruce, 40, 148, 225, 227
Milletto, Matt, 40, 148, 225–231
Mississippi Ave., 88–89
*Mix Magazine*, 201
MJB, 26
Mocha (port), 24
Montevilla Farmers Market, 268
Mr. Green Beans, 132
multiroaster concept, 39, 113, 120–22, 125, 131–32, 256

natural-processed coffees, 235, 246–47
Neuschwander, Hanna, 76, 81
Newberg, Oregon, 195–96
New Seasons, 76
New York, NY, 92
*New York Times Ristretto* blog, 139, 247
Niemyer, Carissa, 289–293, 307
Niemyer, Don, 289–293, 307
Nossa Familia, 261–66
Novak, Brennan, 190
Novel Java, 86

Oblique Coffee, 40, 275–79
Olson, Ken, 251, 252

Oppenheimer, Jana, 76, 118
*Oregonian*, 252
origin of coffee, 31, 32

Pacas coffee, 158
Panther Roasters, 307
Paris, France, coffee industry, 254
Pastor, Andrea, 267–273
Peet, Alfred, 27
Peet's Coffee & Tea, 27
Pendergrast, Mark, 25
percolators, 27
Piccolo, Sammy, 118, 118n
PIDs, 107, 107n, 116
Pikaart, Tom, 231
Pino, 198
Plummer, Todd, 64–65
political issues, 270–71
Pollock, Joel, 76, 307
Pollock, Leticia, 307
Pond (band), 238
Portland, Oregon
   artisan economy, 129
   coffee culture, 17–18, 37–41, 197, 229–230
   diversity of coffee industry, 207, 256, 305
   FoPo neighborhood, 292
   influence on industry, 39, 293, 299, 305–6
   innovations in coffee, 211
   North area, 88–89
   proliferation of roasters/cafés, 191, 241–42, 270, 285–86
   quality of life, 17, 289
   reputation, 97, 255–56, 305
   unemployment rates, 137–38
   Williams neighborhood, 203–4
Portland Development Commission, 89
Portland Global Initiatives, 65
*Portlandia*, 277, 289
Portland Roasting Coffee, 38, 63–70

# Index

Powell's Books, 86
pricing
    competition for beans, 66, 245
    customer sensitivity, 28n, 50
    direct-trade relationships, 35–36, 65, 205–6, 228
    quality and, 30, 35n, 69, 75, 100, 109, 245, 302
Prince, Mark, 115
publications, coffee, 40, 251
public offerings, 57
Purvis, Christine, 167
Purvis, Sam, 161–67
    background, 161–62
    competitions, 40, 138, 139–140, 162–63
    Epipheo, 167
travel to origin, 163–64

quakers, 237

radio ads, 27
Rancilio machines, 216–17
Red E Café, 39, 129–134
Red Wagon Stores, 44, 51
refractometers, 248, 248n
renewable energy, 271
Rhodes, Jason, 111
Ricci, Joth, 80
Rice, Jessica, 95, 115
Ristretto Roasters, 201–10
    Beaumont shop, 203
    Nicolai shop, 201, 204–5
    Williams shop, 203–4, 208–10
roasting community, 240, 268
roasting style
    dark roasting, 31–32, 50
    light roasting, 32, 34, 75–76, 206, 220, 247–48, 247n
    medium roasting, 206, 236, 285
    slow roasting, 227
roasting theory, 236–37
Roberts, Jim, 38, 55–61

Roberts, Patty, 38
Robur, 107
Robusta beans, 59n
Roman Candle, 81
Rommelmann, Nancy, 201–7, 204, 206–7
Rothgeb, Trish Skeie, 23
Royal Coffee, 226
Russell, Michael, 80
Russell, Wes, 281–87
Russia, coffee industry in, 254

San Francisco, 202
Saturday Market (Eugene), 55
SCAA Sustainability Award, 65
scaling up, 165–66
Scandinavian roasting, 227
Schneider, Ann, 195–99
Schneider, Collin, 195–99
Schomer, David, 116, 196n
Schulman, Jim, 116
Schultz, Howard, 27–28, 54
seasonality, 247
2nd Story, 270, 270n
second crack, 236
Second Cup, 57
second-wave coffee, 33
See See Motocycles, 185
sensory experience, 221–24
Serna, Bronwen, 117
Siegl, Zev, 27, 54
single-origin coffees, 32, 206, 215, 220, 228
siphon brewers, 126–27
Skeie, Trish (later, Rothgeb), 23
slurping, 70
Smith, Brett, 29
Smyth, Brandon, 40, 225–231
social entrepreneurship, 35–36
Songer, Paul, 212
Sorenson, Duane, 71–82
    as an artist, 71
    background, 72–73, 82

Sorenson, Duane (*continued*)
  Colombo and, 87–88, 89
  culinary interests, 81
  on expansion, 78–79
  founding Stumptown, 29, 73–74
  influence on industry, 81–82
  on investment, 79, 80
  involvement, 76–77
  quality standards, 38, 74, 77
  relationships with farmers, 31, 38
  Roberts on, 60
  support for *Barista Magazine*, 253
  travel to origin, 99
  treatment of workers, 75
specialty coffee, defined, 16–17, 197, 271, 285, 300. *See also* third-wave coffee
Specialty Coffee Association of America (SCAA), 46
  specialty coffee industry
  communal nature, 307–8
  expansion, 301–4, 307
  hospitality aspect, 156–57, 285, 303, 306
Speedboat Coffee, 289, 291–93
Spella, Andrea, 211–221
  background, 211–13
  cart, 39, 213–14, 218
  future plans, 221
  on Italian espresso, 214–16
  on location, 219
  on single-origin espresso, 220
  on Sorenson, 82
  traditional values, 216–18
  wholesale business, 219–220
Spella Caffè, 216–221
sprudge.com, 40
standards manuals, 100–101
Starbucks
  dark roasts, 31–32, 50
  influence on industry, 54
  overview, 27–29
  Torrefazione Italia buyout, 238

Stark Café, 78
START (Sustainability Tracking and Reporting Tool), 66–67
Stell, Mark, 38, 63–67
Sterling Coffee Roasters
  atmosphere, 197–98
  fashion, 193, 197, 198
  founding of, 39, 181
  overview, 192–94
  Schneider and, 195
stock market, 57
stovetop percolators, 27
Strand, Oliver, 139, 247
Stumptown Coffee, 71–82
  attitude, 74–75
  Brooklyn roastery, 92
  Brown at, 181–83
  Colombo on, 87–88
  devotion to quality, 38–39, 100, 109
  direct-trade relationships, 30, 36, 75, 109
  education, 77, 229, 272
  employee benefits, 183
  equipment requirements, 96
  Ethiopian partnership, 30
  expansion, 77–79, 80, 91, 202
  founding of, 29, 74–75
  Jim & Patty's Coffee, 58
  multiroaster concept, 121–22
  pricing, 100
  reputation, 202–3
  roasting style, 71, 75–76
  Roberts on, 60
  TSG investment, 60n, 79–81, 91–92, 183
  Wilson on, 115
Sufis, 24
Summit Partners, 81
Suprenant, Thomas, 270
sustainability, 38, 63, 65–67, 164–65, 273, 299
Sustainable Harvest, 38
Sutton, Ricky, 284

# Index

Swedish kitchen witches, 53
Sweet Maria's, 267
Swiss Water, 68
syrups, 33, 97, 284

Talboy, Gary, 56
Target, 301
taste balance, 174
tea taxes, 25
temperature control, 107, 107n, 127
third-wave coffee, 16–17, 23, 29–34, 306. *See also* specialty coffee
Three Lions' Café, 238
Tooker, Jeremy, 238, 238n, 307
Torrefazione Italia, 238
training programs
    American Barista & Coffee School, 231–34
    at Lava Java, 95
    at Spella Caffè, 217–18
    standards manuals, 100–101
    time required, 106, 233–34
Tran, Phuong, 93–101
    background, 93–94
    competitions, 39, 95, 101
    as an employer, 98–99
    future plans, 100–101
    Lava Java, 39, 93–97
    reputation, 97, 99
    on Sorenson, 72
    travel to origin, 99–100
    Wilson and, 94–95
triangulation test, 170–71
Trigger, 81
triple bottom line concept, 63
TSG Consumer Products, 183
Tully's, 147
Turkey, coffee trade, 24–25
Turkish coffee, 20

Uncommon Grounds (Pendergrast), 25
United Nations Earth Summit, 64

United States, coffee industry in, 25–26
United States Barista Championship (USBC), 117

vacuum packaging, 26
vacuum pots, 126–27
Vick, Stephen, 253
Vienna, Austria, 25
Vinci, Matthew "Vin", 85–90

Walk for Water, 65
washed process coffees, 246
Water Avenue Coffee, 40, 225–231
Watts, Geoff, 31
websites
    CaffePDX.com, 18n
    CoffeeGeek.com, 115–16
    Coffee Review, 139
    sprudge.com, 40
    Sweet Maria's, 267
Wild, Antony, 24
*Willamette Week* article, 190
*Willamette Week's* Best Labor of Love award, 277
Willbur, Ryan, 250
Wilson, Billy, 113–126
    at Albina Press, 104, 111, 118–19
    background, 113–14
    Barista, 120–26
    Barista Alberta, 123–24
    coffee studies, 115–16
    at Coffeehouse Northwest, 191
    competitions, 39, 104–5, 119
    on employees, 122–23, 126
    at Lava Java, 39, 94–95, 96, 114–15, 117
    multiroaster concept, 113, 120–22, 125, 256
    NASCORE competition, 116–17
    on Sorenson, 77
    at Stumptown, 117–18
witches, Swedish kitchen, 53

Woodsman Tavern, 81
World Barista Championship (WBC), 20

Yli-Luoma, Willie, 243–250
   background, 243–44
   opening Heart, 244–45
   quality control, 248–250
   roasting style, 39, 247–48
   sourcing, 245–46
Young, Marcus
   background, 295–96, 298
   on competitions, 299–300
   on specialty coffee, 301, 302–3
Younger, Don, 74
Youth with a Mission, 114

Zell, Doug, 29, 79
Zheng He, 24
Ziniewicz, Sara, 231
Zoka, 253

www.ingramcontent.com/pod-product-compliance
Lightning Source LLC
Chambersburg PA
CBHW071856290426
44110CB00013B/1166